Kind regards
Rambuyn
Tony Keegan

65/100

First In Service

The story of the Rotary Club, Dublin
No. 1 Club Europe

BY

Tony Keegan

Published by the Rotary Club, Dublin.

First in Service is published by the Rotary Club, Dublin.

© Tony Keegan and the Rotary Club, Dublin 2010.

Inquiries to: Hon. Secretary, 4 Bellevue Park, Greystones, Co. Wicklow.
E-mail: tkedits@eircom.net   Website: www.dublinrotary.org

ISBN 978-0-9566667-0-3

All rights reserved. No part of this publication may be reproduced, stored in a retrieval system or transmitted in any form or by any means, electronic, mechanical, photocopying, recording or otherwise without the prior written permission of the publisher.

This book is sold subject to the condition that it shall not, by way of trade or otherwise, be lent, resold, hired out or otherwise circulated without the publisher's prior consent in any form of binding or cover other than that in which it is published and without a similar condition including this condition being imposed on the subsequent purchaser.

Front cover: the early 20th century picture of Grafton Street Dublin looking towards College Green is taken from the Lawrence Collection held in the National Library of Ireland. William Lawrence classification 'Photographer' was a founder member of the Rotary Club, Dublin with premises at 5,6,7 Sackville Street. The Club established its first office at 116 Grafton Street (on the left of the picture) in 1920.

Printed by Barnaville Print & Graphics Ltd., Freshford, Co. Kilkenny.

Glossary

AIDS: Acquired Immune Deficiency Syndrome
B.A.R.C.: British Association of Rotary Clubs
club: The Rotary Club, Dublin unless otherwise indicated.
DBC: The Dublin Bread Company
DG: District Governor
Dublin Club: Rotary Club, Dublin
ESB: The Electricity Supply Board
GSE: Group Study Exchange
HIV: Human Immunudeficiency virus
HRH: His (Her) Royal Highness
I.A.R.C.: International Association of Rotary Clubs
IPP: Irish Parliamentary Party
IPP: Immediate Past President
PDG: Past District Governor
PP: Past President
RDS: Royal Dublin Society
R.I.: Rotary International
R.I.A.C.: Royal Irish Automobile Club
R.I.B.I.: Rotary International in Great Britain and Ireland
RTE: Radio Telifis Eireann
TCD: Trinity College Dublin
UCD: University College Dublin
UNICEF: The United Nations International Children's Emergency Fund
UNESCO: United Nations Educational, Scientific and Cultural Organisation

Acknowledgements

I would like to thank my wife Deirdre for all her help and encouragement and my sons Fin and Joe for their design and technical assistance.

I also thank the following:
PP James Gorman for all his work in reading through and collating the Club Minutes. PP Victor Hamilton and PP Ethna Fitzgerald for their encouragement and assistance in getting this project off the ground. Rotarians Frank Bannister, Peter McKimm and Pamela O'Loughlin for proof-reading the manuscript and for their many helpful suggestions for improving the text. And to Frank for contributing his memories of recent presidents of the club. President Randal Gray for helping me discover some new information with regard to William Stuart Morrow Catherine and Jim Bourke for their present of '**A Century of Service**' and to Jim for digging, analysis and statistical assistance. PP Peter Evans, our club Photographer, and to PP Ken Hunt, Joan Liuzzi, Hilary Hamilton, PP Finbar Ambrose, PDG Horner Beckett and many others for providing photographs. PP Frank Tate and PDG Horner Beckett for allowing me to catch a glimpse of what the club was like in the nineteen forties and fifties and to Horner for his wonderful Rotary memorabilia.
PP Alan King for information on the foundation of the Inner Wheel Club, Probus and the club's Jubilee celebrations.
PP Michael Larkin and Liam Yendole for an insight into the Pattaya project and to Michael for information regarding his trip to the U.S.
PDG John D. Carroll for the material that he supplied in connection with his year as District Governor.
Rotarian Kenneth Carroll for the original Interact club's Minute Book.
ADG Ted Corcoran for information with regard to Toastmasters International and Rotarian Donald Gordon for information of the life and death of his maternal grandfather, Edward Murphy. To Senator Brian Hillery and PP Paul Loughlin a thank you for sharing with me their experiences as Scholarship students and to Rotarian Derek

Griffith for putting me in touch with Brian. And to Rotarian Peter McGonigal for information on time that he and his wife, Kate, spent in Kenya as volunteers. Thank you to Ally Lett of Actons Solicitors for her help in scanning photographs.

I would like to thank the members of the Rotary Club, Dublin for giving me the opportunity of writing this book and to President Elect Mark Doyle and Actons Solicitors for sponsoring the printing costs of the book.

I would like to thank the staff of the National Library Kildare street and the Dublin City Archives for all their assistance and helpful suggestions.

And lastly a thank you to those members of the Rotary Club, Dublin and their companies who sponsored the writing of this book and thus allowed me to take a year out of my life to write it.

Contents

Glossary iii
Acknowledgements iv
Foreword vii
Preface viii
Chapter One - Paul Percy Harris 1
Chapter Two - The First Clubs 7
Chapter Three - Dublin 1911 18
Chapter Four - Dublin Club 25
Chapter Five - Morrow Goes North 35
Chapter Six - Paul Harris Letter 43
Chapter Seven - War 55
Chapter Eight - 1915/16 67
Chapter Nine - Easter Rising 74
Chapter Ten - Changing Times 85
Chapter Eleven - Turbulent Years 95
Chapter Twelve - Paul Harris Calls 109
Chapter Thirteen - Emergency 123
Chapter Fourteen - Toasts, Stones and Stamps 135
Chapter Fifteen - Golden Jubilee 147
Chapter Sixteen - Community Service 160
Chapter Seventeen - 75th Anniversary 171
Chapter Eighteen - Polio Plus 181
Chapter Nineteen - New Millennium 188
Chapter Twenty - Future 196
Appendix One - Presidents, Hon. Secretaries, Hon Treasurers . 198
Appendix Two - District Governors 203
Appendix Three - Original Constitution 206
Appendix Four - Paul Harris Fellows 212
Appendix Five - Ambassadorial Scholars 214
Appendix Six - Mellow Memories 215
Appendix Seven - Presidential Memories 228
Appendix Eight - Inner Wheel Presidents 239
Appendix Nine - Luncheon Venues 241
Bibliography 242

Foreword

Knowledge of Rotary by the general public is sparse, at the best of times. Many confuse us with other organisations that are more secretive and exclusive while others have an inaccurate idea of the type of work that we undertake. This book is an attempt to explain the origins of the Rotary Club, Dublin and to detail the service that their members have given to the community at home and abroad since 1911. It is set against the background of a society that has changed radically while the need to support those who are less well off is constantly here.

For any group to survive and thrive for one hundred years they must be doing something right. In February 1911, we were the first to raise the Rotary banner on this side of the Atlantic when just thirty-four men came together, not necessarily for the most altruistic of reasons. Since then we have gone about our work quietly and unobtrusively and have seen the Rotary movement expand until today there are seventy-six Rotary clubs throughout Ireland and thirty-two thousand worldwide with one and a quarter million members providing service. While we have not always succeeded, we have myriad achievements to our name where Rotarians, men and women, have decided to give something back to society by identifying needs, and by giving their time and raising funds have contributed to alleviating them.

I hope that in reading this book you will have a better idea of how Rotary began, matured and developed into the strong and vibrant organisation that it is today.

Randal Nelson Gray
President
Rotary Club Dublin

Preface

Rotary is a worldwide organisation in which men and women come together in friendship to provide service to the community at home and abroad. In 2011 the Rotary Club, Dublin celebrates its centenary and this book seeks to show how we provided this service in the context of the changing political, business and social conditions of the past one hundred years. Service can mean many different things. It can mean providing money to support worthwhile projects, it can be the giving of one's time and expertise or it can be the provision of a platform for speakers to explore how society can move forward in its harmony and diversity.

At his District Conference in 1983 our member John D. Carroll who was District Governor that year spoke about the difficult times that come to us all during our lives.

There can come a day for every man when his foundations are shaken and the world is dark and there seems nothing to live for, but when everything else is gone the sense of duty remains. The value of a person lies not in their social status but in their efficiency. The true value lies in the contribution a person can make to their community. The true aristocracy lies not in lineage but in service. All social claims are valueless and baseless unless they are backed by usefulness to the general community. The important thing about any person is not their ancestry but their potential for the future'.

Our club has survived and thrived through two world wars, an insurrection in our own city, a War of Independence and a Civil War and a vastly changed political landscape. Our Rotary District, the island of Ireland, has maintained its unity in difficult circumstances, largely through the friendships that were made and developed between Rotarians north and south.

Following the example of one of our daughter clubs, the Rotary Club of Cork who began this project in 2001, the Dublin Rotary Club launched its first Remembrance Tree at Christmas 2009. Situated inside the north entrance to Dundrum Town Centre, it was manned for a week by an intrepid band of freezing cold volunteers led by Peter McGonigal (Dentistry) and his team. At the beginning, we were not too clear on the idea behind the tree but Peter explained it to us: it gave an opportunity for people to remember their loved ones by inscribing their names and a message on a ribbon that was attached to the base of the tree.

When we began we had no idea as to whether or not the public would respond positively to this rather, for us, unique idea. We should not have worried. From early morning until late at night on the week before Christmas a steady stream of people remembered their loved ones. It was an uplifting and humbling experience to be a conduit for so many thousands to express their love for another person.

Conscious of the effect of the recession on our fellow citizens we designated the Society of Saint Vincent de Paul as our sole charity and over the week we collected over €16,000 for this most worthwhile cause. Over thirty members and their families gave of their time to make this project such a success. The duty roster compiled by Brian George (Packaged Food Distribution) was a work of art in itself and despite lively and good-natured competition from sundry choirs, a train and a very cold wind all who took part felt refreshed and ready for the Christmas festivities.

In January, the ribbons were gathered together and blessed at an Ecumenical Service in the Wesley College Chapel attended by many of those who had taken part in the project.

Although over two hundred man/woman hours are required to make this project work we are committed to repeating it in the coming year. We can only hope for improved weather next Christmas.

The first Rotarians (from left): Silvester Schiele, Paul Harris (pointing to book), Hiram E. Storey and Gustavus H. Loehr.

William Stuart Morrow Organising Secretary of the Dublin, Belfast, Glasgow, Edinburgh, Liverpool and Birmingham Rotary clubs.

William (Bill) McConnell, Stuart Morrow's brother-in-law – founder member, president and honorary secretary, of the Rotary Club, Dublin.

Chapter One

Paul Percy Harris

'Work hard and live honourably' Pamela Harris

Our story begins in the small town of Racine, Wisconsin on the 19th day of April 1868. That day, the second child of George H Harris and Cornelia Harris (nee Bryan) was born. He was christened Paul Percy. George H Harris was not a native of Racine but came from Wallingford, Vermont. He had settled in Racine, in 1864, when he married Cornelia whose father, a lawyer, was one of the leading citizens of Racine and its second Mayor.

George ran a drug store in Racine that had been financed by his own father. George was a man whose ideas and aspirations for himself and his family were in constant conflict with his ability to carry them through to fruition. Eventually George's father's patience and money ran out, the business closed and the young family was split apart. George took Paul, then aged three, and his five-year-old brother Cecil back to his Vermont home. In his biography "*My Road to Rotary: The story of a boy,* a *Vermont community and Rotary*" published in 1948 Paul Harris remembers vividly, stepping off the train in Wallingford and meeting his paternal grandfather, Howard, for the first time. 'The tall man took my clenched fist in his warm, strong hand, which was ever so much larger than father's, with enormous thumbs that made excellent handles for little boys to hold onto'. They walked the short distance to the Harris home where he met his grandmother Pamela, 'a dark-eyed elderly lady, who weighed precisely 89 pounds, never more, never less'.

Paul's father, George, soon headed off following his dreams and from then on Paul considered the Vermont home of his grandparents as his. In later years he spoke of the frugal work ethic of Grandfather Howard and how he exhibited the same tolerance and friendship to the lone Jewish and Roman Catholic families in the village as to his own co-religionists. His grandmother was warm and loving and the first to prepare hot meals and freshly baked bread if another family was in need. The example that he got from observing his grandfather and grandmother was to be an important factor in forming his character.

Paul, was his father's son and he liked to roam the countryside around Wallingford, catching trout, climbing mountains and with his friends engaging in practical jokes and escapades. One evening he exited the house after his nine o'clock bedtime and with a couple of friends rode the cowcatcher on the front of the Wallingford train to nearby Manchester and back. They all remained unscathed but it was a very dangerous activity about which his grandparents knew nothing. Although he had a serious side to his personality, japes, jokes and pranks were always part of his later life.

Paul was an average student and attended the local Wallingford school that is today dedicated to his name. As he grew older his grandfather realised that he would have to provide for the boy's education as this was beyond the capability of his parents. George and Cornelia had attempted to bring the family together but, despite his best efforts, George was unable to hold down a steady job and they had drifted apart again.

Howard enrolled Paul in the Black River Academy but his high spirits did not endear him to its President. Soon after his arrival 'the President of the Academy took an inventory of the good and the bad in me, and concluded that there was insufficient of the good to justify any attempt at salvage'. His grandparents then sent Paul to Vermont Military Academy whose more disciplined approach ensured that Paul knuckled down to his studies and in 1886 he earned admission to the University of Vermont. Eighteen months later disaster struck when he was wrongly accused of misconduct and expelled. Although many years later the University apologised and absolved him from any wrongdoing, this must have had a devastating effect on Paul and his grandparents. However, he managed to bounce back from this calamity and got himself admitted to the prestigious Princeton University in New Jersey where he did well academically. A telegram announcing that his grandfather Howard had been taken ill brought him home in mid-term. Although he had rushed to Wallingford by train immediately on getting word of the illness, he was too late and his grandfather Howard had died before he arrived home.

The loss of his beloved grandfather had a profound effect on Paul and he dropped out of Princeton and took a menial job sweeping floors and cleaning furnaces in the Sheldon Marble Company in nearby Rutland. The work ethic that his grandfather had instilled in him was soon noticed by his boss and he was promoted but it took a year of mourning and thinking about his future before he was ready to move on to the next stage of his life. In a heart to heart talk with his grandmother, Pamela, she reminded him of the high hopes that Howard had had for Paul's own father and how they had been dashed. She went on to tell him how her late husband had seen greatness in his grandson. 'Work hard and live honourably for your grandfather's sake', she concluded. Just over a year later his grandmother Pamela passed away in her sleep.

These words of his Grandmother galvanised Paul into action and in 1889 he enrolled in the University of Iowa Law School in Des Moines. En-route from Vermont he had to change trains in Chicago and he was so impressed by the bustling city that he stayed on for a week. Paul studied hard at Iowa and in 1891 he graduated with a degree in law. At Vermont, Princeton and Iowa Universities Paul made many friends and he kept in touch with them over the intervening years. This network of friends and acquaintances was to be invaluable to him in later years. In 1891 he was a young man setting out on his new career - or was he?

The keynote speaker at his graduation, a respected lawyer who had graduated from Iowa a decade before, recommended that any young lawyer should head for a small town, find his feet and enjoy himself before coming back to the big city and deciding in which area of law he would specialise. This advice made a big impression on Paul and no doubt reinforced by the wanderlust genes of his father, George, he set off on a great adventure.

Firstly, he went to the North Western United States where he hunted and fished until his money ran out. Then he headed for San Francisco where he took a job as a reporter on the Chronicle. A few months later he was picking fruit in Southern California, followed by a teaching position in a Los Angeles Business College, followed by a stint as a night clerk in a hotel on the other side of the United States in Jacksonville, Florida. Whilst there he met George C. Clerk who owned a marble and granite company. They were to remain friends for life. George immediately saw potential in Paul as a salesman and made him a very tempting job offer.

Paul was not yet ready to settle down and set off for Washington D.C., Kentucky and Pennsylvania taking odd jobs as he went. In Philadelphia he noticed an advertisement looking for 'hands on' a cattle boat and the next day he was on board with Liverpool as his destination. It was a totally frightful experience with the conditions and food for the cattle on a par with those of the crew. What was even worse was the fact that when the boat got to Liverpool he had only a day in which to see the city before the voyage back to the United States began. Notwithstanding his experiences, on his return to Philadelphia he immediately found another ship going to England and joined the crew. This was a much more pleasant voyage and after they docked in London, he had ample opportunity to see the British capital, an experience he never forgot. Writing afterwards about travel he commented, 'Travel is a good correction for mental near-sightedness, if the traveller sets aside his prejudices.'

Paul arrived back in the United States in 1893 and immediately took the Exposition Flyer for Chicago to see the World Fair. Originally set to open the previous year to coincide with the 400th Anniversary of Christopher Columbus' discovery of the New World, the Fair was postponed for a year due to the immense construction task involved. Costing $28 million, it was attended by around 27 million people and featured such astounding sights as overhead railways, moving pavements and electrically powered boats traversing the many lakes. It was a showcase for the unfolding American Consumer Society and in addition to many industrial and cultural exhibits; the major focus was on a bewildering display of the latest consumer goods.

The Fair and Chicago in general made a great impression on Paul and it was during this visit that he decided that when his time for exploration and wandering was over that he would make his home in Chicago.

However, he was not ready to settle down just yet. Off he went to New Orleans and got a job picking oranges. In October of 1893 a tidal wave struck the city inundating vast tracts of land and drowning thousands of people. Paul was involved in the rescue operations and many years later he wrote, ' 'Although years have elapsed, the suffering and horror of that night still remains in my memory'.

He then returned to Jacksonville and finally took up the offer of a job from his friend George C. Clerk selling marble and granite. The attraction of this position was threefold. Firstly, it afforded Paul the opportunity for travel as his sales territory covered the southern states of the United States, the Bahamas and Cuba. Secondly, it involved meeting people of every creed and colour and learning about how they lived. And thirdly, it was an opportunity for him to save some money to provide capital for his ultimate ambition of a legal career. He had sold marble and granite for two years and when his five years of wandering was over he informed his friend who ran the business that he intended to go to Chicago and begin his law practice. Despite protestations to the contrary from his employer he persevered with his purpose and in February 1896 he arrived back to Chicago, rented a small office and obtained a licence to practise law in Illinois.

It took Paul a while to build up his legal practice but gradually he began to represent victims of embezzlement, bankruptcy and fraud. He joined the Chicago Association of Commerce and while he met many people he found it difficult to develop friendships among them. His inquiring spirit led him to the unusual practice of eating in different ethnic restaurants on successive evenings. In doing so he experienced the cultural diversities of the Indian, Hungarian, Italian, German, Greek and Chinese communities in the melting pot that was Chicago. He also began to frequent different denominational services each Sunday and learned about the various belief systems of his fellow citizens.

In 1900 a simple event took place that was to have a profound effect on Paul Harris and, subsequently, on many other men and women throughout the world. A fellow attorney, Bob Frank, invited him to dinner in his suburban home and after the meal, both men strolled down the principal street of the suburb. As Bob passed each shop he exchanged greetings with the owners and it became obvious to Paul that each knew each other both as business people and friends. It also became apparent that they had many business concerns in common and that they assisted one another both on a business and on a personal level. This was a real revelation to Paul. This was the sort of camaraderie he had experienced in Vermont and now he saw it in practice in a suburb of Chicago. Over the next number of years he often thought about this phenomenon and wondered how he could replicate it in the city environment.

Chapter Two

The First Clubs

'I have struck a city – a real city – and they call it Chicago. The other places don't count. Having seen it, I urgently desire never to see it again. It is inhabited by savages'. Rudyard Kipling

Chicago in the opening years of the 20th century was a bustling city of over a million and a half people second only to New York in size. Originally built largely of wood on what was effectively a swamp on the shores of Lake Michigan, the Great Fire of 1871 had allowed for a complete re-building. Added to this was the impetus given by the 1893 World Fair and Chicago's unique geographical position. It was the terminus of the newly built Union Pacific Railway and the city that provided the most convenient gateway to a Wild West that was gradually being tamed. Stockyards thronged by tens of thousands of cattle, abattoirs, rendering plants and offal polluted the environment to such an extent that the stench of hydrogen sulphide gas was everywhere. It was also the city where work could be found and it was to Chicago that waves of emigrants went from Central and Eastern Europe, in particular. Tens of thousands of men, women and children flocked there for the promise of a golden future.

Giant skyscrapers were being built alongside the most degraded tenements. Christian, Moslem and Jewish congregations flourished cheek by jowl with bars and brothels. Muggings and murder were commonplace as was trade, commerce, corruption and politics. Courageous lawyers like Clarence Darrow fought corruption at every level and many like-minded men and women supported him. Chicago was a melting pot of humanity in all its most sublime and degrading aspects.

It was popularly known as the Windy City not because of any meteorological phenomenon, but because its citizens were renowned for their propensity to talk endlessly on any subject under the sun. There were clubs to cater for a complete range of special interests including sporting, trade, religious, union affiliations, ethnic groups and political parties. Although these institutions existed, it was considered not to be the done thing to utilise membership of such clubs to promote business interests. No doubt business was done between members but it would have been done privately between members, not overtly.

By 1905 Paul Harris had built up his legal practice to such an extent that he had a steady stream of clients. One such client was Silvester Schiele, a coal merchant, for whom Paul had collected some bad debts. From time to time they talked and Silvester shared with Paul reminiscences from his youth in rural Indiana. Paul found a resonance with his own youthful experiences in Vermont, particularly with regard to the community spirit and neighbourliness of the people. They talked about how this spirit could be transferred into Chicago and they considered the business advantages that could accrue if a number of men could come together in friendship to their mutual advantage.

In the late afternoon of Thursday February 23rd 1905 the two men dined together in Madame Galli's Italian restaurant and again mulled over the idea of a friendship and business booster club. They had shared their notion with a mutual business acquaintance Gustavus H. Loehr, a mining engineer, who was so enthusiastic that he had invited them to his office to discuss the matter further. So, that evening Paul Harris a lawyer, Silvester Schiele a coal merchant and Gustavus H. Loehr a mining engineer, met in Loehr's office on the seventh floor of the Unity Building at 127 Dearborn Street. Hiram Storey a merchant tailor and a friend of Loehr's joined them. It was a small room with a single bulb, a desk, some uncomfortable chairs, a coat rack in the corner and an engineering chart on the wall.

The four men talked about their family and business backgrounds and they shared experiences of what it was like to be doing business in

Chicago. Paul spoke of the emptiness that he found in having no true friends in the city, his indignation at the cutthroat business practices and the lack of trust in business and commercial life. He proposed that they form a club that would have at its centre, friendship and mutual co-operation in business. It would be different from other clubs in that just one man from each recognised business or profession would be a member and an existing member would vouch for their integrity.

The next day Paul met Harry Ruggles, a young printer whom he used in his legal practice and told him about the meeting the previous evening. Harry was very enthusiastic about the idea and became the, yet unnamed Club's, fifth member. The second meeting[1] was held in Paul's office and the original four were joined by Harry Ruggles, Bill Jensen a real estate broker and Al White an organ manufacturer.

Silvester Schiele hosted the third meeting on March 23rd at his coal yard office and there were fifteen men present. This was, in effect, the first business meeting of the new organisation in that it considered matters that are still part of our Rotary heritage today.

The first item that they discussed was by what name should the Club be known. Many suggestions were made reflecting the friendship, business and geographical standing of their new venture. These included Windy City Roundup, Chicago Fellowship, Chicago Circle, the Lake Club, Chicago Civic Club, Booster Club, Friends in Business, Men with Friends, the FFF (Food, Fun and Fellowship) and the Trade and Talk Club. Other suggestions included the Blue Boys, the Conspirators, and the Round Table. All had their adherents but none a majority. Paul Harris proposed that, because of their practice of rotating their meetings between the offices of the different members, they should be called the Rotation Club. After more discussion this was refined to Rotary Club and this name received unanimous approval.

It was further decided that there should be no dues: any expenses should be met from fines on members for such misdemeanours as missing a meeting. To miss four meetings in a row would result in loss of membership. Membership was to be for one year only and could only be renewed by a vote of 75% of the other members. A single negative vote from an existing member would prevent a new member joining. All members were to be known by their first name and anyone using the appellation of 'Mister' would incur a fine. A Board of Directors was then elected with Silvester Schiele as President, Paul Harris having declined the position. He preferred to work on the business of attracting new members. By October 1905 when Harry Ruggles printed the first Roster the Club had thirty members. A little more than a year later it had eighty.

For the next couple of years the Chicago Rotary Club met for dinner in various hotels and conducted business afterwards in often over crowded bedrooms with members perched on radiators, beds and uncomfortable chairs. Apart from the friendship, the most important part of the Club's business was reciprocal business arrangements between members. The most important officer was the Club Statistician whose task it was to record business deals between members, having received details by postcard. He made a report to each Club meeting. In fact the Club's Constitution adopted in 1905 included just two Objects. These were:

The promotion of the business interests of its members.
The promotion of good fellowship and other desiderata ordinarily incident to social clubs.

By 1907 when Paul Harris took on the Presidency, the Club had settled into the Sherman Hotel and except for a period when it was being renovated this remained their venue. Having decided on a permanent meeting place the issue of the name arose again and there was pressure to alter it to a Booster Club. This attempt was defeated and the Rotary name has remained to this day.

Around this time also, scattered press reports began to appear castigating members of the Chicago Club for, in effect, organising a closed shop trade system among themselves. Paul Harris himself had been thinking about how the Club could contribute to the welfare of the citizens and he used this negative publicity to suggest that they should be involved in doing some good in the community. In 1906 a patent attorney by the name of Donald Carter had joined and he had a vision that the Club should ' do something of some benefit to the people apart from its own members'. The following year, with Paul Harris' support, he persuaded its members to adopt a third Object. This was:

The advancement of the best interests of Chicago and the spreading of the spirit of civic pride and loyalty among its citizens.

Following on from this the Club identified the lack of a public convenience in the city. Despite the opposition of many storekeepers who charged for the use of their restrooms they were instrumental in having such a facility installed. This was followed up by helping disadvantaged children, packing food parcels and delivering them to impoverished slum dwellers. Thus, Community Service was born.

By 1908 the Chicago Club was prospering. It was now a registered non-profit corporation, had 140 members who had gained significantly from their membership and was becoming a potent force for good in its own city. But Paul Harris' restless mind still was not easy.

'Why', he thought to himself, 'could not the idea be also taken up in New York or even Jacksonville where his friend George C. Clark was in business'.

When he floated this idea to members of the Chicago Club, he got a very cool reception. They had joined to have a bit of fun, to increase their turnover and later on to do some good in their native city. What had they got to do with places most had never even seen? Any such venture would cost money and would likely end in failure.

Quietly, in his own way, Paul bided his time. It happened that a young salesman friend of his, Manuel Manoz, was being sent to San Francisco on a business trip. Paul told him about how Rotary operated in Chicago and asked him to sound out businessmen in San Francisco about the idea of starting a club in that city. What appeared to have been a casual request changed the face of Rotary forever.

When Manuel Manoz arrived in his hotel in San Francisco he spent the first evening in the foyer planning his schedule of calls for the next day. The city was still rebuilding after the disastrous earthquake of two years previously and he naturally asked the man sitting across from him for some directions. This man turned out to be Homer Wood, a local attorney. After obtaining the directions that he required, the conversation turned naturally to one another's business and personal lives. Manuel remembered Paul Harris' request regarding spreading the Rotary message, told Homer about the way the Chicago Club operated and the great business advantages to be derived from membership. Homer Wood was very interested and at Manuel's prompting he wrote to Paul Harris in Chicago.

Paul was delighted to get word from the West Coast. He sent Homer a copy of the Chicago Constitution and other relevant documents. After further correspondence Homer called a meeting of some five friends in his office and they firmly embraced the idea of founding a Rotary Club in their city. The new Club was launched at a Banquet in the Saint Francis Hotel on the 12th November 1908 attended by many leading San Franscisco citizens including General M. H. de Young, the publisher of the Chronicle. Hardly had the Banquet begun than Homer heard that Charles M Schwab, America's most prominent steel magnate, was dining in another part of the hotel. He immediately went and spoke to Schwab, acquainted him with what was happening in another part of the same establishment and invited him to address the gathering. Schwab agreed and made an inspiring speech. The next day's Chronicle featured the story of the new Rotary Club and their inspirational speaker. Homer, who had been elected President, bought up 1,000 copies of the newspaper and sent them on to Paul Harris in Chicago to be used as promotional material to help spread the idea of Rotary to other cities throughout the United States.

Within a month Homer had started a club across the bay in Oakland and the following year, following on from a business trip he made to Seattle, a club was founded there.

Chapter One

Paul Percy Harris

'Work hard and live honourably' Pamela Harris

Our story begins in the small town of Racine, Wisconsin on the 19th day of April 1868. That day, the second child of George H Harris and Cornelia Harris (nee Bryan) was born. He was christened Paul Percy. George H Harris was not a native of Racine but came from Wallingford, Vermont. He had settled in Racine, in 1864, when he married Cornelia whose father, a lawyer, was one of the leading citizens of Racine and its second Mayor.

George ran a drug store in Racine that had been financed by his own father. George was a man whose ideas and aspirations for himself and his family were in constant conflict with his ability to carry them through to fruition. Eventually George's father's patience and money ran out, the business closed and the young family was split apart. George took Paul, then aged three, and his five-year-old brother Cecil back to his Vermont home. In his biography "*My Road to Rotary: The story of a boy, a Vermont community and Rotary*" published in 1948 Paul Harris remembers vividly, stepping off the train in Wallingford and meeting his paternal grandfather, Howard, for the first time. 'The tall man took my clenched fist in his warm, strong hand, which was ever so much larger than father's, with enormous thumbs that made excellent handles for little boys to hold onto'. They walked the short distance to the Harris home where he met his grandmother Pamela, 'a dark-eyed elderly lady, who weighed precisely 89 pounds, never more, never less'.

Paul's father, George, soon headed off following his dreams and from then on Paul considered the Vermont home of his grandparents as his. In later years he spoke of the frugal work ethic of Grandfather Howard and how he exhibited the same tolerance and friendship to the lone Jewish and Roman Catholic families in the village as to his own co-religionists. His grandmother was warm and loving and the first to prepare hot meals and freshly baked bread if another family was in need. The example that he got from observing his grandfather and grandmother was to be an important factor in forming his character.

Paul, was his father's son and he liked to roam the countryside around Wallingford, catching trout, climbing mountains and with his friends engaging in practical jokes and escapades. One evening he exited the house after his nine o'clock bedtime and with a couple of friends rode the cowcatcher on the front of the Wallingford train to nearby Manchester and back. They all remained unscathed but it was a very dangerous activity about which his grandparents knew nothing. Although he had a serious side to his personality, japes, jokes and pranks were always part of his later life.

Paul was an average student and attended the local Wallingford school that is today dedicated to his name. As he grew older his grandfather realised that he would have to provide for the boy's education as this was beyond the capability of his parents. George and Cornelia had attempted to bring the family together but, despite his best efforts, George was unable to hold down a steady job and they had drifted apart again.

Howard enrolled Paul in the Black River Academy but his high spirits did not endear him to its President. Soon after his arrival 'the President of the Academy took an inventory of the good and the bad in me, and concluded that there was insufficient of the good to justify any attempt at salvage'. His grandparents then sent Paul to Vermont Military Academy whose more disciplined approach ensured that Paul knuckled down to his studies and in 1886 he earned admission to the University of Vermont. Eighteen months later disaster struck when he was wrongly accused of misconduct and expelled. Although many years later the University apologised and absolved him from any wrongdoing, this must have had a devastating effect on Paul and his grandparents. However, he managed to bounce back from this calamity

Meanwhile back in Chicago a very significant man in the history and the spread of the Rotary message had joined the Club. Chesley R. Perry, born in 1872, came from a completely different background from Paul Harris. He was a Chicago City boy, born and bred. He had enlisted in the Illinois National Guard at the outbreak of the Spanish American war and had seen service in Cuba, attained the rank of captain and had become fluent in Spanish. He had also acted as a war correspondent for the Chicago Times-Herald. After the war he had worked in the local library and then in business. He had a good business sense and many of his investments had paid off handsomely. By 1908 he was working with a cement-brick machinery manufacturer and, through his friend Harry Ruggles, was introduced to the Chicago Club. On the same evening Arthur Sheldon who had founded a 'School of Scientific Salesmanship' and who coined many of Rotary's early slogans, also joined. It soon became obvious to all that Chesley Perry's skills lay in his organisational abilities.

However all was not well in the Los Angeles area. The Los Angeles Club had been formed from San Francisco in the same manner that San Francisco itself had been founded. The difference was that the two prime movers, Walton Wood and Irwin Muma, did not have the time out of their busy business lives to continue the work of canvassing for members. They employed Hiram C. Quick, a professional organiser, who was as good as his name. He knew every manager and proprietor and he built up the membership rapidly. For reasons that are unknown, differences arose between Quick and the Los Angeles Club Board and he was fired. Quick, however, discovered that the Los Angeles Club had not registered their name with the California Secretary of State and thus, officially, did not exist. He registered the name 'National Rotary Club' and proceeded to canvas for members. Unsurprisingly, given his talents he was very successful and soon there were two competing clubs in the same city. Although relations between them were less than harmonious Quick was doing very well financially. He then tried to repeat the registration idea in Seattle but the Rotarians there were tipped off by San Francisco and managed to get their own club registration in before him. Soon after that he had a disagreement with the Board of the Los Angeles Club that he had founded and was sacked and never heard of again. The two rival clubs agreed to merge in 1912 and, with three hundred members, became the largest in the country.

Following the foundation of the San Francisco Club, Los Angeles and the other clubs on the West Coast the Chicago Club had, whether they liked it or not, to embrace the idea that the Rotary movement was beginning to have a life of its own. If they were to have any influence on its development they were going to have to become involved in how and where it would spread. Soon after he joined, Chesley Perry was appointed Extension Officer and after a hard day's work he would go to Paul Harris' office and they would work together for many hours corresponding with and assisting the foundation of Rotary Clubs right across the United States.

By 1910 there were sixteen Rotary Clubs in the United States and Chesley Perry decided that it would be a good idea to have a Convention to cement the bonds between the clubs and chart a way forward for the burgeoning movement. Sixty delegates registered from fourteen Clubs with one delegate per fifty members. When you included wives and guests over one hundred and fifty turned up for the event. The members of Chicago laid on red carpet treatment for all their visitors. They were met at the railway station and ferried in open-top cars to their hotels. Banquets were held and the delegates worked hard at laying down a foundation for the growing Rotary movement.

Topics discussed included: social activities, membership qualification and growth, dues, business reciprocity between members, an emblem, compensation for officers (many clubs paid their secretaries a percentage of the membership dues), population of cities eligible for a Rotary Club and the number of Clubs that a city might support.

At the first meeting presided over by Paul Harris, Chesley Perry was elected Chairman. It was then decided to form the National Association of Rotary Clubs and a Board of Directors was appointed. At the conclusion of the first Convention the Board of Directors met and appointed Perry as its General Secretary, a post that he was to hold for the next thirty–two years. A platform had been created to facilitate the spread of the Rotary idea.

The following year the Convention was held in Portland, Oregon. They decided to set five objectives for the fledging organisation to replace the three that the Chicago Club had formulated. These were:

- To organise new clubs.
- To promote the common good of all clubs.
- To encourage civic pride and loyalty.
- To promote honourable business methods.
- To advance the business interests of individual members.

Paul Harris also engineered the abolition of the post of Statistician. He saw this move as the beginning of a shift away from self to service. At the conclusion of the Convention he stepped down as President and agreed to accept the title of President Emeritus.

The Portland delegates also decided that a Rotary magazine was needed. Perry was instructed to set about publishing such a magazine. Unfortunately for Perry they only voted a levy of 25 cent per member to fund the project and he was left acting as Editor, Advertising Salesman and Publisher of the new venture.

When the 'Rotarian' began to be published monthly in 1912 Chesley Perry emphasised the shift to service by publicising club projects throughout the United States. These included:

The Los Angeles Club giving Christmas gifts to 15,000 needy people.
The Portland, Oregon Club exposing corruption
The Lincoln, Nebraska Club funding a local hospital.

The move towards being a service organisation for the Community had begun. Even so Clubs valued their independence and it was some years before there was a uniformity of purpose in this regard.

Meanwhile on the West Coast, William Stuart Morrow, a native of Dublin City, was an early member of the San Francisco Club. Born on February 20th 1856, Morrow was baptised in the Ormond Quay Presbyterian Church on May 4th of that year. His parents were Robert and Margaret Morrow (nee Barnes) and at that time they were living at

12 Westland Row. He was educated at the Royal School Armagh and had graduated from Trinity College Dublin in 1876 with a Senior Moderatorship and a Gold Medal for Logic and Ethics. Following graduation he had enrolled as a law student in the Middle Temple in London but a failure of his eyesight prevented him from continuing his work at the Bar. He returned to Dublin where his father Robert operated a business as booksellers, stationers and circulating librarians on the corner of Nassau and South Frederick Streets. Morrow began to make his way in the commercial life of the city and was the youngest person to have been appointed a Justice of the Peace. In 1887 he was a member of the Executive Committee of the Queen's Jubilee Citizens Committee formed to mark the fiftieth anniversary of the accession, in 1837, of Queen Victoria to the British throne. He is listed in the Thoms Directory of that year as living at 15 Charleville Road, off the North Circular Road with his business address given as South Frederick Street. Morrow married Alice Mary Parker in St. Mary's Church of Ireland church in Limerick on the 23rd of November 1887 and according to the 1911 census he was the father of three children. Over the next twenty years he appears to have spent a considerable amount of time in the United States although there is evidence that he travelled back to Ireland on a number of occasions. The SS Baltic's manifest has him travelling from Liverpool to the U.S in 1905 as an American citizen with an address at 2067 Central Avenue Allandar(maybe Almeda) California. His classification in the San Francisco Club was 'Law and Collections'. In late 1910, following on the dissolution of his business partnership, he returned to his native Dublin.

Meanwhile, the Rotary movement had spread across the border to Canada with the formation of the Winnipeg Club and Paul Harris had plans to found the first club outside of North America in London. The Chairman of the Extension Committee who succeeded Chesley Perry was Harvey C. Wheeler of Initial Services Ltd. His London associate was Arthur Bigelow to whom Harvey described the idea and benefits of Rotary. Arthur undertook to call together a meeting of business acquaintances and told them about Rotary and how it had spread through North America. There was agreement to form a Club in London and the inaugural Dinner took place on August 3rd 1911.

London received its charter in August 1912. As far as Paul Harris and the Extension Committee were concerned this was the first Club to be formed outside of North America, but they had not taken into account, nor even known about William Stuart Morrow. They were soon to discover the special talents and energy of this remarkable Irishman.

[1] *Rotary Histories are silent on what precisely was discussed at, what are considered to be, the first two meetings of the Chicago Club. It is likely that no Minutes were kept until the third meeting in Silvester Schiele's coalyard.*

[2] ***A Century of Service****: the story of Rotary International by David C Forward*

[3] ***The Hub of the Wheel****: The story of the Rotary Movement in Ireland District 1160 (earlier 16) compiled by Terence S Duncan A.C.I.I., F.C.I.B.*

Chapter Three

Dublin 1911

OBEDIENTIA CIVIUM URBIS FELICITAS

(Obedient citizens make for a happy city)
Motto of Dublin City

William Stuart Morrow returned to a city with a population of 375,000 most of whom lived between the Royal Canal north of the city and the Grand Canal in the south. In the latter half of the nineteenth century suburbs outside of the ring provided by the canals had begun to emerge. North of the River Liffey these were largely in Drumcondra and along the shore of Dublin Bay through Fairview. South of the river Ballsbridge, Donnybrook, Ranelagh, Rathmines, Rathgar and Terenure began to be developed.

Dublin had been the administrative Capital of Ireland since British rule was imposed following the Norman invasion in 1169. Thanks to Henry Grattan backed by the Volunteer movement, during the latter half of the 18th century, its Parliament based in Dublin's College Green had been able to exercise greater authority vis a vis its Westminster counterpart. Dublin had become a fashionable place to live and the Irish aristocracy of the time had invested heavily in real estate to provide themselves with suitable accommodation in the capital. In the second half of the 18th century great squares such as Rutland (Parnell) Square, north of the river, Merrion and Fitzwilliam Squares to the south, provided town houses for the nobility and gentry. The decision of the Duke of Leinster in 1745 to situate his Dublin residence south of the river shifted the centre of gravity of the city southward. In 1801 the Irish Parliament was abolished following the Act of Union. One effect of this was to shift the focus away from Dublin to London and the nineteenth century, in contrast to the eighteenth, was a period of decline for the city. Many of the grand houses fell into disrepair and, particularly north of the river Liffey, were converted ultimately into one room tenement accommodation. By 1911 there were 5,000 one-room dwellings in Dublin with up to fifteen persons in each.

By the nineteenth century also, Dublin had become a major port. Up to that time a sand bar at its entrance had inhibited larger vessels from entering. Goods had had to be transported overland from firstly Dalkey Sound and latterly Howth. The building of the South and North Walls and quays enabled much larger vessels to dock. Alexandra Basin was completed in the opening years of the 20th century. The first railway in Ireland was opened in 1834 linking Dublin and Kingstown (Dun Laoghaire). Thereafter railways were built throughout the whole of Ireland. By 1911 there was 3,500 miles of track linking the capital and its port to every corner of the country.

The existence of this transport system ensured that most of Ireland's exports and imports passed through Dublin Port. In 1911, exports were largely of the food and beverage variety. Nearly one million live cattle and horses were exported that year, with many of these being herded by drovers through the city streets to the docks. Food and other agricultural products, porter, whiskey and processed tobacco made up the rest of the total. Imports included coal and fuel, grains, machinery, household goods and raw tobacco.

The internal transport system in Dublin was largely based on the tram. In 1911 there were three hundred trams operating on sixty miles of track radiating from Sackville Street. The tracks were built into the roads and provided a good and efficient service connecting the suburbs with the city centre. Suburban trains ran to Howth on the North side and Bray and Greystones on the South. There was an additional line linking Harcourt Street with Bray through Dundrum.

There was very little manufacturing industry in Dublin, in contrast to Belfast that was rapidly developed in the nineteenth century as the manufacturing and shipbuilding capital of Ireland. Manufacturing capacity in Dublin was largely confined to brewing, distilling, biscuit and mineral water manufacturing, building and locomotive engineering. Outside of these sectors retail, commercial, medical, law, central and local administration provided the principal employment in the City.

In 1911 there were, for instance, 3,500 persons employed as civil and public servants in central and local administration. Those employed in the sectors mentioned above were the lucky ones. Tens of thousand of the lower classes were simply unemployed or eked out a living as casual labourers and others, mostly female, acted as servants to the middle classes.

Local administration was centred on the City Hall. Pembroke Urban District Council administered the Ballsbridge and Donnybrook areas and Rathmines Town Council looked after Rathmines, Ranelagh and Rathgar and had its own dedicated water supply from the Glenasmole Reservoir above Bohernabreena. These councils were integrated into the Dublin City Council in 1930.

The Local Government franchise based on property had been extended to women by the eighteen nineties. By 1911 men over twenty-one had a vote at national elections. This was extended to women aged thirty in 1918 and to all citizens of the Irish Free State over twenty-one years of age by 1922 Constitution.

Politically, the Irish Parliamentary Party (IPP) that had split after the fall of Parnell in 1892 dominated Dublin: it had reunited under John Redmond in 1900. In 1911, Dublin City was represented at Westminster by four Members of Parliament from the IPP and two Unionists, one of whom was Sir Edward Carson, represented Trinity College. There was a concerted move orchestrated by the IPP, relying on its pivotal position vis a vis the incumbent Liberal Government, toward Home Rule. The Unionist minority both in parts of Ulster and the rest of Ireland was opposing this measure. The argument for a form of Home Rule was backed up by the fact that there was more revenue raised in Ireland than was spent there.

The Dublin Chamber of Commerce, founded in 1783, was the voice of the business community. It acted as spokesman and lobbyist on behalf of Dublin's employers and was a respected and influential body. It had numerous contacts with the administration in Dublin Castle.

While Dublin and Ireland was ruled from London there was a certain devolution of power. The Viceroy, Lord Aberdeen appointed in 1905, representing the King Emperor, resided in the Vice Regal Lodge (now Aras an Uactharain) in the Phoenix Park while political power was exercised by the Chief Secretary, Augustine Birrell, who had a seat in the British Cabinet. The Under Secretary, a permanent civil servant, headed the administration in Dublin Castle. There was a vice regal court with quaintly named gentlemen, rather grandly dressed in colourful outfits. Grand balls and banquets were arranged and if you were rich and influential enough you could have your daughter presented to the Viceroy at an appropriate ceremony. The Blue Hussars, a mounted cavalry detachment provided the necessary pageantry that such ceremonial occasions expected.

If you had a good income, Dublin was a pleasant place in which to live. If you were poor, however, it was pretty unpleasant. The employer classes were not very interested in sharing any of their wealth with those lower down the social scale. In 1907 James Larkin had arrived in the city and set about organising the working classes into trade unions to better protect and extend their rights and working conditions. His arrival and subsequent activities did not go down well with the owners of capital. One leading businessman in particular took grave exception to Larkin and all he stood for. This man was William Martin Murphy.

Born in Cork into a prosperous family of building contractors Murphy moved to Dublin in the 1870's. He was elected as a Member of Parliament for the St. Patrick's Ward in 1885, opposed Parnell at the split and lost his seat in 1892. Despite his best efforts he never regained it. By 1911, he was the leading businessman in Dublin. His interests included the Dublin United Tramway Company, the Great Southern and Western Railway Co., Clerys Department store and the Irish Independent newspaper. Murphy also had extensive interests abroad and was a leading member of the Dublin Chamber of Commerce. He was its President in 1912/13. It is indicative of the position of Dublin as a non-manufacturing area that its leading businessman should largely have obtained his wealth from retail and service companies.

Electricity had begun to be introduced into Dublin in the 1890s and the Corporation had Power Stations in Fleet Street and the Pigeon House east of Ringsend. Limited street lighting had been introduced with around 500 lamps in operation in 1911 at a cost of £560,000. Gas, however, was how the majority of those houses that could afford it were lit and powered. The Dublin and Alliance Gas Company had a network of pipes throughout the city and supplied them from its plant situated between Macken Street and Misery Hill near Ringsend. Both the electricity and gas plants used imported coal as their power source.

There was a telephone service of sorts with the Central Exchange at Crown Alley off Fleet Street that was considered rather unreliable. In fact, even to obtain an instrument, never mind to get it to work, it appeared you had to know the right person. The postal service centred on the General Post Office (GPO) in Sackville (O'Connell) Street was much more reliable. Letters and postcards were usually used while telegrams were common. The reliability of the postal service was such that you could be certain that a letter posted in, for instance, Westport Co. Mayo before 2pm would arrive at its destination in London before noon the next day.

As the wealth of the middle classes grew they began to travel to a greater extent. Initially, day trips to the seaside and then longer holidays to the developing resorts at the railheads at Tramore, Ballybunion, Salthill and Killarney were the norm. This increasing travel was further facilitated by the introduction of a timetable for the first time in 1880, using Dublin Meantime as the standard throughout Ireland. Ireland, however, remained twenty-five minutes behind London until Greenwich Meantime was extended to all of Great Britain and Ireland in 1916. There were 5058 motor cars registered in Ireland in 1911 the vast majority of which were garaged in Dublin.

Jaunting cars, as a mode of transport, were much more prevalent in Dublin and remained so until well after the First World War.

Theatres such as the Royal, the Gaiety and the Empire Palace (now the Olympia) provided entertainment for all classes featuring musical and variety performances on a daily basis. In 1911 the Chairman of the Empire Palace was Willie Findlater who was to be a founder member of the Dublin Rotary Club with the classification of Grocer and Wine Merchant. Reflecting the Gaelic revival movement the Abbey Theatre had presented its first performance of William Butler Yeats' 'On Baile's Strand' and Lady Gregory's 'Spreading the News' on December 27th 1904. In February 1911 they were presenting the 'Land of Heart's Desire' by W.B. Yeats. Two years previously in 1909 the Volta, the first emporium showing moving pictures, opened in Mary Street managed by the soon to be well known literary figure, James Joyce.

Dublin in 1911 was well served by parks and public spaces. The Phoenix Park had been opened to the public in 1745 and with 1760 acres was and still is the largest city park in Europe. It housed the Zoological Society's collection of animals and was a favourite place for the citizens of Dublin to visit. The nearby People's Park provided lawns, flower beds, shrubs and herbaceous borders to delight the eye and the nose. The Botanic Gardens in Glasnevin, an off-shoot from the Royal Dublin Society, preserved exotic species of trees, roses, plants and orchids from every corner of the globe. Saint Stephen's Green laid out and presented to the people of Ireland by Sir Arthur Guinness (afterwards Lord Ardilaun) in 1877 was a favourite place to go and relax and listen to the military band, feed the ducks and generally take things easy. The Fusiliers' Arch at the north west entrance had been erected four years earlier in 1907 to commemorate those Irishmen killed in the lately finished Boer War.

As regards cultural activities the Royal Dublin Society (founded in 1732) was based in Leinster House with buildings also located in Ballsbridge where a successful sporting and social event, the Dublin Horse Show, was held each August. The RDS had, since its foundation gathered together a rather large collection of books, works of art and artefacts. They had donated these to the State in the 1870s and 1880s and they were housed in the new buildings of the National Library, Museum and National Gallery adjoining Leinster House. The builders of this prestigious set of buildings were J&W Beckett and Co.[1] based in Ringsend.

The Dublin of 1911 to which William Stuart Morrow returned was a mixture of crushing poverty and increasing wealth among the middle and upper middle classes. It was a city whose politics were dominated by the Irish Parliamentary Party with a strong and influential Unionist minority. Secretly, however, the physical force nationalists were beginning to regroup and in five years from the foundation of our club a cataclysmic event would shake the city. If there was to be a Rotary club in Dublin it would have to be formed largely from the commercial and professional classes. This was the task that Morrow faced in January 1911.

[1] *Their principal, Walter Beckett, was a Founder Member of the Dublin Club with the classification of Builder and Contractor. His nephew Past District Governor Charles Horner Beckett is today an honorary member of the club having joined in 1944 He was President in 1956/7 and was District Governor in 1971/72.*

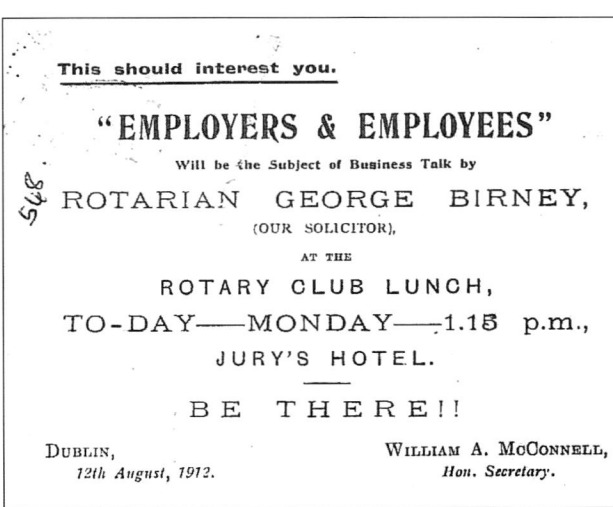

Sample of card sent weekly to members to encourage them to attend the Dublin club luncheon.

Chapter Four

Dublin Club

*'Large streams from little fountains flow
Tall oaks from little acorns grow'*
David Everett

When William Stuart Morrow arrived in his native Dublin in January 1911 he had no job lined up for himself. It is possible that he thought that he could begin to make a living collecting debts for clients, but that business would of necessity take a while to get going. He did, however, have one major advantage in that his sister, Ada Margaret, was married to William Alexander McConnell, Manager of the Caledonian Insurance Company with offices in Dame Street, the commercial heart of Dublin.

Morrow naturally told his brother-in-law McConnell about the Rotary club of which he had been a member in San Francisco. As he described how the idea of Rotary worked to bring businessmen together in friendship to their mutual advantage it became obvious to both men that it was possible, just possible, that such an idea could be transferred to Dublin to the advantage of both of them. William McConnell, known to his business acquaintances and friends as Bill, introduced his brother in law to some of his clients over an informal lunch in early February 1911. Morrow explained the basic principles of Rotary to them. Some were interested and some were not. It was, in modern day parlance, a hard sell. It was a completely new idea and it took some getting used to. Over the next days and weeks Morrow persevered, and through McConnell and his clients, was introduced to more and more business people in Dublin. He spoke to them wherever he could and told them about the Rotary phenomenon that was sweeping through North America.

By the third week in February he considered that he had enough businessmen interested to call a formal meeting and that took place at 1.15pm in Jurys Hotel, College Green on Wednesday, February 22nd. The news page of The Irish Times gives us an idea of the concerns that people were interested in at that time. It is reported that the Parliamentary Irish Party had had a meeting the day before at which a statement was received from the Irish Women's franchise League – no action was to be taken. The next item on their Agenda was the forthcoming coronation of George V. The principle of non attendance at such events was upheld while it was felt that His Majesty would receive a warm welcome on his visit to Ireland. Trouser skirts had been seen in Berlin and in Madrid what are described as Harem skirts had caused riots. Junket was napped to win the Wednesday Hurdle at Windsor

Morrow presided at that February 22nd meeting and the Minute Book is described on the inside front cover in his own hand as 'Rotary Club Dublin – Minute Book No. 1'. On page one under the heading 'Rotary Club' Morrow has recorded the Entrance Fee as £2.2.0 and the Annual Dues as £1.1.0. The temporary headquarters are noted as Jurys Hotel and the Organising Secretary as W. Stuart Morrow. Those present then signed in their own hand under the following inscription.

We, the undersigned hereby agree to become members of the Rotary Club and to pay the Entrance Fee of £2.2.0 as soon as Twenty members shall have been enrolled therein.

Name	Address	Classification
W.H. Lane	*20 Nassau Street*	*Tailors*
J.L. Phillips	*(Trading as Lane and Phillips)*	
Thos S. Ryan	*14 College Green*	*Jewellers etc.*
	(J R Ryan & Co.)	
Henry D Jury	*7 College Green*	*Caterer*
W. Findlater	*30 Upper Sackville St.*	*Grocer & Wine Merchant*
Thomas Hempenstall	*12 Suffolk St.*	*Optical goods*
	(Dixon & Hempenstall)	

William A. McConnell	31 Dame St.	Insurance
	(Caledonian Insurance)	
E.W. Fannin	3 Rutland Square	M.D

There follows the Minutes of the February 22nd meeting:

Minutes of the Meeting held at Jurys Hotel on Wednesday February 22nd 1911 at 1.15pm.

W. Stuart Morrow Organizing Secretary Presiding.

Present	Wm. Findlater	Alex. Findlater & Co.	Groceries
	T. S. Ryan	JR Ryan & Co.	Jewellery
	Wm. H. Lane	Lane & Phillips	Tailoring
	Wm. A. McConnell	Caledonian Ins. Co.	Insurance
	Wm. Mitchell	Hodges & Sons	Kitchen Utensils
	Henry D Jury	Jurys Hotel	Hotel
	C. W. McDermott	Belfast Linen Co.	Linens
	R. Dobbyn	Greenmount Oil Co.	Oils
	Dr. Walsh	JJ Graham & Co.	Drugs

There are a number of discrepancies between the two lists. Firstly, Lane the Tailor seems to have signed for his Business Partner Phillips as well as himself. Secondly Mitchell and Dr. Walsh who are recorded by Morrow as being present at the meeting did not append their signatures. Notwithstanding this omission they were considered by the Club as having joined at that meeting. Thirdly, C. W. McDermott and R. Dobbyn who appear on both lists were never heard of again, did not pay any Entrance Fee and were not considered as Members. Fourthly note how Willie Findlater who became our President in 1913/14 described himself as Grocer and Wine Merchant. Morrow entered Groceries against his name. Classifications were important and Morrow, no doubt, wanted to keep them as tightly allocated as possible. Why allow a member to have two classifications when he could get someone else to join and pay an Entrance Fee for the second one. He was thinking ahead.

The next item on Morrow's Agenda was a reading of a paper that he had prepared himself.

A paper was read by Mr. Morrow after which the following resolution was proposed by Mr. Lane, seconded by Mr. Ryan and unanimously adopted.

Resolution. That having listened to a statement of the history, aims and methods of the Rotary Clubs now in operation in the principal cities of America, we approve of the attempt to establish a Rotary Club in Dublin.

The following resolution was proposed by Mr Ryan seconded by Wm. McConnell and unanimously adopted.
Resolution. That the Entrance Fee to the Rotary Club be fixed at £2.2.0. The dues at 10/- per quarter and that the Organizing Secretary receives in lieu of salary one half of the Entrance Fee for each member that he obtains.

The following Resolution was proposed by Wm. McConnell, seconded by Mr. Jury and unanimously adopted.
Resolution. That the first General Meeting and Dinner of the Rotary Club for the election of Officers for the ensuing year be held on Tuesday March 14th 1911 at 6.30pm at Jurys Hotel.

This latter Resolution setting the venue for the Club's first dinner in Jurys Hotel seconded by its owner is the first European application of the then First Object of Rotary: the promotion of the business interests of its members. Also note the American spelling of the word 'organising'.

The Minutes concluded:

In consequence of Wednesday February 29th being Ash Wednesday it was decided to have the next Meeting and lunch on Tuesday February 28th and the Meeting was adjourned.

Read and approved February 28 1911
William S. Morrow - Chairman

In their excitement establishing the new venture those present obviously had forgotten that 1911 was not a Leap Year and the following Wednesday was actually March 1st. In any event the next meeting was not held on a Wednesday but on Tuesday February 28th again in Jurys Hotel. These Minutes read:

Rotary Club
Minutes of the Meeting held at Jurys Hotel on Tuesday February 28th 1911.
W. Stuart Morrow, Organizing Secretary, Presiding.
Members present
Mr TS Ryan, JR Ryan & Co., Jewellery
Mr. Wm H. Lane, Lane & Phillips, Tailoring
Mr. Wm. A. McConnell, Caledonian Insurance, Insurance
Mr. Henry D. Jury, Jurys Hotel, Catering
Mr. Thomas Hempenstall, Dixon & Hempenstall, Optical goods
Visitors present
Mr. R.J. White, 45 Fleet St., Printer
Mr. J.W. Chancellor, 7 Grafton St., Photographer
Mr. Arthur Webb, 12 Westmoreland St., Boots & shoes
Mr. Robt. Carlyle, 12 College Green, Stocks & Bonds
Mr Keatinge, 42 Grafton St., Painter & Decorator
Mr Mansfield, Nassau St., Leather Goods

The Minutes of the Meeting of February 22nd were read and approved. The Organizing Secretary separately introduced each member who had signed the Roll of the Rotary Club since the last meeting. The visitors were given any information any of them desired regarding the aims and methods of the Rotary Club. Several names of suitable members were suggested to the Organizing Secretary and the Meeting adjourned until Tuesday March 7th.
Read and approved
W Stuart Morrow
Chairman March 7th 1911

The original [1]Minute Book No. 1 has the Minutes of all the early meetings of the Club both of lunches and Council recorded on the right hand page only. The left-hand page remained blank except for those opposite the first two meetings on February 22 and February 28th. On those Pages we find the Membership Roll referred to by Morrow in the Meeting of February 28th. There are thirty-five names recorded there. On succeeding pages Morrow has entered in pencil seventy names of the leading businessmen operating in Dublin at the time. Some of these would have been the names referred to in the Minutes of February 28th and others were probably gleaned from Trade Directories such as Thoms. In any event, William Stuart Morrow was going about his task of obtaining members for the Club in a thorough and painstaking fashion. Half of two guineas was not to be sneezed at. In fact he has recorded in pencil on the right hand page, opposite the Inside Front Cover under the heading Commissions -dates, names and monies due to him.

The third meeting took place the following Tuesday.

Rotary Club
Minutes of the Meeting held at Jurys Hotel on Tuesday March 7th 1911.
W Stuart Morrow Organizing Secretary Presiding.
Members present
Mr. Wm H Lane, Lane & Phillips , Tailoring
Mr Henry D Jury, Jurys Hotel, Catering
Mr. William Findlater, Alex Findlater and Co, Groceries
Mr. Thos. Henpenstall, Dixon & Henpenstall, Optical goods
Mr. Wm. A McConnell, Caledonian Insurance, Insurance
Mr Richard White, R.T. White, Printing
Mr. Arthur Webb, 12 Westmoreland St., Boots & shoes
Mr W.J. Arnold, F Sanderson & Sons, Coachbuilding
Mr Robt. H. Carlyle, 12 College Green , Government Stockbroker
Visitors
Mr J. Robertson Coade, Managing Director, Mineral Waters - Cantrell & Cochrane

Mr. W.B. Crawford, 29 Dawson St., Motor Supplies
Mr J Walter Beckett, Sth Docks Works Ringsend, Builder
Mr R. A. Foley, 17 Nassau St., Underwood Typewriters
Mr. Robt. Perrin, College Green , Journalist
Mr Geo. L. O'Connor, 42b Molesworth St., Architect
Mr Humphreys, Dame St., Rubber stamps and dies

The Minutes of the February 29th meeting were read and approved.
The Chairman separately introduced each member who had signed the Roll of the Rotary Club since the last meeting.
The following Resolution was proposed by the Chairman, seconded by Mr Wm. McConnell and unanimously adopted.
Resolved. That the dues for the Rotary Club be fixed at £1.1.0 per annum instead of 10/- per quarter.
The following resolution was proposed by the Chairman, seconded by Mr. White and unanimously adopted.
Resolved. That the First General Monthly Meeting and Dinner of the Rotary Club for the election of its officers for the ensuing year be held on Tuesday March 21st at 6.30pm at Jurys Hotel.
For the information of the visitors present the Chairman read a paper on the objects and methods of the Rotary Club and the meeting adjourned until Tuesday March 14th.
Read and approved
W Stuart Morrow Chairman
March 14/11.

In arranging a Dinner for March 21st Morrow was following the example of his previous Club in San Francisco that, the reader may remember, held a very successful Banquet at which their first President and Officers were elected. However it will be noted that unlike San Francisco Morrow had, as yet, not managed to induct into membership any influential Newspaper Editor.

The fourth, of what I would call Information Meetings, took place in Jurys Hotel the following Tuesday.

Rotary Club
Minutes of the Meeting held at Jurys Hotel on Tuesday March 14th 1911.
Members present
Mr Geo Birney, 16 Lr. Sackville Street, Solicitor
Mr Arthur H Walker, Cooper Kenny & Co., Incorporated Accountants
Mr Geo L. O'Connor, 42 Great Brunswick Street, Architect
Mr. James R. Coade, Managing Director, Cantrell & Cochrane Mineral Waters
Mr. J Walter Beckett, Sth Docks Works Ringsend, Builder
Mr. Ed. C. Pelissier, 9 Rutland Square, Dentist
Mr Wm. Findlater, Alex Findlater & Co, Groceries
Mr Thos Hempenstall, Dixon & Hempenstall, Optical goods
Mr Wm. A McConnell, Caledonian Insurance, Insurance
Mr. Arthur Webb, 12 Westmoreland St., Boots & Shoes
Mr R Humphreys, 71 Dame Street, Stamps and Stencils
Mr W.H. Lane, Lane & Phillips, Tailors
Mr Richard White, 45 Fleet St., Printers
Visitors present
Mr Walker, J Morgan, 9 Grafton St., Hats
Dr. Edmund Smith, 124 St. Stephens Green, Surgical Instruments
Mr. J. Kavanagh, Star Blds., Canadian Produce Broker.

The Minutes of the Meeting of March 7th were read and approved.
The Chairman separately introduced each member who had signed the Roll of the Rotary Club since the last meeting.
The Chairman announced that by arrangement with Mr Jury the Waiters tips at the Rotary Club luncheons was fixed at one penny and that members were particularly requested not to exceed that amount so that uniformity might be observed.
The Chairman announced that the mineral waters supplied at this lunch had been donated by Mr. Coade of Cantrell & Cochrane and that the Menu Cards had been executed by Mr. Foley of the Underwood Typewriter Co. and both Members were thanked accordingly and the

*Meeting adjourned until Tuesday evening March 21st at 6.30pm.
Read and approved
W Stuart Morrow
Chairman March 21/11*

The supply of mineral waters and menu cards, an early example of product placement, shows how business and fellowship can overlap seamlessly in a social setting. Of the seven visitors at the previous meeting Morrow had managed to convert five – Coade, Beckett, Foley, O'Connor and Humphreys into members within a week. And although Foley was not present he had managed to get his name and his company mentioned.

By the Inaugural Dinner on March 21st Morrow had managed to obtain entrance fees from Mr Robt. Perrin 12 College Green -Irish Investors Journal, Mr Edward W Howe Robt Morrow & Son, St. - Pictures and Frames, Mr Albert R Wayte –Bicycles, Mr. Wm. B Crawford 29 Dawson St.- Motor Accessories, Mr. Fredk. Earle Kilkenny Woodworkers – Furniture and Mr. J.H. Fleming Belfast Banking Co. – Bank, There were no visitors recorded as being present as is the norm at general meetings. When the previous minutes had been read and passed there was a Ballot for the office of President and J.H. Fleming (see Appendix 6) who appears to have joined in the week preceding was elected. William Findlater (see Appendix 6) was elected Vice President. Stuart Morrow was elected Secretary and James Coade (see Appendix 6) was elected Hon. Treasurer. The following members were elected to a Committee[2]: Arthur H Walkey, Geo Birney, Arthur Webb, W.H. Lane and Richard White (see Appendix 6).

After President Fleming had taken the chair he proposed a toast to 'The King' and this was 'duly honoured'. There is an alteration in the Minutes at this point. In what appears to be Morrow's handwriting there is 'which was drunk with enthusiasm by all the members present'. The latter phrase is crossed out and 'duly honoured' inserted. The alteration is not initialled and there is no indication when it was made. The health of the newly installed President was toasted and the new elected Council was detailed to meet at 4.30pm on Tuesday March

23rd at 4.30pm. The new Rotary Club had been established with thirty-six members with an average age of forty-two.

[1] *The original Minute Book of the Dublin Club was purchased by Morrow for 3s/6d, measures 23cm x 18cm and is bound in red cloth. In addition to noting the Commissions due to him (half the Entrance Fee for each new member) he has filled pages at the back of the book with names, addresses and classifications, all recorded in pencil.*

[2] *The early Minutes of the Club describe its controlling committee as the Committee whereas the Constitution tells us it is the Council. Throughout the text I have referred to it as the Council and subsidiary bodies as committees and sub-committees.*

```
T   ake this hint, if you are wise

A   dvertise, friend, advertise!

G   rit, and business enterprise

R   arely fail the man who tries,

E   very day to win some prize.

H   asten then - for e'en "Time flies",

A   nd in waiting, failure lies -

N   ow's the time to advertise!


            (Sent to a Rotarian this morning)
                    23/12/'12.
```

Notice sent to all members of the Dublin club from Tom Grehan Advertisement Manager the Irish Independent. Grehan had joined the club in April 1911.

Chapter Five

Morrow goes North

'He profits most who serves best' Arthur Sheldon

At the Meetings of the Council on March 23rd and 30th the members set about organising the necessary tasks that any club must undertake to be successful. Morrow, as Secretary, was to continue to receive, in lieu of salary, one half of the Entrance Fee of two guineas for each new member that he obtained. The Secretary was instructed to prepare and have printed a draft Constitution for the new club. It was further resolved that any Member wishing to bring a visitor to lunch should so inform the Secretary in advance. A quorum of three was agreed for future Council Meetings and Morrow proposed four businessmen for membership. Three were accepted with the fourth Dr. Harvey being referred to Dr. Fannin for his comments. Dr. Harvey turned out to be Mr. Harvey, a surgeon, and was admitted as a member. Morrow then submitted a list of businessmen that he proposed to contact and the Council members having considered it, agreed that he should do so.

By the next Meeting on April 10th it was obvious that Morrow had been busy in the intervening time. He had seven men to propose for membership. Six were approved; the seventh a Mr Godkin was deferred. The Treasurer paid Morrow.

The Council and Morrow were pretty active because the next meeting was held just ten days later on April 20th and this time Morrow had twelve applications for membership. Eight were admitted unanimously with two who were related to one another and in similar businesses being deferred so that one or the other could agree to join. One could be a member, but not both. Bodkin, who had been proposed at the April 10th meeting was turned down for membership because his classification would conflict with that of an existing member. This is the first instance where a member's classification caused a prospective member to be denied entry to the club. This was to be the first of many such instances and would cause a great deal of discussion over the coming years. Ireton P Jones who went on to be a very active member applied to have his classification changed from that of 'Auctioneer' to 'Nurseryman' and this was agreed. More names were suggested to the ever active Morrow and the meeting adjourned.

A Dinner was arranged for April 26th instead of the usual lunch and the proposed Constitution was discussed in detail, revised and Morrow was requested to have it reprinted in time for the next monthly dinner. Business having been concluded, the attendance was entertained by three members with songs accompanied by another on the piano.

Luncheons continued in Jurys Hotel College Green at 1.15pm every week with attendance ranging from twenty to forty. There seemed to have been speakers at most lunches including Hempenstall on Optical Goods, Foley on Typewriters, Smith – surgical instruments, Walker – hats, Lawrence – photos, Birney – the advantages of bookkeeping, Earle – Kilkenny Woodworkers, Walsh – drugs and chemicals, Webb – boots and shoes, Walkey – private companies, White – printing, Stewart – stationery, McConnell – insurance and Grehan – advertising. The members were introducing themselves and their businesses to one another in accordance with the First Object of the Club. One, however, would have one's doubts about the topic of surgical instruments at a luncheon!

Entertainment and Fraternal sub committees were formed and on July 4th a sum of £1 was given to Mr Robert Woods of Williams & Woods Great Britain (Parnell) Street towards an excursion for poor children. This is the first instance and the beginning of Service to the Community recorded. A Mr. William Wallace, of Cantrell & Cochrane Belfast, was a visitor at the July 11th lunch.

From the foundation of the Dublin Club in February Morrow had worked very hard at persuading the leading businessmen of the city of the advantages of joining the Rotary Club, Dublin. Despite some objections from existing members of a conflict of business interest, by June he managed to obtain a further fifty Members to add to the thirty-six that had signed the original Roll. By mid July there were one hundred members of Rotary in Dublin. To jog members' memory he had compiled and circulated a list of classifications and invited Members to write in individual businessmen's names and addresses opposite each classification. This, however, also resulted in correspondence from members in the form of a pre-emptive strike in that objections were raised to the inclusion of classifications that might impinge on their business. On July 10th Mr. R. N. Tweedy of William Coates & Son, classification 'Electrical Engineer', wrote to Stuart Morrow, Secretary of the Club:

Re/. Classifications not yet represented.

Dear Sir,
We note that this list circulated contains the classification 'electric signs' and we beg to inform you that we should object to any other firm being elected on this classification as we either supply or make every kind of electrical apparatus.
We are sure that this point only needs to be brought to your attention in order to be corrected.
Yours faithfully
R. N. Tweedy

On the obverse of the page Mr. Tweedy wrote in red ink:

I notice another heading 'Gas Engines'. I suppose that would include 'Gas Producers'. Now Coates Ltd are sole agents in Ireland for the largest makers in the world – the Power Gas Corporation of Stockton-on-Tees, who work the Maid Patents.

If I can persuade them to apply for Membership could it be arranged that I should represent them at the meetings? Of course I could nominate one of many assistants if necessary.

We are also sole agents for R. Maygood & Co the lift makers, and the same question applies here, although you have omitted lift makers from your list.
Initialled RNT

At the Council Meeting on July 14th this letter was considered and it was decided to take 'no action'. This decision can better be understood in light of another letter dated July 13th received from William Stuart Morrow announcing his resignation. There is no letter in the file but it has been written in Morrow's own hand into the Minute Book as follows:

Jurys Hotel College Green
Dublin July 13th 1911

The Committee, Rotary Club, Dublin.

Gentlemen,
It is with the sincerest regret that I am obliged to tender to you my resignation as Secretary. I find it absolutely necessary that I should take in more money to meet expenses, and as no employment has presented itself in Dublin, I have decided to remove to Belfast, where my first efforts will be devoted to establishing a Rotary Club in the city. It is possible that I may, before long, receive some offer of employment that will bring me back to Dublin, in which event, my services will be at your disposal should you desire them.
In the meanwhile, I desire to express my appreciation of the numerous courtesies received at your hands, and to wish you and all the members of the Dublin Rotary Club every possible success and happiness.
Yours very truly
W. Stuart Morrow

The Minutes continue

After the resignation had been duly accepted Mr. Morrow was asked to send out notices of a special Committee Meeting for Monday July 17th *at 3.30pm and to state on the Notices that the appointment of a Secretary would come up for consideration. Mr Morrow was also asked to prepare cards for the luncheon on July 18th and deliver same to the President, together with the Minute Book and such papers and stationery relating to the Club as were in his possession.*

A list of the members who had not yet paid their Entrance Fees, and on which list if paid, there would be a sum of £18.18.0 coming to the Secretary was submitted and referred to the Treasurer for further action and
The Committee adjourned.
Signed J. H. Fleming
17.7.1911

There is no indication that the Council of the Club had any prior warning of Morrow's resignation although it is likely that his brother-in-law William McConnell must have known the way his mind was working. Looking through the Minute Book and the letter files of the period it is obvious that sooner or later, given that Rotary membership revolved around classification, Morrow would find it more and more difficult to enrol new members. He appears to have taken in something in the region of between seventy and eighty pounds in the five months since February. In terms of a hundred years later this would be around €12,000.

Of course, another option for him would have been to establish a second club in Dublin. It is quite certain that the existing members of the club would have vehemently opposed any proposal along these lines. Morrow would have been aware of a similar situation where the San Francisco Club had been instrumental in establishing a club across the Bay in Oakland. It is not known whether or not he considered this option. If he did, he dismissed almost at once, and decided that his future lay elsewhere. In fact, no other club was established in the Dublin area until the Dun Laoghaire club was chartered fifty-four years later in 1965.

At the next meeting of the Council on July 17th a payment of £10 was authorised for Morrow. Mr. Walkey, classification Accountant (Cooper

& Kenny), was appointed Secretary on a temporary basis. The question of remuneration was 'left open' with Walkey suggesting a possible bonus.

Walkey's appointment did not last long as at the next Meeting of Council on July 24th it was decided to appoint a Mr. Charles M. Coghlan who was in attendance at the meeting. His salary was fixed at £25 per annum plus half the entrance fee. He was to attend club dinners at the club's expense but would be required to pay for his lunches.

On the same day, July 24th, the indefatigable W. Stuart Morrow penned the following letter from the Royal Avenue Hotel Belfast using their headed notepaper:

Arthur H. Walkey Esq.
Secretary, Rotary Club, Dubin

Dear Mr. Walkey,
Will you please announce at tomorrow's luncheon that I held a preliminary meeting today at the above hotel. It was attended by fourteen of the leading business men of Belfast, and resolutions approving of the establishment of a Rotary Club in Belfast and fixing the same charges as are made in Dublin were carried unanimously.
Yours very truly
W. Stuart Morrow

On August 14th the William Wallace who had attended the July 11th luncheon of the Dublin Club, as a visitor, was elected President and the second club in Europe had been founded. An office with a telephone was rented and a girl attendant was employed at 5 shillings per week. Morrow had negotiated the same terms as he had had in Dublin and by January the following year he had built the Belfast membership up to 124.

Back in Dublin one of the members wondered whether, being in the Dublin Club, he was also a member of Belfast. There was no comment from other members recorded, but it is interesting to note the sense of collegiality, or maybe business acumen, that was developing.

Business topics were quite naturally, to the forefront of minds of members. J. Sheridan (Beef Extracts) who headed up the Bovril organisation in Dublin wrote a long and detailed letter to the Secretary in which he outlined how he would like to see the club develop. He suggested that speakers should be found to speak on the following topics: the quantity and quality of advertising, the best advertising mediums, competition and how to deal with it, methods of soliciting orders, cutting of prices, collecting of accounts, giving or refusing credit, railway carriage and exhibitions as a means of advertising. A businessman's concerns have not changed a lot in the past one hundred years. The Council took these suggestions to heart and individual members were asked to speak on these subjects over the following months.

Two suggestions were made at the September meeting. One, from T. A. Grehan was that the time had arrived for holding a Business Exhibition in Dublin and the other from Ireton Jones that 'members wear a button bearing their name and club number'. Neither of these suggestions were put to the meeting but were to be a fruitful source of discussion in the coming months.

As the summer ended it was decided to undertake the first Club outing. A number of suggestions had been made including a visit to Mr. Ireton Jones Nursery and Gardens in Delgany but it was finally decided that a visit to Howth by train and tram would be made on Saturday September 8th. It is a remarkable fact that this excursion was reported in the Irish Independent as a news item. Perhaps there was not a lot of other news that day but the likelihood is that T. A. Grehan who was Advertisement Manager with Independent Newspapers and who had joined in April organised the inclusion. The cutting from the newspaper is pasted into the minute book:

Dublin Rotary Club

On Saturday afternoon a party of the Club to about forty, consisting of Members and their friends, left Amiens Street by 3pm train for the Howth Summit. After a quick run to Sutton the party boarded one of the Summit tram cars, the top of which had been reserved for their use by the railway company, and proceeded by the Sutton route to the top of the Hill. Having enjoyed afternoon tea at the pavilion, they made their way to the Bailey Lighthouse, surveying much of that interesting structure. Retracing their steps to the Summit the members took different routes – some going by the famous cliff track, some by the inland road – whilst the less robust, availing of the car, made their way to the Claremont Hotel, where dinner was partaken of and much enjoyed. Some musical items contributed by the party after dinner added much to the pleasures of the evening. Returning to town by the 10 o'clock train, the party dispersed, much pleased with the first afternoon's outing of the Club.

This is the first reference to the Rotary Club, Dublin in the national press and it is indicative of the ethos of the club at the time that the news report should concern the fellowship aspect of Rotary rather than any service of which there was very little.

In October, Robertson Coade the Hon Treasurer and Managing Director of Cantrell & Cochrane Ltd., classification Mineral Waters, visited the Belfast Club for lunch. He received a warm welcome and the Belfast President was invited to our next Dinner. Thus began the friendly and cordial relations that have to this day existed between the two clubs.

Chapter Six

Paul Harris letter

'What do Rotarians do? – They go to lunch'. George Bernard Shaw

There were some teething troubles as the first year drew to a close. Ireton Jones, the nurseryman from Delgany, in his enthusiasm to promote business between members, had printed a little booklet with members' names, addresses and telephone numbers. Apparently telephone numbers were not included in the Club Directory. This initiative from Jones prompted an outraged letter from Robert Carlyle, the Rotary Government Stockbroker announcing his resignation. The problem, apparently, was that it was unethical for him to provide his telephone number publicly. When it was explained that the booklet with a heading 'Rotary Telephone Directory' was not, in fact, a publication of the club he was somewhat mollified and agreed to withdraw his intention to resign. The following motion was passed by Council on January 25th 1912 and circulated to members:

No printed matter, circular or other document bearing the title of the Rotary Club Dublin be issued or circulated without the authority of the Committee

The previous week Stuart Morrow informed the club, by letter, that he had decided to leave Belfast and go to Glasgow to found a Rotary Club there. He asked that Members should give him the names of any business contacts that they might have in that city. He had completed just six months in Belfast and no doubt the pool from which new members could be drawn was beginning to dry up. Glasgow, the industrial capital of Scotland, had a similar business profile to Belfast and it appears that he thought it to be fertile ground for the Rotary message. Morrow was absolutely right in his analysis and the Glasgow Club was founded in March 1912 and by the following year had over one hundred members. On 2nd September of that year our member Gerard Black, classification Dental Surgeon brought greetings from the members of the Glasgow Club to our lunch. By that time the untiring Morrow was in Edinburgh where he had founded yet another club.

On the 6th February 1912 Council had before it a letter from Paul P. Harris himself. It was addressed to Mr. J. H. Fleming, Manager of the Belfast Bank of Dublin, Dublin, Ireland and was dated January 23rd 1912

Dear Sir,

We have just learned of the existence of the Rotary Club of Dublin. We are extremely desirous of becoming better acquainted and we trust the secretary of your organisation will find it practicable to keep in touch with Mr. Chesley R. Perry, Secretary of the National Association of Rotary Clubs.

We expect that the National Association will become the International Association in August. It is extremely gratifying to us to note the interest in Rotary which is shown abroad. We look forward to the day when the International Association of Rotary Clubs may render the members of the various organisations it represents and the countries from which it springs, great service, by bringing business men of different countries into closer business relationship and into better understanding of each other.

Mr. W. Stewart *(sic)* **Morrow, secretary of the Belfast Club, informs us that his next step in the extension of Rotary will be to Glasgow. We are already in correspondence with Mr. H. Waller, manager for Scotland for Lever Brothers Ltd., proprietors of the Port Sunlight Soap Business. We hope to interest the managers of that company in all countries.**

Mr. A. F. Sheldon, head of the great school of scientific salesmanship, who has opened up headquarters in London, will make a tour through Great Britain in the not far distant future. He

is a great speaker and I trust that your Club will have opportunity to hear him.

I suppose that you are in touch with Arthur R. Bigelow 49 Great Sutton St. England, vice president of the Rotary Club of London. I hope that the Rotary Clubs of Great Britain will keep in frequent communication with each other and with us.

Trusting to hear from you in the near future, I beg to remain, with kind regards.

Yours very truly

Signed Paul P. Harris

That the significance of the letter was appreciated by the Council can be gauged by the fact that they directed the Secretary to enter the Club's reply in the Minutes. The reply is marked 'appended' but unfortunately it is not there now and we do not know its content.

There are a number of points that should be borne in mind in considering the Paul Harris letter. Morrow had founded the Dublin and Belfast Clubs without any reference whatsoever to San Francisco, Chicago or even Paul Harris. The first Harris had learned about Morrow's activities on this side of the Atlantic was when he received a letter from him telling what he was about and, probably, asking for business contacts for his next venture in Glasgow.

In the very first paragraph Harris asks that the Dublin Club keep in touch with his Organising Secretary Chesley Perry. Harris knew what had happened on the West Coast of the United States when a club, calling itself Rotary, had tried to set itself up. He did not want this to happen here. From the first time he heard about the Irish clubs he wanted them to be integrated into the, soon to be world-wide, Rotary Association. The second paragraph outlines the benefits to be obtained from the International Association of businessmen and the third gives an indication of how his and Perry's minds were working as they

OFFICERS:
PAUL P. HARRIS, CHICAGO
PRESIDENT

R. R. DENNY, SEATTLE
1ST VICE-PRESIDENT

J. E. FITZWILSON, BOSTON
2ND VICE-PRESIDENT

MAC MARTIN, MINNEAPOLIS
TREASURER

WERNER HENCKE, ST. LOUIS
SERGEANT AT ARMS

National Association of Rotary Clubs
of America

CHESLEY R. PERRY, SECRETARY
911 FIRST NAT'L BANK BLDG., CHICAGO
TELEPHONE RANDOLPH 608

OFFICE OF PAUL P. HARRIS, PRESIDENT
1317 NO. 127 NORTH DEARBORN ST., CHICAGO
TELEPHONES: CENTRAL 2018 AUTOMATIC 41-530

DIRECTORS:
WM. J. BOVARD,
NEW ORLEANS
C. W. HILL,
LOS ANGELES
E. G. MAC CAN
NEW YORK CITY
GLENN C. MEAD
PHILADELPHIA
LEE B. METTLER,
KANSAS CITY
A. R. STAFFORD,
ST. LOUIS
W. G. STEARNS
TACOMA
L. Q. SWETLAND,
PORTLAND (ORE.)
F. L. THRESHER,
MINNEAPOLIS

Jan. 23, 1912.

Mr. J. H. Fleming,
Manager of the Belfast Bank of Dublin,
Dublin, Ireland.

Dear Sir:

    We have just learned of the existence of the Rotary Club of Dublin. We are extremely desirous of becoming better acquainted and we trust that the secretary of your organization will find it practicable to keep in touch with Mr. Chesley R. Perry, Secretary of the National Association of Rotary Clubs.

    We expect that the National Association will become the International association in August. It is extremely gratifying to us to note the interest in Rotary which is shown abroad. We look forward to the day when the International association of Rotary Clubs may render the members of the various organizations it represents and the countries from which it springs, great service, by bringing business men of different countries into closer business relationship and into a better understanding of each other.

    Mr. W. Stewart Morrow, secretary of the Belfast Club, informs us that his next step in the extention of Rotary will be to Glasgow. We are already in correspondence with Mr. H. Waller, manager for Scotland of Lever Brothers, Ltd., proprietors of the Port Sunlight Soap Business. We hope to interest the managers of that company in all countries.

    Mr. A. F. Sheldon, head of the great school of scientific salesmanship, who has opened up head quarters in London, will make a tour through Great Britain in the not far distant future. He is a great speaker and I trust that you club will have opportunity to hear him.

    I suppose you are in touch with Mr. Arthur P. Bigelow, 49 Great Sutton St., England, vice president of the Rotary Club of London. I hope that the Rotary Clubs of Great Britain will keep in frequent communication with each other and with us.

    Trusting to hear from you in the near future, I beg to remain, with kind regards.

              Yours very truly,
                    Paul P. Harris

Letter received from Paul Harris early in 1912.

planned Rotary's extension throughout the world: they intended to use the multinational network of U.S. companies to spread the Rotary message.

There is not a businessman in the world who would not like to increase his sales and who better to advise how to achieve this elusive objective than Arthur F. Sheldon, the leading exponent of salesmanship, who just happened to be a member of the Chicago Club. The letter ends with a hope that the 'British Clubs' will communicate with each other and Chicago frequently.

Of course, it should be remembered that Paul Harris was a successful lawyer and knew how to get his important points across in writing: these were that there are benefits to be got for Rotarians in having a Federation of Clubs. He was inviting us to join.

It took another year before the rather important matter of Affiliation Fees could be worked out. At the Duluth, Minnesota, Convention in

Wounded troops and Rotarians on an Outing to Powerscourt Waterfall in the Summer of 1915. Walter Beckett who organised the Outing and who was president of the Dublin club in 1925/26 is on the running board of the car on the extreme left.

August 1912 the name of the parent body was changed, as Paul Harris had predicted, to the International Association of Rotary Clubs with Chesley Perry confirmed as Secretary. Perry was looking for an Affiliation Fee of $1 per member from the newly established clubs on this side of the Atlantic and London had already paid this amount. Negotiations took place and following a visit to Chicago by Hugh Boyd Hon. Secretary of the Belfast Club a fee of 25 cents per member was suggested and agreed. There is no record as to whether or not the London Club obtained a refund! On April 4th 1913 the President of the Rotary Club, Dublin William Findlater and its Secretary William A. McConnell signed the agreement to affiliate. A Dollar draft was procured and it and the documents were despatched to Chicago. On 13th July 1913 Wm. Findlater wrote to the Hon. Secretary Wm. McConnell.

My dear McConnell,
I enclose you herewith letter from Mr. Perry and the charter – I think you might drop him a line to say that you have received it.
What about having it suitably framed?
Yours faithfully
Signed   Wm. Findlater

The Dublin Club had officially become a member of the Rotary family. I believe from older members that the charter was indeed framed and hung for many years in the Club's Office in Westmoreland Street. Unfortunately it is not now in our possession. There is no letter from Perry in the files.

Over a year before this event we had acquired our first club crest. Suggested and designed by G. L. O'Connor F.R.I. A. I. classification Architect it was accepted by the Council in January 1912 and used on all correspondence thereafter. Its significance was described by O'Connor:

'General character of design; Celtic Wheel – suggesting progress

Original crest Rotary Club, Dublin.

**Cross – suggesting faith (in ourselves and our work)
Laurel Wreath – Victory and Success.
Irish crown on top'**

The motto was suggested to be 'sic virescit industria' which O'Connor helpfully translated as 'thus flourishes industry'.

In early January also, Morrow had told us about the new style Directory that Belfast had produced featuring photographs of the Members. Dublin decided to follow suit and W. Lawrence the Rotary Photographer was contacted for a quotation. Wm. Findlater agreed to have his photograph taken for the 'Roster', although he wrote;

Personally I look upon the 'Roster' as a bit of a farce but am willing to fall in with it if a sufficient number of other members are equally foolish.

It is not recorded whether or not this photographic record of the early members was actually printed. There are certainly no copies in the archives.

In May, another outing for members and their wives was organised. This time it was to Wicklow. They travelled by train to Greystones were they were met by cars that brought them to Ireton Jones' Gardens and Nursery in Delgany where afternoon tea was partaken. Dinner was in the Grand Hotel in Greystones and some of the party visited the newly opened electric light station nearby – courtesy of the same Mr. Tweedy who had queried the list of classifications. After the ladies withdrew, business was transacted and then members rejoined their wives for songs and entertainment. The return ticket on the train was 1s, the car to Delgany and back 1s and the Dinner 3s. The 5s total was considered most satisfactory. Menu cards were kindly supplied by Mr. Howe, Ireton Jones gave table decorations and buttonholes, Savoy chocolates for the ladies and cigarettes for the gentlemen were supplied by M.M. Murphy and Vine Sanderson respectively and Mr Spielman announced that he would present each of the ladies with a 'coshime'.

As with all organisations, members resigned for all sorts of reasons most of which were not actually recorded. Other members had their membership terminated due to non-payment of Annual Subscription 'despite many requests'. Consequently new members had to be sought constantly. One such was James Adams of the well-known Auctioneers and Valuers then based in Merrion Row. He did not want to join and put an alternative view of the value of the Number One Object of the Club. On July 17th 1913 he wrote:

Dear Mr. Jones,

          Thanks for your kind offer of nomination for membership of the Rotary Club. I am too busy to give time to the meetings of the Club. Neither of my sons seems to care about joining.
    I am sure the objects of the club are very praiseworthy but where business is concerned I think every man should only rely on such merit as he possesses for getting business rather than on the influence of fellow members of a club.
    Any club which limits its membership to only one business or profession must prove very limited indeed.
    I only make these observations as they occur to me on glancing at the rules. Again thanking you and wishing you every success now and always.
       Yours truly
   Signed J. Adams

Adams did not join, but many did. However, classifications remained a thorny issue. Fred Elvery, Elephant House 46 & 47 Lower Sackville Street was interested in joining the club, but there were difficulties.

Dear Mr McConnell,

          With reference to our conversation today on the Classification for the 'Rotary Club'. I regret that I cannot see my way to confine myself to one CLASSIFICATION – we pose as WEATHERPROOFERS and SPORTS OUTFITTERS, so

consequently must go as such. Taking for instance – if I go as a 'Sports Outfitter', the following comes under heading: Riding, Hunting, Driving, Motor, Fishing and Shooting coats, Cycling coats and capes, Driving Aprons and Golf Coats.

For tourists on pleasure - tourist coats and light weights.

I class most of our Waterproofs with our sports, and therefore cannot see my way to change the two – after all it is only dividing two departments in a business. I may mention that the coats named above are both ladies and gents.

Yours faithfully

Signed Fred Elvery

The Council dealt with this by deferring consideration of the application in order to see if they could get a waterproofer member who was not a sports outfitter. This ploy having failed to materialise a suitable candidate, Fred Elvery the consummate salesman was admitted as a member under both the Waterproofer and Sports Outfitter Classification.

Food is, and has always been, a perennial subject for discussion at Rotary meetings. Henry Jury, the proprietor of Jurys Hotel, was a founder member of the club, but he never took a position on a committee and there is no correspondence from him in the files. The Council accepted his resignation on May 7th 1912 with no comment. Stuart Morrow resigned from the Dublin Club on the same day but most definitely continued his Rotary membership.

Complaints had been made by members to the Council concerning both the quality and quantity of food served at Jurys luncheons and these difficulties came to a head in May 1912 when fifteen Members appended their signatures to the following letter to the Manager of Jurys Hotel:

We, the undersigned, wish to draw your attention to the way in which the weekly luncheon is served. The meat is usually cold when we get it, and the bit they give you is too small and no good; also the lunch is never served at 1.15 as it ought to be'.

The Officers of the club made strenuous efforts with Jurys to improve matters as it proved to be not easy to find alternative accommodation. Jurys were willing to add an extra waiter if the club would pay 5s but this was not acceptable. The Central, Wicklow, Hibernian Hotels and the Savoy Restaurant were contacted to no avail. Eventually after a good deal of effort on the part of the President and Hon. Secretary the Dolphin Hotel in Essex Street offered a private room for the lunch and the club held its first meeting there on Monday September **23rd** 1912.

In October of that year the club had a Speaker at lunch on a rather obscure topic – **The Irish League of the Empire**. This was not, as one might suppose, an organisation to cement Irish links with the King Emperor, George V. Rather, its primary object was to 'ascertain and press forward Irish Imperial needs and to promote and further Irish Imperial Interests'. In the document supplied to the Secretary of the club, H. W. Farrell, the League's Organising Secretary advocated the 're-opening of Irish ports and the establishment of direct links with all parts of the Empire and the holding of Conferences, assemblies and Meetings of Irish Imperial interest'. Following his talk Farrell attempted to persuade the club to become involved in his project but, thankfully, his offer was declined. No more was heard of Farrell or his League.

In September 1912 Kevin Kenny, principal of Kennys Advertising Agency, suggested having a Business Exhibition through which members could introduce their goods and services to the public at large. A small Committee was formed to assess the practicality of the idea and reported two weeks later that such an Exhibition was quite feasible. Income was estimated to be £580 and expenditure £425 and it was decided to go ahead with organising a 'Commerce Exhibition' provided that guarantees of £500 were in place. By October 20th the Committee reported that the guarantees had been pledged, the Rotunda Rink[1] was booked and the Exhibition was scheduled to take place for a week from November 18th.

On that day following a lunch attended by sixty-one members and many visitors Her Grace the Countess of Aberdeen[2], the wife of the

Lord Lieutenant cut the ribbon and declared the Exhibition open. The opening ceremony was presided over by William Martin Murphy, President of the Dublin Chamber of Commerce who complimented the Dublin Club on having mounted such an impressive exhibition in such a short space of time. He went on to say that every available space had been let and that it was assured of success.

The club purchased a Silver Cup from the Rotary Jeweller Morton for ten guineas and it was to be presented to the 'champion typewriter'. Other prizes were presented by members also. William Martin Murphy was quite right in his assessment of the success of the 'Commerce Exhibition' in that when the Committee reported in January 1913 they were able to announce a profit of £30 that was to be set-aside for a similar event in the future.

It is an indication of the prestige of the club and its members that in just over a year from its foundation they were able to organise such an exhibition and have the leading businessman in Ireland preside over its opening by the wife of the principal subject in the land. There is no indication as to whether or not it was confined to Rotary members but it is likely that non Rotarians were allotted exhibition space after the Rotary members' needs had been satisfied. The Exhibition was certainly a success and was followed within twenty months by a much larger and grander event- the Civic Exhibition of 1914.

[1] *The Rotunda Rink was part of the Rotunda Group of buildings and pleasure Gardens at the north end of Sackville Street, originally designed to provide an income for the Lying In Hospital next door. The Irish Volunteers were formed here in November 1913. Up to recently the Ambassador Cinema occupied the premises.*

[2] *Isabel Maria, Countess of Aberdeen, the wife of the Lord Lieutenant was indefatigable in her work of promoting goods of Irish manufacture. She gave her support to any venture that would support employment and the manufacture of quality Irish produce.*

Afternoon outing of Dublin club to Pennicks Nurseries Delgany followed by Dinner and a Musical Evening in the Grand Hotel Greystones in June 1912. The president Dr. J.J. Walsh is seated in the centre of the front row.

Chapter Seven

War

'The lights are going out all over Europe and I doubt we will see them go on again in our lifetime'.
Edward Grey 1st Viscount Grey of Falledon Secretary of State for Foreign Affairs

In May 1913 a request was received from Chicago for a contribution towards the relief of victims of the Dayton Flood disaster. As there was no existing mechanism in the club to respond to this type of request an ad hoc committee was formed. On May 26th a draft for $125 was sent to Chicago. This was the first International Service action by the Dublin Club. $25,000 was contributed in total by Rotary clubs on both sides of the Atlantic.

A new scheme, a Booster Week, also made its appearance at this time. Each week a name of a member was drawn and all members of the club were expected to give their business to that person in the coming week. This idea resulted in varying degrees of success for the lucky winners. At the AGM on March 23rd a motion was passed:

'That inasmuch as the Rotary Club exists to promote the business interests of its members, and as every member is anxious to know what the particular business interest of each fellow Rotarian might be, each available weekly lunch meeting should be addressed by a member on the business he represents or on some subject related thereto'.

The 'Booster'scheme continued for fifteen months and appears to have been discontinued, without explanation,

On July 1st a special banquet was held by the club in honour of the visit by Frank Mulholland, Vice President of the I.A.R.C. Mulholland was a special representative of Paul Harris and the Dublin Club was his first stop on a planned tour of the Rotary Club's in Britain and Ireland. Looking back on this visit many years later William McConnell saw this visit as a '**definite turning point in our history**'. The message that Mulholland brought was that '**Rotary had been conceived in selfishness but baptised in service**'. It took some years before the import of these words brought about the change in attitude that they heralded. It was the beginning of a journey on a road that would bring service to the community both at home and abroad to the forefront of Rotary thinking.

In the summer of that year thoughts turned to the upcoming International Convention in Buffalo New York. After a long discussion on the merits of sending delegates it was finally decided that a subvention of £15 would be given to Mr. John Sheridan, Managing Director of Bovril Ltd., classification Beef Extracts, who was travelling to the United States at the time of the Convention. Seventy-four clubs were represented at the Buffalo Convention representing ten thousand members in six countries. The hospitality and friendliness of the American Rotarians that he met overwhelmed Sheridan. In August 1913 he wrote:

My dear McConnell
I have no time to write any particulars now-I have had the most strenuous week of my life, but it was worth fifty times the amount of energy I put in. I am glad to be able to tell you that the 'hit' of the occasion was the delegation from Great Britain and Ireland and please, please do not misunderstand me when I say that Ireland was second to none. When I tell you that last night Frank Mulholland presented me with a prepaid Sleeping Car ticket to Toledo to be his guest in that town, as I sat with President Meade on the platform at the Banquet and which I had to refuse. When I tell you that Will Stephens of California presiding over an informal gathering of the Los Angeles boys invited me to his town with the statement that the trip was not to cost me one cent until I arrived again in New York. When I tell you that I am travelling tonight to Washington by Special Pullman, as the guest of John

Dolph, for the express purpose of shaking hands with the President of the United States (*Woodrow Wilson – an honorary Rotarian*) tomorrow you may, perhaps be able to conceive a small idea of what Rotary means in this country.

Buffalo is a favourite place for conventions owing to its proximity to Niagara, but it is admitted here that no such gathering of men and gentlemen has ever before assembled in the town.

I am pressed for time just now and besides I don't want to spoil my little story at the Dolphin by my sending news in advance so I shall conclude by telling you that Findlater is the International Director and Pentland of Edinburgh is the International vice President and that were it not for your instructions I could so easily have made Findlater VP and Pentland Director – I say this because there were five delegates from Great Britain one or two of whom left their native towns apparently under the belief that they were all powerful in the selection of the International Officers. I hope Findlater will be pleased, because he was elected unanimously and on my personal account, while the other vice Presidents were balloted for.

The New York boys are all right and I hope to attend their dinner on Tuesday night.

Please excuse this hurried scroll – a namesake of mine (the manager of a big advertising business here) who saw my name in the local papers is waiting on me – his father came from Co. Cavan and he wants to talk over the family history.

Yours faithfully
Signed J. Sheridan

There is no record of any further Report by Sheridan of his Buffalo visit.

At the September 25th Monthly Meeting Morrow popped up again, this time as the Secretary of the Liverpool Club that he had founded the previous March. The principal item on the Agenda was how the Dublin Club should react to the exorbitant railway rates and the decision of Cunard and the White Star Line to curtail their Queenstown (Cobh) service.

In September 1913 two rotten tenement houses collapsed in Church Street causing death and destruction. There was no mention of this, or in succeeding meetings in 1913, of the disorder and riots in the City occasioned by the lock out of unionised members of staff of the Dublin United Tramway Company. Sympathetic action on the behalf of other workers led to widespread unrest in the city. The employers led by William Martin Murphy eventually starved the workers, led by Jim Larkin, back to work.

For unspecified reasons, members wished once again change the luncheon venue. The Imperial Hotel, in Sackville Street, was contacted and the first meeting took place there on September 25th with a Table d'hôte lunch provided for two shillings. At the first meeting there, two new club committees were formed to assist the Council in the running of the club. These were termed Internal and External and had twelve members each.

In November 1913 the first edition of the club magazine 'Cogs' appeared. It was printed by Rotarian Richard White on an A3 sheet folded to give four pages of A4 and contained eight strip advertisements from club members at a cost of two shillings each. It consisted of short articles poking gentle humour at some members, an Announcement that an Editor was required, details of upcoming speakers, new members and a listing of 'British Rotary Clubs'. Belfast is listed as having 146 members, Dublin 126, Edinburgh 144, Glasgow 200, Liverpool 140, London 80, Manchester 65 and Birmingham with the peripatetic Stuart Morrow as Secretary and listed as being 'in process of formation'.

Following a meeting in Liverpool on October 30th attended by representatives of all the 'British' Clubs it was decided, subject to agreement from the members of the individual Clubs, to form the

British Association of Rotary Clubs. Their President Wm. Findlater and Hon Secretary Wm. McConnell represented Dublin. The monthly meeting of Dublin members on November 17th endorsed the decision of the President and Hon. Secretary and voted £5 towards the cost of the establishment of the new body.

The year ended with the Monthly Dinner on December 29th featuring a Christmas Tree donated by Ireton Jones illuminated by R. N. Tweedy decorated with over seventy presents provided by members of the club. As the number of presents easily exceeded the attendance there was definitely one for everyone. The meeting was adjudged 'one of the best ever'.

The early part of the New Year, 1914, was enlivened by the visit of over forty members of the Belfast Club for a joint celebration of the 9th anniversary of the foundation of Rotary. Described by the 'Daily Express' as a unique occasion in that it was considered to be 'the first time that such a large body of leading Belfast business and professional men travelled down especially to be guests of Dublin businessmen'. One hundred and thirty sat down to dinner in the Imperial Hotel and it was noted that there were now over 100 Rotary Clubs in the United States and Canada and that plans are afoot to extend the movement to Australia, South Africa, France, Germany and Russia. Events later that year were to have a profound effect on these plans for expansion. The Dublin Club returned the Belfast visit at the end of October the same year travelling by the Great Northern Railway from Amiens Street Station.

In the spring of that year the proposed constitution of the British Association of Rotary Clubs was circulated. The Dublin Club proposed that the name of the organisation should be either the 'Association of Rotary Clubs of Great Britain and Ireland' or the 'Associated Rotary Clubs of Great Britain and Ireland'. Neither suggestion was adopted by the new organisation.

At the March Annual General Meeting it was proposed to alter the Club Constitution so that the Rotary Year should begin on November

1st. This was carried, as was the proposal that there should be two subscriptions paid that year – one in March and the other in November. It was noted that the club could well do with the extra income as *'the income hardly meets the expenditure'*. These changes were made to bring our year into conformance with the other Clubs in the soon to be formed 'British Association of Rotary Clubs'. The newly elected President, J.P. McKnight, therefore held office for just eight months and a new President, R.H. White, was elected in November 1914. The Immediate Past President was added to Council at the same time.

The British Association of Rotary Clubs (B.A.R.C.) was constituted at a meeting in Liverpool on May 4th 1914 attended by sixteen delegates representing eight clubs. Dublin was represented by their President J.P. McKnight and PP William Findlater Vice President of the I.A.R.C. who was therefore the first Rotarian in Europe to hold international office. W. Stuart Morrow also attended the inaugural meeting, this time as a member of the Birmingham Club. In addition to the two already named the other clubs represented at the meeting were, Belfast, London, Manchester, Glasgow, Edinburgh and Liverpool.

The Houston Convention in June of that year was attended by twelve hundred and twenty eight Rotarians representing over one hundred clubs. Among them was Thomas Stephenson Secretary of the Edinburgh Club who entertained the assemblies with Scottish airs in the manner of Sir Harry Lauder, himself a member of the Glasgow Club. Unfortunately Rotarian Stephenson was too free with his opinions to reporters and his views on women and the Irish question appeared in the Houston Chronicle. Sheridan, who had represented the Club at the previous years Convention in Buffalo, got wind of the interview and communicated its content to the Dublin Club. A special meeting was called to discuss the matter and correspondence between the Dublin President and Stephenson was tabled. The upshot was that Stephenson wrote to the Houston Chronicle stating that what he had said on 'Women hindering their Own Cause' and the 'Irish Question' were his own views, had nothing to do with the Houston Convention and were not meant for publication. The letter was published in the September 2nd edition and the Dublin Council expressed the outcome to be satisfactory. Both Votes for Women and Home Rule for Ireland were the burning political issues of the time and were quite outside the remit of Rotary that espoused the dictum that there should be no Religion or Politics discussed.

Cordial relations were resumed with Stephenson and the following year he attended the club Dinner and showed slides and moving pictures of his U.S. visit. The equipment to facilitate this show was provided by our new member Thos. H. Mason, classification Lanterns and Slides.

Following on from the success of the Business Exhibition organised by the club in November 1912 the Civics Institute[1] now proposed to hold a much larger Civic Exhibition from July 15th to August 31st at the Linenhall Building and Grounds. The Dublin Club agreed to become involved, officially, and George L. O'Connor, classification Architect, was appointed director and Kevin Kenny of Kennys Advertising Agency – Advertising Agent was appointed commercial manager while other members served on the organising committee under the Presidency of His Excellency the Lord Lieutenant the Earl of Aberdeen. Lady Aberdeen, well known for her good works in promoting Irish manufacture was chairman.

Over twenty members immediately agreed to take space at the Exhibition at a cost of 4 shillings per square foot. Plans were made to have the principal avenue in the hall designated 'Rotary Avenue' with all stands being taken by members of the Dublin Club. The silver cup provided by the Club for the typewriting competition at the 'Commerce Exhibition' was again presented. Other competitions were organised, including one for 'salesmanship'.

The Civics Exhibition was organised on a much grander and more impressive basis than the much smaller exhibition put on by the club the previous year. A large number of carriages led by the Lord Lieutenant, flanked by the a detachment of the Blue Hussars and the Lord Major of Dublin and many dignitaries proceeded to the Linenhall Buildings[2] situated between Constitution Hill and North King Street

Delegates attending the meeting constituting the British Association of Rotary Clubs May 4th 1914. Back row (left to right): H. Boyd (Belfast), J.S. Proctor (Glasgow), C.E. Dolby (Liverpool), P. Thomason (Manchester), C.B. Penwarden (Manchester), C.H. Dewey (London), W.L. Sleigh (Edinburgh), W. Stuart Morrow (Birmingham), T.H. Stephenson (Edinburgh). Front row (left to right): J. Dobbie (Edinburgh), G.J. Pratt (Liverpool), D.F. Cooke (London), R.W. Pentland (Edinburgh), J.P. McKnight (Dublin), Wm. Findlater (Dublin) and W.H. Alexander (Belfast). W. Stuart Morrow who had founded the Dublin, Belfast, Glasgow, Edinburgh and Liverpool clubs had by 1914 progressed to Birmingham.

where His Excellency declared the event open. It was scheduled to run for six weeks and incorporated everything the public could desire. The object of the exhibition, according to the organisers, the Civics Institute, was to foster in the community a higher and a nobler concentration of their civic duties and responsibilities. The advertisement in the daily papers the following day gives some indication of what was on offer.

Civic Exhibition

Open daily 12noon to 10pm at the Linen Hall Buildings and Grounds Dublin.

Great variety of Interesting exhibitions and attractions.

Ten acres of superb buildings and beautiful promenade grounds.

Easily accessible by special trams from College Green and Nelsons Pillar.

Splendid Industrial and Commerce Exhibition.

Display of the Department of Agriculture and Technical Instruction

Town Planning, Housing, Garden Cities and Suburbs.

Industrial Schools Display	**Bands Military and local**
Torchlight Tattoos and pipers	**Concerts and varied entertainment**
Ballroom and children's dances	**Diningroom and open air Tea Garden**

Competitions. Admission one shilling all day, 6d in the evening.

Season Tickets 7/6

While the Civic Exhibition was taking place events of a much wider significance, that were to have a lasting effect of tens of thousands of Irishmen and women, were beginning to unfold across Europe.

The assassination of the Archduke Franz Ferdinand of Austria in Sarajevo by the Serbian, Gavrilo Princip, on June 28th resulted, due to interlocking alliances, in Britain declaring war on Germany on August 4th. This in turn led to the postponement, until the conclusion of the war, of Home Rule for Ireland that had been passed by the British House of Commons in 1912. The

Poster advertising the Civic Exhibition held in Dublin July 1914.

Irish Parliamentary Party under John Redmond had procured this long promised measure by its crucial support of the minority Liberal Government. The House of Lords had delayed its implementation but their veto power had been curtailed by the Parliament Act of 1911 and was due to run out in late 1914. The mere promise of Home Rule, however, had resulted in the formation of the Ulster Volunteers, under Sir Edward Carson M. P. for Trinity College Dublin, to oppose it. This action had been mirrored in Dublin by the formation of the Irish Volunteers in November 1913, under Professor Eoin McNeill, to defend its implementation. There were three other armies of varying sizes and degrees of discipline in Ireland. They were the British army, the refusal of whose officers to act against the importation of arms by the Ulster Volunteers had resulted in the Curragh mutiny. The Citizen Army led by James Connolly that was initially formed to protect the workers of Dublin during the 1913 Lockout and Irish Republican Brotherhood (IRB), formerly known as the Fenians. The IRB had infiltrated the leadership of the Irish Volunteers from its inception and after it split in November 1914, following John Redmond's call at Woodenbridge to its members to enlist in the British Army to defend the small nations of Europe, they held a dominant, yet secret, position.

The Dublin Club's reaction to the outbreak of hostilities was to appoint a special sub committee to investigate, report and assist members in securing trade that they consider could more profitably executed by home manufacturers. This followed on from a luncheon discussion as to the capturing of German trade.

Towards the end of 1914 a letter was received from Frank Mulholland, who had become President of the International Association of Rotary Clubs (I.A.R.C.) referring to the need to clear the debt that had arisen from the early years of the organisation. While it was expressly stated in the letter that the British Clubs would not be required to participate in this effort it was agreed to send a contribution to the I.A.R.C. of 1/- per member.

A Christmas Party was held again with Christmas tree and lights but the difference this year was that instead of presents for the members there was a collection for the new Red Cross hospital that had been set up in Dublin Castle for those soldiers wounded in the War. This is the first substantial fundraising effort carried out by the club for an Irish project and £50 was raised for this worthwhile cause.

By this time relations with the hotel manager in the Imperial were at a low ebb. He was not happy that the club was holding its monthly dinner elsewhere and they were requested to find an alternative venue for lunch. The Metropole on the other side of Sackville Street was interested in providing a venue and the first lunch was held there in February 1915. The next Council Meeting was told that the manager of the Imperial had been replaced and the new manager wanted the club to return. They decided to stay where they were.

That month also saw the first President's Night to celebrate the 10th Anniversary of the foundation of Rotary. It was held in Mills Hall, Merrion Row. This was a black tie function and Mr. W. Percy French, 'the Celebrated Irish Humourist', provided the entertainment at a cost of three guineas. The tickets were 3/- each, excluding wine. The circular advising of the function advised that *'It is hoped that all Rotarians who possibly can do so will attend, and that they will bring as guests their lady relatives and friends. Mere men guests are also permissible'*.

[1] The Civics Institute of Ireland was founded in 1914 and fostered the concept of Town Planning. They set up the Dublin Civic Survey Committee. In the 1930s they established playgrounds for disadvantaged children. They co-operated with TCD in founding a Social Science course. They disbanded in 1960.

2 The Linen Hall Buildings had been unoccupied for some time prior to the Civic Exhibition and were destroyed by fire during the 1916 Rebellion. Its grounds have been incorporated into the Park in front of the Kings Inns Building.

Chapter Eight

1915/16

'Service Above Self'
Rotarian Ben Collins Minneapolis Club

By the end of 1914 William Stuart Morrow had achieved his self-imposed task of establishing two Rotary Clubs each in Ireland, Scotland and England. The regard in which Morrow was held in the U.S. at the time can be gauged from Resolution 15 passed at the Houston Texas Convention in 1914: to '**express the appreciation of the International Association of Rotary Clubs to Mr. W. Stuart Morrow for his work in organizing Rotary Clubs in Great Britain and Ireland**'. As can be seen from the membership numbers quoted in the first edition of Cogs the London Club, with the largest population to draw from, had the lowest membership. They approached Morrow and enlisted his help in attracting new members. He went about his task with customary zeal, even though he was now sixty years of age. He had some success in obtaining new members but matters came to a head when he opened a 'Rotary Bureau' in the Strand without the permission of the club. The B.A.R.C. advised the Dublin Club of this unauthorised activity and the club decided '*to take no action*'. The last that we hear of Morrow in the minutes is when he asked the Dublin Club to sponsor him on a trip to the United States introducing Irish manufactured goods to U.S. Rotarians. The club decided not to become involved in this scheme. The pioneering days of Rotary were coming to an end and there would be no place for the restless spirit of Morrow in the new environment. It should be noted, however, that Morrow's club forming days were not over. In 1921 we find him canvassing for members for the Optimists Club in Oakland, California. The Optimists were and are an organisation dedicated to improving the lot of underprivileged and deprived young people. Like Rotary its membership was confined to businessmen. One day he called on one of the city's Business Colleges to seek to interest its manager, whom he assumed to be a man, in joining the Club. The Manager turned out to be a woman and was disappointed to learn that she was ineligible for membership of the organisation. Following this meeting Morrow got to thinking about the idea of a club for women in business and on May 31st 1921 the first meeting of the Soroptimists Club was held in Oakland California. Both the Optimists and Soroptimists are thriving organisations today. William Stuart Morrow died in 1942 at San Mateo, California, aged eighty-six.

In April 1915 classifications were still causing trouble. A wheelwright was proposed for membership, but it transpired that his principal business was coach building and Sanderson was the Rotary Coachbuilder. He was turned down for membership and offered a place on the waiting list.

An article in the Rotarian magazine asked each club to have a discussion amongst its members as to whether or not the strict Classification Rule 111should be relaxed. The club duly discussed the matter and by a narrow margin the proposal to relax Rule 111 was defeated. All the indications were that the members were benefiting to a great extent from their membership of the club and they wanted to keep it that way.

A rather more difficult matter came to the fore around the same time. R.A Foley, classification Typewriters, who was a Founder Member declined to pay his Annual Subscription because he disapproved of the practice of:

'…the singing of any anthem at any Club function. If anthems be allowed now we shall eventually have hymns, subjects and matters foreign to the purpose for which the Dublin Rotary Club was established are now frequently introduced – questions on which not all members are agreed, and this is one reason why I cannot attend meetings under existing conditions.

On a previous occasion I protested against the drinking of toasts at Rotary Club functions, and the practice was not persisted in.

On hearing from the Committee that anthem-singing and controversial subjects will be barred, I shall be glad to forward cheque to Mr. Coade.
    Kind regards
    Yours faithfully
    Signed R. A. Foley.

The Council considered this letter carefully. They wrote advising Mr. Foley that in their opinion all club functions were organised within the letter and spirit of Rotary. Foley did not pay his subscription and his name was removed from the Roll of Members.

It is difficult to be absolutely certain as to what anthem Foley was referring to in his letter May 3rd, but it is probable that he was referring to the British anthem. Patriotic favour for the allied cause in the Great War permeated all sections of society and it is probable that many members had sons and brothers in the armed forces prosecuting the war. This becomes obvious in later years when Motions of Condolence are passed by the club on the death of sons and brothers of members. There was certainly a toast to the king proposed at the first President's Night in February of that year. Foley could have been referring to that event in his letter. An interesting sidelight on this matter is that forty years later the question of toasts was to come to the fore again in a more direct and dramatic manner.

At the invitation of the War Services League the club took on the task of entertaining wounded soldiers by bringing them on an outing to Powerscourt Waterfall. The train was to be met at Bray Station and cars provided to bring the soldiers to the Waterfall where tea and refreshments would be provided. The practical nature of the businessmen in the club was evident in that before undertaking this venture they ensured that there was adequate insurance cover in place. Later that year an invitation was accepted from the Royal Irish Automobile Club to join their committee organising entertainment and treats for wounded soldiers in the Royal Dublin Society premises in Ballsbridge. The Rotary Club took responsibility for every second Wednesday and to further support the war the club decided to invest £100 of its funds in the government's War Loan bond.

T. A. Grehan, advertisement manager of the Irish Independent, was certainly one Rotarian who believed strongly in the early Rotary slogan – 'He who serves best, profits most'. Hardly a month would go by without him hatching some scheme or other to entice members of the club to take out advertisements in one or other of his newspapers. One idea that he had was to set aside a page per month (or per week if required) for just advertisements from Rotarians, at a special rate, of course. On July 13th 1915 he received a letter from Paul P Harris written on the notepaper of his firm of attorneys – Harris, Kagy & Vanier, 127 North Dearborn Street, Chicago:

My Dear Mr Grehan,

I beg to acknowledge receipt of your announcement of the establishment of the 'First Rotary Newspaper in Europe'. I thank you very sincerely for your thoughtfulness in informing me.

I feel somewhat of a stranger to the Dublin Club, not having heard directly from many of you. I have, however, observed with interest and satisfaction the records of the development of your organisation, and hope that I may have the pleasure of the personal acquaintance of yourself and other members of the Rotary Club of Dublin.

With kind regards to yourself and best wishes to all, I beg to remain

Yours very sincerely

Signed Paul P Harris

This was a non-committal, yet friendly letter. It was to be another thirteen years before Dublin Rotarians were to have the pleasure of meeting Paul Harris personally.

The club decided not to send a representative to the 1915 International Convention held in San Francisco from July 18th to 23rd at which a number of significant decisions were made. Although he still kept in touch with the work of Rotary, Paul Harris had retired from active participation in the organisation's affairs at this time and had assumed the title of President Emeritus. The process that he had begun in moving Rotary away from a purely business oriented movement to a more broadly based one that included service to the community continued. This was evidenced in the adoption at the San Francisco Convention of a revised set of 'Objects of Rotary'. These were:

To promote the recognition of the worthiness of all legitimate occupations and to dignify the occupation of each member as affording him an opportunity to serve society.
To encourage high ethical standards in business and professions.
To increase the efficiency of each member by the development of improved ideas and business methods.
To stimulate the desire of each member to be of service to his fellow man and society in general.
To promote the scientising of acquaintance as an opportunity for service and an aid to success.
To quicken the interest of each member in the public welfare of his community, and to co-operate with others in its civic, social, commercial and industrial development.

The Convention also voted $500 (£100) towards extension work by the B.A.R.C. and for the first time organised the clubs into Districts. Of the nineteen districts, fifteen were in the United States, three in Canada and District 19 comprised Britain and Ireland with J.S. Proctor of Glasgow as Governor.

The deliberations and decisions of each convention were highlighted in the following edition of the Rotary magazine, were published in booklet form and were available for clubs to purchase for a nominal sum. Gradually Rotary was beginning to move away from being an introverted organisation to one that would embrace the needs of all.

As the year drew to a close it was decided not to hold a special Christmas dinner but instead toapproach Temple and Harcourt Street Children's Hospitals with a view to ascertaining whether or not they would like the Club to provide a Christmas tree and presents for the children. The managers of both Hospitals gladly agreed to the Dublin Club's proposal and thus began a tradition of visiting Children's Hospitals at Christmas time that is still carried on to this day. There were eighty children in Temple Street and forty in Harcourt Street and each got a present, drinks, cakes and sweets that were provided by the wives and sisters of members and a fully decorated Christmas tree was erected in each hospital.

At the final meting of Council on December 15th 1915 the following motion was passed unanimously on the proposal of President Coade and seconded by Mr. Drought:

That Leave of Absence be granted to those members away on Military Service viz. Dr. E. M. Fannin and Mr. E.S. Robinson, with consequent relief from Club Subscription during the period of their service with the Colours.

Meanwhile a major extension drive was underway in Britain with plans to found Rotary Clubs in Leeds, Bradford, Portsmouth, Leicester, Bristol, Derby and Dundee. The club sent a cheque for £10 to support the B.A.R.C. in this work. The possibility of founding a club in Cork was raised by a number of the members and the President and Hon. Secretary agreed to sound out some business acquaintances in that city on this topic. Having been raised at a number of meetings it was decided to invite any Cork businessmen who happened to be in Dublin to attend one of the club lunches and see how Rotary operated. Nothing more came of this idea of extending Rotary to the South of Ireland at that time. It was not until 1926 that the Cork Club was founded.

In early 1916 the club was faced with a major dilemma: a lady who was in an executive position in business applied to join. The Council were at a loss as to how to deal with the issue and decided to write to the B.A.R.C. and Rotary headquarters in Chicago for guidance. It was to be some months before a definitive reply was received.

On February 17th S. J. Riordan classification Showcard and Ticket Writer wrote to the Hon. Secretary complaining that five members who had used his services at the Rotary Avenue in the Civic Exhibition the previous August had not cleared their account with him. The Council considered the matter and decided that:

'it could not take any responsibility therewith'.

Commercial matters would have to take their own course. Whereas Council felt unable to offer any succour to Riordan on this matter it would not be long before they would come to his aid in a more substantial fashion.

Soon, however, the Dublin Club and its members had to deal with a truly cataclysmic event: the Easter Rising of 1916 and its aftermath.

The Rotary Butcher Michael Reid (fourth from right) with some of his staff outside his business premises 11/12 Chatham Street, Dublin

Chapter Nine

Easter Rising

'I write it out in a verse-
MacDonagh and McBride
And Connolly and Pearse
Now and in time to be,
Wherever green is worn
Are changed, changed utterly:
A terrible beauty is born'.

'Easter 1916' William Butler Yeats

The events of the week following Easter 1916 had a traumatic effect on the citizens of Dublin. Whole swathes of the city were destroyed, many people totally unconnected with the military action were killed, businesses and livelihoods wiped out and a spark lit a fuse that eventually led to independence and the establishment of the Irish Republic.

When the Irish Volunteers split following the Woodenbridge speech by the Irish Parliamentary Party's leader John Redmond urging Irishmen to enlist in the British army, a minority of about ten thousand remained with their Chief of Staff Eoin MacNeill. O'Neill's view was that the organisation should not engage in any overt military action unless conscription was imposed on Ireland. The members of the Irish Republican Brotherhood who had infiltrated the Irish Volunteers' leadership had other ideas and planned a nation-wide insurrection on Easter Sunday 1916. Arms and ammunition had been procured via the Asgard the previous year and more were expected when Sir Roger Casement returned from Germany on the Aud. Unfortunately for the plans of the I.R.B. Casement and the Aud were intercepted in Kerry and he was arrested. Notwithstanding this setback, the I.R.B.

leadership still intended to launch their insurrection throughout Ireland under the cover of planned manoeuvres. MacNeill discovered their plans and after listening to a variety of conflicting arguments he issued an order calling off the Easter Sunday manoeuvres. This was published in the Sunday Independent of April 23rd. The effect of this countermanding order was to throw the Volunteers into confusion. It also had the effect of indicating to the Dublin Castle authorities that nothing was now planned for that weekend and that they could relax and set about enjoying themselves. The I.R.B., however, persevered with their intention and decided to act on the following day, Easter Monday.

On that morning around a thousand to twelve hundred Irish Volunteers, members of the Citizen's Army and Cumann na mBan occupied the General Post Office on Sackville Street, Boland's Mill's, Jacob's Factory, St. Stephen's Green, the South Dublin Union, the Four Courts and the City Hall. At 12 noon Commandant General Padraig Pearse read the Proclamation of the Irish Republic outside the G.P.O.

The weather was warm and sunny that day and many Dubliners had either gone to attend the Irish Grand National at Fairyhouse or had taken the train to the seaside with their families. It was a day for relaxing and taking it easy.

On that same Easter Monday morning Alfred Fannin, Managing Director of Fannin's Medical Supply Company 41 Grafton Street, who had joined the Dublin Club the previous February with the classification of Surgical Instruments, was playing golf in Greystones Golf Club. Alfred was the brother of Dr. Edwin, also a member of the Dublin club, who had been given leave of absence by Council in December 1915 when he had joined the Royal Army Medical Corps and been posted to Malta. Alfred played nine holes in the morning and as he was taking lunch in the Clubhouse he learned that the telephone lines to Dublin had been cut and that Sinn Fein[1] was causing some trouble in the city. His attitude to this news can be gauged from the fact that he played another nine holes with his cousin Edwin Booth[2] and his wife Edith before driving back safely to his home at 32 Herbert Park.

The next day Alfred found it impossible to go to his place of business and decided to keep a record of events[3] as they unfolded to send to his brother Edwin in Malta.

Alfred's brother-in-law was Dr. Alfred Parsons; a surgeon attached to the Royal City of Dublin Hospital at Baggot Street. From Monday of that week he slept in the hospital and dealt with the many casualties as best as he could.

Alfred wrote that someone called Dolores (Eamon DeValera) had taken control of Boland's Mill. The first engagement that Alfred learned of involved a detachment of the Georgious Rex, a band of ex rugby players and British Army veterans who were returning from a route march in the Dublin Hills to their base at Beggar's Bush Barracks. They carried rifles but were unarmed and were affectionately known to Dubliners as the Gorgeous Wrecks. As they marched down Northumberland Rd. they were fired upon from houses on the corner of Haddington Rd. Many were killed and others severely injured while others escaped through back gardens to the relative safety of their barracks. The shooting could be heard quite clearly in Herbert Park and it was all Alfred could do to calm his family.

Smith, his Manager, opened the Grafton Street shop, as usual on the Tuesday, and went out to Herbert Park and reported that all the staff, except one whom he thought to be a Sinn Feiner, had turned up for work. This man did take part in the Rising but was carried, dead, into Dr. Steevan's Hospital. Smith told Fannin that the military had taken over the telephone system and they were only receiving officially allowed calls from hospitals. They were unable to make telephone calls themselves. Some surgical dressings had been sent to the Richmond Hospital and the messenger boy had had to obtain a permit from the rebels to allow him to get through the barricades in Sackville Street. The staff was sent home early. On that day also, just around the corner from Fannin's premises, Edward Murphy, a civilian, the maternal grandfather of our current member Donald Gordon, was shot in the head and killed as he walked past 'Smyth's On The Green'. Murphy, who lived in Pembroke Street and had survived the Canadian Gold

Rush and the Boer War, had just doffed his hat to a member of the staff of Smyth's when he was shot.

On the Wednesday, Fannin went as far as Baggot Street and could hear heavy guns being fired. Although he did not know it at the time these were being fired by the Helga, a fishery protection vessel that had been brought up the Liffey to below Butt Bridge. From the Tuesday onwards it wrought havoc and destruction on all the buildings between the north quays above Butt Bridge and the G.P.O. On the first day, shells from the Helga destroyed buildings on Eden Quay including the premises of S. J. Riordan the club's Attendance Officer who had been trying to get his accounts paid some months previously. All his stock and equipment were burned as were all our Attendance Records and he was left without premises or the means to carry on his business.

On the same day, Liberty Hall in Beresford Place where the Provisional Government had met on the morning of the previous day before heading for the G.P.O. was hit by shells and burned out. A systematic destruction of all buildings within the range of the guns aiming towards the G.P.O. began. The Royal Hibernian Academy in Lower Abbey Street was destroyed and then the Metropole to which the club had transferred our luncheons the previous year. All the member's badges and the President's gavel were destroyed and the club would have to look for a new luncheon venue.

Fannin went as far as the Methodist Centenary Church on the south side of Saint Stephen's Green. He went up onto the roof and observed a republican flag flying over the College of Surgeons whilst the park attendant in the green was feeding the ducks. There was a barricade of motor cars at the Russell Hotel and shooting between the rebels in the College of Surgeons and the British army in the Shelbourne Hotel. On the same evening he saw shooting between troops marching in from Kingstown and the rebels who occupied Carisbrook House at the junction of Pembroke Rd and Northumberland Rd. The rebels also occupied the Trinity College Botanic Gardens[4].

On Thursday, Fannin had a close shave when bullets passed quite close to him in Ballsbridge. He did not impart this information to his family in Herbert Park. Later that day the Herbert Park residents were reassured by the long lines of troops marching along Morehampton Road towards the city. Many pieces of artillery added to the level of confidence that the Sinn Feiners would soon be beaten. He chatted to troops billeted in Herbert Park and his daughter, Sylvia, brought out some fruit for them.

Provisions were running low and it was necessary for Fannin to carry back potatoes and vegetables and other grocery items from whatever shops he could find. He was able to go with other men from the neighbourhood to the back entrance of the Johnston Mooney and O'Brien Bakery in Ballsbridge to obtain bread. This was a most unaccustomed activity for a middle class man and he mentioned it particularly in his report to his brother Edwin.

While Alfred Fannin was seeing what he could of the action around the south of the city another Rotarian William Findlater who rejoiced in the appellation of being the 'Second Rotarian in Europe' was guarding his shop premises. William had been Club President in 1913/4 and, as we saw, was elected International Director at the Buffalo Convention in 1913. Findlaters was the leading retailer of groceries, wines and spirits in Dublin and had several branches. Its headquarters was at 39-42 Upper Sackville Street

When the Irish Volunteers occupied the G.P.O. on the Monday of Easter Week and began firing at anyone in uniform the Dublin Metropolitan Police, who were unarmed, had been withdrawn. This left the way open for hundreds of looters to emerge from the tenements between Sackville Street and the North Strand, smash windows of shops that had not been damaged and carry away what merchandise they could get their hands on. Alert to the danger William Findlater, a bluff, larger than life character with a great sense of humour, sat himself down on a chair outside his premises with a loaded blunderbuss resting across his knees. From time to time senior members of the staff relieved him. All week a watch was kept and by the time the fighting was over, Findlaters was the only premises on Sackville Street to escape the looters.

On Friday, Fannin managed to get into his Grafton Street premises under military escort and got much needed supplies for Baggot Street Hospital where many of the wounded were being treated. On Saturday, he paid all the staff for a full week's work although little or no business had been done. He was a good employer and appreciated the fact that the staff had turned up for work under very trying conditions. Alfred Fannin sent a covering letter to his brother Edwin enclosing the Diary he had kept and some newspapers:

…The papers will give you a good idea of what took place but the feelings of those who went through it must be imagined. The experiences of the G. Rs. were very tragic. I explained what happened to the lot that went by Northumberland Road. The other lot, Harris's, were fired on between Shelbourne Road and the front gate of Beggars Bush. One or two were killed and the remainder got to the gate or over the wall. To defend Beggars Bush there were seven soldiers, mostly crocks, There were 100 or so of G. Rs. with only 13 rifles amongst the lot. They tried to make the live rifles look as many as they could. But if the Sinn Feiners rushed them they could easily have wiped them out. George Beckett and Connell[5] of the Belfast Bank were among them. They had to lie all night under the walls of the Barracks in the hope that if the SFs came they might knock in their heads at close quarters before they could shoot. Late on Tuesday afternoon an armoured car came into the Barracks with rifles and on Wednesday a party of the Sherwood Foresters fought their way into the Barracks but until Wednesday of next week they could not leave the Barracks and were being sniped at all the time…..

As the week ended the British army closed in on the G.P.O which was abandoned while it was burning on Friday. Pearse surrendered unconditionally at the corner of Moore Street and Great Britain (Parnell) Street on Saturday. Over the course of the weekend the other outposts followed suit.

Between the 3rd and 12th of May fifteen leaders of the rising were executed following Field Courts-Martial. All the signatories of the

Proclamation and all the Commandants with the exception of De Valera and Countess Markievicz were shot in Kilmainham Jail.

On May 8th it is recorded that our club received a letter of sympathy from the British Association of Rotary Clubs. On May 12th Council met in President Coade's office in Cantrell & Cochrane Ltd. in Nassau Place and it was directed that lunch should be held the following Monday in Mills Restaurant in Merrion Row. New badges were ordered from the Dundalgan Press and $5 sent towards a presentation to the outgoing President of I.A.R.C. It was business as usual as far as possible.

Our attendance officer who had lost his business on Eden Quay and who was now trying to operate out of a room in Gardiner Place expressed a rather straightforward view in a letter dated May 6th and addressed to Wm. McConnell Hon. Secretary of the club:

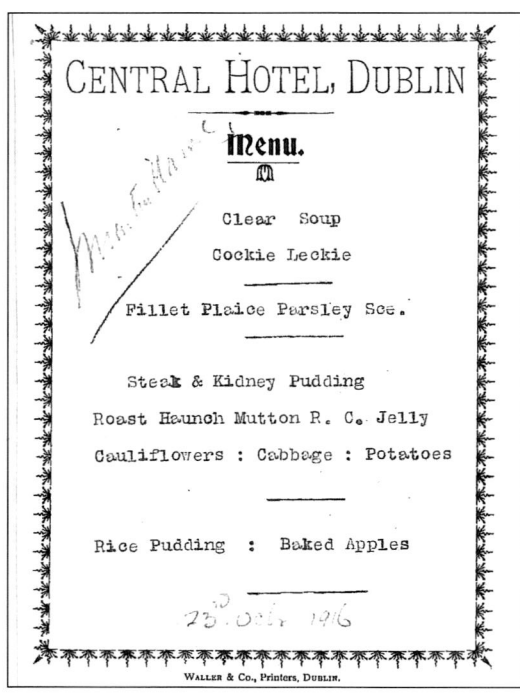

Central Hotel luncheon menu for the Dublin club October 1916

My dear McConnell,
                    Here I am in Gardiner's Place with one large room for temporary premises-all my property of dyes, colours, bronzes, card boards etc at 7 Eden Quay (are) gone in consequence of the foolish attempt of the Sinn Fein party to gain their ends. Big heads and little wit, that explains the movement.

I regret that the Rotary Record Book is amongst the ruins – I kept it at my business place for convenience, of course. As I am perplexed and worried please excuse my absence from lunch at present.

I see several Rotarians in the list – Lawrence, Kapp, Taylor, Elvery and Findlater's branch house in Upper Dorset Street. Perhaps there are others. It pains a fellow more to see Rotary people getting a 'Knockout' because of the close acquaintance.
I trust that you pulled through yourself without mishap.
I notice that the leaders are dispatched day after day and that is how it ought to be.
with kind remembrance, believe me
dear McConnell
Yours in Rotary
Signed S. J. Riordan

In writing 'I see that the leaders are dispatched day after day and that is how it ought to be' he was agreeing with the leader writer of the Irish Independent who wrote on May 10th calling for the execution of the worst of the leaders of the Rising. Two days later James Connolly and Sean McDermott were executed.

At the Mills Restaurant lunch it was announced that the club were making inquiries re lunch at the Café Cairo, the Gresham, Jurys and the Dolphin with regard to future luncheon venues.

As Hon. Sect. McConnell's instigation a circular was issued to all members of the Club advising them of Riordan's situation following on from the destruction of his business. Over a period of three weeks over £85 was raised which in today's terms is in excess of €10,000. Thanks to the generous and immediate response of members he was able to get back into business and remained a member for many more years. Only one member is recorded as having to decline to support Riordan's fund. Fred Elvery of 46/47 Lower Sackville Street felt that he had to decline. He wrote to Hon. Secretary Wm. McConnell on June 13th

…I would be very pleased indeed to help in this case but at the present moment I am nearly as badly off. Being in business yourself you will understand the circumstances under which I am situated at present and trust that you will excuse me on this occasion….

By June 10th Wm. McConnell, our Hon. Secretary, was writing to William Martin Murphy who in addition to his chairmanship of Independent Newspapers and the Dublin United Tramway Company had also taken upon himself the duty of chairing the Dublin Fire and Property Losses Association 1916. William McConnell forwarded to William Martin Murphy a copy of a resolution passed by the British Association of Rotary Clubs to strengthen Murphy's hand in dealing with the Government. The Resolution in the names of the Rotary Clubs of the cities of Belfast, Birmingham, Dublin, Edinburgh, Glasgow, Leeds, Liverpool, Manchester and Newcastle-upon-Tyne called upon the Government to ensure that compensation for losses incurred in the recent insurrection in Dublin should be commensurate with the actual losses sustained irrespective of any protective arrangements (i.e. insurance) made by the sufferers for ordinary contingencies. The letter to Martin Murphy indicates that copies of the Resolution had been forwarded also to the Prime Minister Herbert Asquith, Home Secretary Herbert Samuel and Sir Robert Chalmers Under Secretary for Ireland. The four Dublin papers also got copies. There is no indication of the outcome of their endeavours. Interestingly it may be noted that, for whatever reason, there is no mention of the London Club, founded in August 1911, in the listing of clubs supporting the Resolution. It may be an oversight.

As the year passed there was a gradual change in people's attitude to the events of Easter Week 1916, even among some of the employer and Unionist class. Sir Maurice Dockrell was not a members of the Rotary Club but Dockrells were represented by James A McMahon classification House and Estate Agent.

A William Breen was in the G.P.O garrison during Easter Week, was interned in Frongoch in Wales, and after his release at the end of 1916 he went back to work in Dockrell's. The heads of the various departments and other employees went as a deputation to Sir Maurice Dockrell and told him that they would not continue to work in the same firm as Breen. Sir Maurice replied saying that Breen had fought according to his colour and they themselves were able-bodied men who should be in khaki fighting at the front, and if they did not want to work with Breen they knew their way out.

My own grandfather, Edward Keegan, was not so fortunate. Having survived being wounded in the defence of the South Dublin Union he was dismissed for 'disloyalty' when he tried to return to his job in 'The Irish Times'. Attitudes were changing, but slowly.

[1] *Sinn Fein, the public face of Irish nationalism, was founded by Arthur Griffith in 1905. He was active in seeking a separate government for Ireland under a dual monarchy with Britain similar to the system that existed in Austria and Hungary.*

[2]*Edwin Booth joined the club in 1920 and is the paternal grandfather of our current member David Booth.*

[3] *Letters from Dublin, Easter 1916 – Alfred Fannin's Diary of the Rising Edited by Adrian and Sally Warwick-Haller and published by the Irish Academic Press in 1995*

[4]*The Botanic Gardens were situated on the corner of Lansdowne Road and Pembroke Road. The site is currently occupied by the D4 Hotel (formerly Jurys where we met for lunch from 1970 to 2007).*

[5] *George Beckett, an Architect, was an Uncle of our Hon. Member PDG Horner Becket . J. W. Connell was elected a member of the Dublin Club in April 1917 with the classification of Banking in place of our first President J. H. Fleming who had died. Connell had succeeded Fleming as Manager of the Belfast Banking Co.*

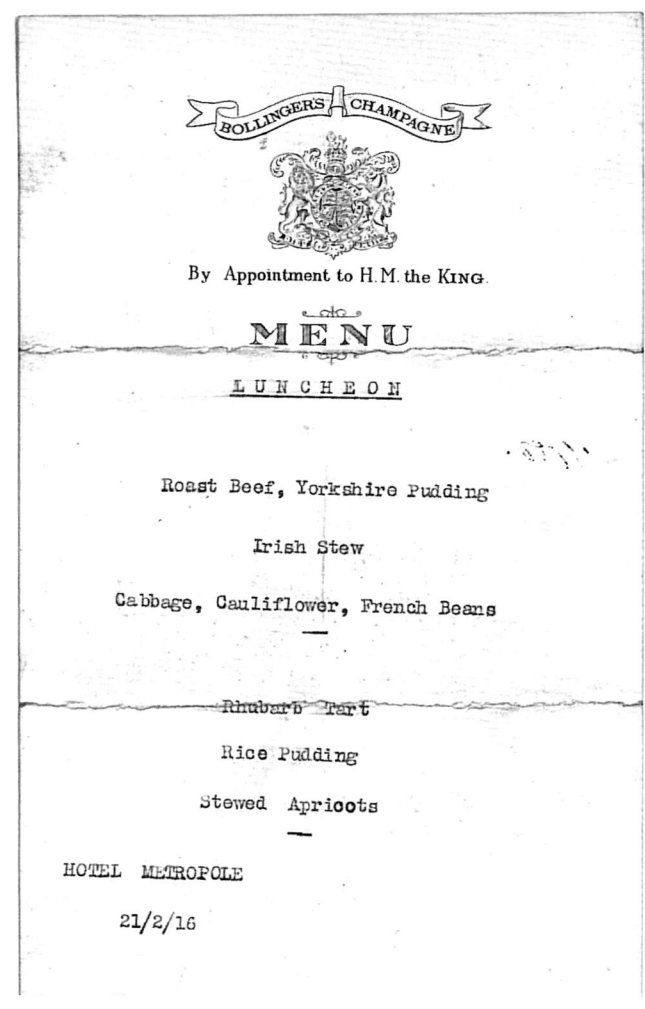

Menu Hotel Metropole 1916

Chapter Ten

Changing times

'When its doors are open to women and to Trade Unions it will become the most powerful influence for breaking down class prejudices and social barriers'.
Rotarian R.N.T. Tweedy August 1918

The changing times following the Easter Rising and the resulting executions polarised the country and the members of the club found themselves in the middle of a political landscape that was beginning to change radically. The first evidence of this shift in public opinion is to be found in the Minutes of the Council of June 30th and the Monthly meeting of the club on July 3rd 1916. Both meetings considered the possibility of holding a members' summer outing on the same lines of those held in former years to Howth and Greystones and in the case of both meetings they decided against this idea. More tellingly, however, the July 3rd meeting of Members considered and decided against having an outing for wounded soldiers, like the one to Powerscourt Waterfall in August 1915. On the recommendation of Council this proposal was withdrawn because of the *'existing circumstances'*. The club's support for the Red Cross Hospital in Dublin Castle[1] was continued, as was their involvement in the entertainment of wounded soldiers that they had undertaken in conjunction with the R.I.A.C. in the R.D.S. premises in Ballsbridge.

All of the members, being in business in Dublin, would have been in daily contact with members of the public from diverse backgrounds. They would have been aware of the changing public attitude and whilst almost all of their private views would have been firmly on the side of law and order and the army, they had to make a living and the public were their customers. James Stephens[2], writing during the Rising noted the differences between how men and women dealt with the events of Easter week as they unfolded. The men tended to be more guarded in their comments while the women expressed themselves forcefully for one side or the other, generally against the insurgents.

As the week went on, Stephens noticed a grudging acceptance of the fact that the rebels were putting up a good fight and that while they were not likely to win they were doing a good deal better than expected. The murder of crusading pacifist Sheehy Skeffington and two other totally innocent men in Portobello Barracks on the orders of Capt. Bowen-Colthurst and the manner in which the military dealt with this outrage further undermined many people's respect for the authorities. There was, as yet, no way this alteration in the public mood could be measured yet there is no doubt that the astute businessmen in the Dublin Club could see that there was change in the air.

On the French/Belgium border the Battle of the Somme began on July 1st 1916. In the bombardment preceding it, Bernard Reid, the son of Michael Reid of McDonagh's of Chatham Street, classification Victualler, was killed. Like many other young men at the front he had been a member of the Irish Volunteers and had, in fact, been one of the organisers of the Rotunda enlistment meeting in 1913 and had signed many of the membership cards of those involved in the rising. He was one of many sons and relatives of members killed in the conflict.

In July, Lord Wimborne, who had resigned as Lord Lieutenant in the aftermath of the Easter rising, was re-appointed. The Club decided that a loyal address was not appropriate as *'His Excellency was re-entering as Viceroy'*[5]

At the September monthly meeting the thorny question of a woman applying to join the club was again on the Agenda[3]. The I.A.R.C. had replied and guidance had been received.

'A letter dated 25th July 1916 was read from the International Association of Rotary Clubs intimating, in reply to our enquiries, that the Board of Directors was not in favour of the admission of women members and that there was no wish on the part of any Club that women should be admitted.

The letter also referred to the formation in certain cities of the United States of Clubs of Business Women using the word 'Rotary' in their title[4]. They mentioned that the Board of Directors of the I.A.R.C. did not think it would be necessary for them to resort to the Courts to have this practice on the part of the organisations referred to, discontinued.

It was resolved by the meeting not to consider applications for membership from ladies and it was further resolved on the motion of Ireton Jones, seconded by Mr. Beckett that the Dublin Club would recommend to the Board of the I.A.R.C. that they should take steps to safeguard the title of Rotary in Great Britain and Ireland.'

It was to be another seventy-three years before women in business were admitted to Rotary and this was only achieved following a court challenge in the United States.

At the request of the B.A.R.C a discussion was held at the October meeting with regard to the pros and cons of the metric system. Following on from this the following resolution was passed:

'That the Dublin Rotary Club is of the opinion that in the interests of both education and commerce it is desirable that steps be taken as soon as circumstances permit for the adoption of the metric system of money, weights and measures in the British Isles.'

It was to be some decades before this proposal was adopted in Britain and Ireland.

Towards the end of 1916 hundreds of those who had been interned following the rising began to be released and were welcomed back at the railway stations by crowds. In July 1917, a bye-election was called for the east Clare constituency to return a Member of Parliament to Westminster. Eamon deValera representing Sinn Fein, who had been released from Lewes Jail just two days before the voting took place, defeated the Irish Parliamentary Party candidate taking 70% of the votes. The change in public mood noted by the Club the previous year had now become manifest. In October of that year deValera succeeded Arthur Griffith as President of Sinn Fein.

Since its foundation attendance at club luncheons had not been good. This was despite many endeavours on the part of Council to encourage the participation of all members. Printed postcards were sent each week reminding members of the lunch with the name and subject of the speaker. Each Council and Committee member was given a number of members' names and encouraged to telephone them each week to remind them to turn up to meetings. Attendance competitions were held on the basis of dividing the membership into two teams of 'Always Present' and 'Never Absent' giving a point to each team for members that turned up for lunch. The winning team after two months would buy the lunch for the other. Cups were awarded on a similar basis.

At the annual general meeting of 1916 only thirty-one members were present. The Committees that reported are listed although we do not have their individual reports. The Committees were: Attendance, Publications, Proceedings, Public Affairs and Business Interests, Fraternal and Wounded Soldiers Entertainment.

The Harcourt and Temple Children's hospitals were again to be provided with Christmas trees and presents with the Orthopaedic hospital in upper Merrion Street and the Children's Ward of Cork Street hospital added to the list. Members who had subscribed and their wives were to be invited to take part in the festivities at the three hospitals between 3 and 6pm on the Friday before Christmas.

George Russell[6] (AE) was a high profile speaker at the monthly dinner early in 1917 talking on the subject of 'Food Production as a Business'. He described the work being carried on in organising farmers into Co-operatives and spoke about the cost and methods of production. His address attained *'a very high level, with an earnest appeal for the laying aside of all those differences which were the chief obstacle of all progress in Ireland'*.

Business continued as usual throughout the year with new members joining, resignations being accepted, memberships being terminated and difficulties with classifications remaining. In November C. J.

Ryder Managing Director of W & A Gilbey Wine Importers and Distillers, classification Wines, tendered his resignation for a completely new reason:

... I feel deeply that the Rotary Club should have been used by certain members to propagate their temperance fads, and that they should have so far forgotten the principles of Rotary as to make an attack on any trade represented on the list. But no doubt they thought the opportunity too good to be lost to try to convince the members of my trade that they were not only 'publicans' but also 'sinners'.

Emollient words from the Hon. Secretary had no effect on Ryder and eventually the Council was forced to accept his resignation, with regret. It should be remembered that at this time the temperance movement was sweeping through the United States and that over the following twelve months thirty six states would support the eighteenth amendment resulting in the introduction of Prohibition in 1920.

The charitable work of the club continued to grow and in 1918 it undertook the organisation of a section of the Whitsun Fair held in the grounds of Saint Helen's between Booterstown and Mount Merrion. It was arranged with Mr Toft that he would supply merry-go-rounds and side-shows, that the club would provide some personnel and that the gross profits would be split on a 50/50 basis after a deduction for some prizes. The President was able to announce at the June Council that £273.14.7 had been raised for the Red Cross from this venture.

The following year the club was again invited to participate in the Fair and this time the proceeds were to go to Mercer's Hospital. At its February meeting Council decided that '*the Club section should not include gaming tables and that the Club should not in any way be connected therewith*'. Notwithstanding this decision, £292.9.0 was raised for the hospital.

In August 1918 Robert Tweedy felt obliged to offer his resignation as he had been given a technical commission in the Royal Air Force to **'supervise the electrical staffs of all the aerodromes in Ireland'**.

In a second letter dated the same day – August 14th Tweedy wrote to the Hon. Secretary:
… **I joined the Club in its earliest days, and have watched it develop – without being able to do much to assist – from an obscure and somewhat scorned body to a position of almost incredible power for good.**

I believe and I believe ever since I became a member, that Rotary is destined to leaven the whole mass of society with its doctrine of good-will more than any other Association, Society, Chamber or Union of which I have knowledge.

When its doors are open to women and to Trade Unions it will become the most powerful influence for breaking down class prejudices and social barriers, and for promoting that spirit of tolerance and justice which is no more than a name through all the grades from Autocrat to Bolshevik.

Until that state of Universal Perfection arrives:-
'LET ROTARY FLOURISH'

Tweedy persisted in his intention to resign in order that he might take up his new position. Allowing for some hyperbole in his description of the position the Dublin Club had achieved in just seven years, there is every indication that because of the calibre of its members, it had made a positive impact on Dublin society.

Though publicly the club was making its presence felt for good, the perennial problem of food, or rather the lack of it was still to the fore. Notwithstanding the fact that G.K. Chesterton the novelist and short story writer had given an excellent talk at lunch Burton Phillipson classification Motor Car Dealer wrote:
… **I was simply disgusted yesterday, at the lunch provided. We had a plate of soup, which I admit was not bad, but could by no freak of imagination be called good. I then had a cold plate, with a bit of lukewarm beef and a drop of coloured hot water thrown at me by a hurried waiter; after this, 'on the watch', I waited for ten**

minutes; by this time what few particles of fat floated on the gravy, were frozen to the edge of the plate. I was then passed down a dish containing badly boiled and roughly chopped up greens; after asking about seven or eight times I got a hard potato and when I attempted to eat the combined mess my palate failed me. Following this there was a so-called milk pudding with bit of apple 'mush' thrown over it, which I refused, and for this I had the privilege of paying 2/6, hence my protest.

This was followed up by an observation from T. A. Grehan that:

...For 1/2d (less than half the price of the Central lunch) you could have an excellent lunch in the Red Bank Restaurant...

The difference, of course, was that the club had a room to themselves in the Central, they all arrived at the same time and the management could not know, in advance how many would turn up for lunch. Council advised the Kitchen Committee of what, no doubt, they already knew – the members were dissatisfied and they would have to talk to the management of the Central Hotel.

The monthly meeting for November 1918 was held on the 11th, Armistice Day. The United States had become involved on the side of the allies in 1917 and had made a major contribution to the defeat of the German and the Austro-Hungarian Empires. That evening the Club sent telegrams of congratulations to King George V, President Wilson, Marshal Foch, Admiral Beatty, Sir Douglas Haig, General Pershing, the Prime Minister and the President of the International Association of Rotary Clubs.

A war that had been confidently expected to last a few months had gone on for over four years. There had been terrible carnage on both sides and a revolution in Russia had brought the Bolseviks to power. Although there had never been conscription in Ireland, over a quarter of a million young men had enlisted. The club had done its best to support the War Office's advertising campaign and had held a special lunch in 1915 to publicise their recruitment effort. Over fifty thousand young Irishmen had perished and an entire generation had been scarred by the experience of trench warfare. Those returning from the front, where many of their comrades had made the supreme sacrifice of their lives, came back to a Dublin whose people, by and large, turned their backs on them.

In December 1918 a general election was held and Sinn Fein won seventy-three seats, the Irish Parliamentary Party returning just one member, Capt. Willie Redmond for Waterford, was wiped out. Thirty Unionists were elected including Sir Maurice Dockrell for Rathmines. The newly elected Sinn Fein members decided not to attend the British Parliament and met instead in the Round Room of the Mansion House, Dublin on January 21st 1919, constituted themselves as the First Dail and declared an Irish Republic. Events had been set in train that were to have major consequences for all the people on the island of Ireland.

By the December 30th monthly meeting replies to the club telegrams had been received from H.M. The King, Marshal Foch, Admiral Sir David Beatty, Field Marshal Sir Douglas Haig, General Pershing and John Poole President of the I.A.R.C.

At the March Meeting the next year a letter was read from the Management of the Central Hotel stating that they would not be able to cater for the Club after March 31st. We were on the move again.

[1] *This was the Hospital in which James Connolly was held, having been wounded in the fighting in the G.P.O. He was taken from there and brought to Kilmainham Jail where he was executed while strapped to a chair.*

[2] *'**The Insurrection in Dublin**' by James Stephens in 1916. Stephens, a poet and author, was at that time Registrar of the National Gallery and lived in a flat in Fitzwilliam Square.*

[3] *This application to join the Club should be viewed in the context of the movement to extend the franchise to women. The Women's Social and Political Union led by Emily Pankhurst had campaigned*

vigorously for 'Votes for Women. Although this campaign had been suspended for the duration of the War the feeling among many women and some men was that women were entitled to equal status with men. The Irish Women's Franchise League had been formed in 1908.

[4] *The I.A.R.C. was referring to the Minneapolis Women's Rotary Club established in 1911 and the Women's Rotary Club of Duluth. The I.A.R.C. denied accreditation to both of these Clubs although Ida Buell of Duluth was allowed to address the 1912 Convention in Duluth, Minnesota. She was described as 'an interesting and entertaining speaker'.*

[5] *Lord Wimborne had followed Lord Aberdeen as Viceroy in February 1915. There is no record in the Minutes of a loyal address being presented to him on that occasion.*

[6] *George Russell who wrote under the pseudonym of AE was one of the leading poets and writers of the day. He was a friend of W. B. Yeats who recommended him to Sir Horace Plunkett for the post of organiser of the Co-operative movement in Ireland. He was at this time editor of the Irish Homestead magazine.*

Outside Westminster Abbey London November 15th 1921. A delegation of Rotarians from Dublin, London and Paris clubs before they laid a tribute on the tomb of the Unknown Warrior on behalf of Rotary International. William McConnell, a founder member of the Dublin club in 1911, President of the Association of Rotary Clubs of Great Britain and Ireland and Governor of the 24th District of Rotary International is fourth from the right.

Chapter Eleven

Turbulent years

'I had a little bird
Its name was Enza
I opened the window
And in-flu-enza'.

Children's skipping rhyme 1919

The 'Spanish Flu' pandemic of 1918/19 was simply the most virulent and deadly disease the world has ever experienced. Worldwide the A virus strain of subtype H1N1 killed about 75 million people between the spring of 1918 and the end of 1919. In Ireland, although data is difficult to come by, the best estimates are that it accounted for 180,000 deaths. An unusual feature of the flu was that it seemed to target young healthy adults in the twenty to forty year age groups. Onset was rapid and many people were dead within twenty-four hours. With an average age in the early forties the Dublin Club could not have been immune from what was occurring in the general population and there is evidence in the Minutes of an increased number of deaths among members and their families at this time. The great movement of troops and peoples as the Great War ended would have contributed to the spread of this terrible disease. Posters went up insisting that all those who had cold and flu symptoms should on no account appear in public. At its height, most public events involving crowds were cancelled. Notwithstanding this unusual and frightening pandemic, business and social life continued.

Initially the new luncheon venue was the Dublin Bread Company (DBC) Restaurant on Saint Stephen's Green. This, however, was considered to be only a temporary arrangement and in July of 1919 the club moved to the newly opened Kidd's Restaurant at 46 Nassau

Street[1]. W.M. Kidd, the proprietor, became a member in November of that year with the classification of Restaurant.

In May 1919 the Executive Council of the British Association of Rotary Clubs held their Annual Meeting in Bristol. It was not quite a full blown Conference but, nevertheless, many Dublin Rotarians and their wives attended, in addition to the accredited delegates. Arch Klumph who had been President of the International Association of Rotary Clubs in 1916/17 and Estes Snedecor who was to become its President in 1920/21 represented the I.A.R.C. Snedecor put forward the idea that 'the International Association should enlarge its scope and include the work of International Associations such as the B.A.R.C'. The B.A.R.C. was, in fact, the only International Association in the Rotary movement and although all its Clubs eventually adopted the Standard Rotary Constitution it still remains as Rotary International in Great Britain and Ireland (R.I.B.I.) the only such quasi independent body in the Rotary world. Snedecor's attempt to bring about the full integration of the British and Irish Clubs into the International Rotary organisation was followed, on many occasions, over the years by like efforts all of which have resulted in the status quo being maintained.

The following year the first proper B.A.R.C Conference was held in Harrogate attended by the representatives of thirty-two Clubs including a delegation from Dublin led by its President Edwin Fannin. Chesley Perry the Secretary of the I.A.R.C also attended and the following week paid a visit to the Dublin Club where he was presented with a dozen poplar ties as a memento of his stay in Ireland.

As 1919 wore on, the political situation in Ireland became unstable. Sinn Fein Courts, under the control of Dail Eireann, began to take over the administration of justice in large areas of the country outside the major cities. It became more difficult for central government to collect taxes and attacks began to be made on isolated Royal Irish Constabulary barracks. Gradually a guerrilla war developed as the British army in Ireland found itself engaged in a conflict with an armed force supported by a large proportion of the civilian population. The British had never encountered such insurgency before and their army was quite unprepared for the multi-faceted response that was required. Their recourse to auxiliary forces, often lacking discipline and training, did not help matters. In 1920 the Westminster authorities responded to the violent unrest by attempting to impose their own solution. The Government of Ireland Act 1920 was enacted allowing for the setting up of two Parliaments in Ireland: one in Belfast, the other in Dublin. The Ulster Unionists who had vehemently opposed Home Rule for the whole island accepted it for six counties of the province of Ulster and Sir James Craig became their Prime Minister, The Act was rejected out of hand by Sinn Fein and the bloodshed continued. After two years of fighting a stalemate situation existed and, through intermediaries, a Truce came into operation in July 1921. Tortuous negotiations followed and eventually a Treaty was signed in London in December 1921. It was ratified by Dail Eireann January 7th 1922 after days of bitter debate. A large minority of the members of the Dail, led by Eamon deValera, withdrew from the Dail, citing the Oath of Allegiance to King George V and their allegiance to the Republic as their principal sticking points. Arthur Griffith was elected President of the Provisional Government and the new administration set about the mammoth task of establishing itself in control of the new nation.

The effect of the Treaty was that the British Army was withdrawn, over the following eleven months, from what they termed Southern Ireland and from the point of view of the many Unionists in the new State they were left to fend for themselves. It is likely that many members of the Dublin Club fell into this category.

During these turbulent years the club continued its work of friendship and charity. In November 1918 following the sinking of the R.M.S. Leinster[2] they contributed over €10,000 in today's money to the Relief Fund. They continued to provide Christmas entertainment and presents for the children in Dublin Hospitals and supported the Saint John's Ambulance. The Orange Bag that first made its appearance at lunch some years previously as an ad hoc means of collecting funds for charitable purposes was put on a more permanent footing with the opening in 1921 of a No.2 Bank Account to be used for charitable purposes only.

In 1919 Lionel Smith-Gordon who had joined the club in 1916 with the classification of Librarian (Scientific and Research) accepted a post on the committee of the Land Bank. Robert Barton, Director of Agriculture, had established the Land Bank in the new Sinn Fein administration. A fellow committee member was Erskine Childers who was to be executed in the Civil War. One of the Land Bank's principal aims was to start a process of re-forestation and farmers were to be encouraged to plant sixteen trees on their land, one to commemorate each man executed in 1916. This is the earliest example I could find of any member of the club co-operating with the newly established Dail.

Over the years there had been discussions on a number of occasions as to whether or not the club should have a permanent home and become something like the Gentlemen's Clubs on Saint Stephen's Green. Nothing concrete had ever been done to bring this about but in the spring of 1920 Council resolved that the club needed an Office. A room had become vacant in the same building, at 116 Grafton Street, in which the Hon. Secretary William McConnell carried on his insurance business. The lease was signed and the deposit paid with the residue that the club held from the successful Commerce Exhibition held in 1912. Twelve office chairs were purchased from Messrs Millar and Beatty at a cost of 23/6 each and Sheridan donated a floor mat with the motto "No Politics" emblazoned on it. The Council held their first meeting there on May 27th 1920.

June 1921 was an exciting time for Rotarians in Britain and Ireland. An intensive extension campaign had paid off and there were now fifty clubs in the B.A.R.C. Edinburgh had been chosen as the venue for the International Convention and two ocean liners had been chartered by U.S. Rotarians for the event. Attended by 2,523 delegates from twenty-five countries the Convention decided to add another clause to the Objects of Rotary:

To aid the advancement of international peace and goodwill through a fellowship of business and professional men of all nations united in the Rotary ideal of Service.

Various Committees reported on the work that Rotary was engaged in throughout the world. Immediately following these reports President Snedecor introduced the songleader[3] who proceeded to lead the delegates in an all action rendition of 'Old McDonald's Farm', a novelty song published in the U.S. four years previously. To the astonishment of all the non United States delegates, the songleader emitted quacks, snorts and moos and invited all present to imitate him. The final chorus was reported to have 'lifted the roof off'. Unfortunately, the gentlemen of the Press zoomed in on this lighthearted intermission and the newspapers the following day were replete with references to farmyard noises rather than the more serious work undertaken by the Rotarians. The Convention finished with a grand parade through the streets of Edinburgh featuring each nation represented. A novel feature of the Convention was the action of Edinburgh Rotarians in inviting the delegates and their wives into their homes for afternoon tea. Home hospitality has become the norm at Rotary gatherings today but had never been experienced by American Rotarians before this time. For them it was a totally unexpected and unforgettable experience.

In November 15th 1921, William McConnell who was at that time President of the B.A.R.C and Governor of the 24th District of Rotary International (comprising Britain and Ireland) together with members of the London and Paris Clubs presented a bronze tablet to the Dean of Westminster Abbey. This tablet was given on behalf of Rotary International to honour the memory of the Unknown Warrior[4] who had been laid to rest in the Abbey twelve months previously. It was inscribed with the words 'Service not Self' and 'To the Unknown Warrior from Rotary International'. On the same occasion Charles Waecter Hon. Secretary of the Paris Club laid a floral tribute. Looking back, in 1955 on forty-four years membership of the Dublin Club, McConnell recalled this event as the most solemn of his time in Rotary.

The International Convention held in Los Angeles in June 1922, attended by William McConnell President of the B.A.R.C., decided to ratify a new Constitution and Bye Laws which would be binding on all clubs joining after that date. At this time also the name of the organisation was changed. Charles E. White who had been Belfast President in 1920/21 and District Chairman in 1921/22 was appointed a member of a Committee charged with drafting the new rules. He suggested that the International Association of Rotary Clubs should become Rotary International. He heard no more of this until, without any preamble, Past International President Frank Mulholland proposed this change. It was immediately agreed without dissension and remains the name of the international Rotary organisation to this day. Looking back in 1955, White remarked that a 'Chairman of a District in Ireland saved Rotary thousands of words and thousands of pages of print'. Subsequently, later in 1922, the B.A.R.C became Rotary International in Great Britain and Ireland (R.I.B.I.).

In July 1922 the third club in Ireland, Londonderry, was chartered. On his way home from the Edinburgh Convention, Joe Hamilton, a Rotarian from Delaware U.S.A. visited a relative in Londonderry and met up with John Crockett, a hardware merchant in his early twenties. Having told him why he was in Europe, Joe undertook to send John some literature on Rotary when he returned home. This duly arrived and John contacted a number of businessmen with whom he was acquainted and general interest was expressed in starting a Rotary Club in the city. By this time the Belfast club had heard of their endeavours and with Belfast's assistance the first meeting was held in April 1922 and the club received its Charter on July 17th of that year.

As 1922 unfolded the political situation in Ireland deteriorated. In March of that year anti-Treaty forces occupied the Four Courts complex and remained there unmolested by the new government. In June a general election resulted in a large majority of members being returned who supported the Treaty and on June 25th, under pressure from the British government to act, Irish government forces began to shell the Four Courts. Two days later the occupying force under Rory O'Connor surrendered. Throughout the country fighting broke out between the two sides and in Dublin street gun battles took place. The Irregulars, as the anti-Treaty forces became known, controlled most of Munster and Michael Collins who headed up the Free State army brought hundreds of men and equipment by sea into Cork and captured the city. On August 12th 1922 Arthur Griffith President of the Executive Council died of a brain haemorrhage brought on by the stress of the situation in which he found himself. On the 18th of August the Dublin Rotary Council passed the following motion proposed by PP J.R. Coade and seconded by Immediate Past President Charles McGloughlin:

'That the action of the Hon. Officers in cancelling the meeting on the 14th inst. out of respect to the late Mr. Arthur Griffith, President of the Irish Free State, and their action in attending the Funeral as representatives of the Rotary Club is approved of.'

Ten days after Griffith's death Michael Collins, Commander in Chief of the Free State army, was killed in an ambush at Beal na Blath in Cork. The Civil War dragged on for another nine months with atrocities being committed on both sides. In May 1923 de Valera wrote to his followers ordering them to dump arms. The war was over. Bitterness caused by the Civil War remained a factor in the political and personal lives of many Irish people for generations after 1923.

On February 1923 a request was received from the Detroit club asking that the Dublin club should send them an Irish flag.

It was decided to reply explaining the different flags and the present position in conjunction with the matter.

Although no copy of this letter exists in the files this minute brings into focus the rapidly changing political conditions in which the club had to operate. Walking a fine line between varying allegiances would not be easy. The new political reality did not interfere with the close relations that existed between the Dublin and Belfast clubs. By September 1929 matters had stabilised somewhat as the club felt able to order

A Free State flag for Club use from Messrs Atkinson for £6.2.6 less 10% discount complete with cord and tassels.

In February 1924, a postal vote was held to determine whether or not the luncheon venue should be changed. Twenty percent of the membership of one hundred and eighty six did not vote and 80% of the remainder cast their ballot in favour of Clerys Restaurant with 20% favouring Kidd's. Council decided on a three-month trial in Clerys in O'Connell Street.

The following year, when Michael Rowan was President, the Rotary year was changed again. The reader may remember that in 1914 J.P. McKnight acted as President of the club for just eight months from March to November of that year. R.I. decided to move the Rotary year back to its original date and therefore Rowan was President from November 1925 to March 1927 when Major Bryan Cooper succeeded him.

In this decade, as Rotary expanded throughout the world and began to attract attention, it also attracted some criticism. Sinclair Lewis in his widely read novel 'Babbit' successfully lampooned the networking aspect of some of the early clubs. R.I. reacted to this and other criticism by reinforcing its ethical foundation and publicising its extensive charitable works. In August 1928, Cogs, at that time the Official Organ of the Rotary Clubs of Saorsat Eireann[5], carried the following message:

Inasmuch as the Rotary movement is intended among other things to encourage and foster high ethical standards in business and professions, the Board of Directors of Rotary International at its recent meeting agreed that the following should be regarded as unethical: -

The use of Official Rotary Directories or Rosters for advertising or commercial purposes.
The offering of special prices, privileges or discounts to Rotarians that are not allowed to the general public.
Advertising appeals based upon Rotary membership.
Solicitation of business upon the representation of Rotary membership.

As the 1920s wore on the club became more involved with the charitable work that is its hallmark today. In January 1925 twenty-five motor cars carrying twenty-two members of the club and the cast of the Gaiety Theatre Pantomime set out for Glencree in the Wicklow Mountains.

Rotarians face snow to entertain Dublin children

Members of the Dublin Rotary Club and many artistes appearing in the pantomime at the Gaiety Theatre visited Saint Kevin's Training School Glencree and entertained the boys. They travelled in twenty-five motors and set off from the Russell Hotel, starting at 3pm. When Enniskerry was reached it was found that there had been a heavy fall of snow. From the village to the school a snowplough had been put into operation, and with the help of the boys, a fairway had been made through eighteen inches of snow. Despite the prevailing thaw the country at the high altitude of Glencree remained snow covered. Here the first contingent of visitors was received by the Very Rev. J. Hughes O.M.I. manager of the school and members of the community. A few cars had minor casualties on the way but these arrived safely later.

In the dining hall of the institution Fr. Hughes expressed appreciation of the visitors in providing the treat for the boys and remarked that ' *it was a very happy thing that their visit coincided with the change of the name from Glencree Reformatory to St. Kevin's Training School. If the object of Rotary was more recognised there would be less trouble, jealously and war and more happiness in the world'.*

Mr. J.W. Beckett, President, replying on behalf of the Club acknowledged the welcome.

A Star Bill

The concert programme consisted of a 'star' bill, amongst those contributing being, Mr. Joseph O'Meara who sang tenor, Mr. P. Gillespie, Feis Ceol Gold Medallist, who, with others, was

deservedly recalled: Mr. Sealy Jeffares (humourist), The McNaughtons, Scholey & Scholey, Varney & Butte, Sakers' Jazz Band, The Moselle Sparkling Eight dancers also performed. Mr. Herbert Bailey took charge of the stage arrangements and Rotarian Ashley James of the Gaiety Theatre directed the artistes. Mr. Frederick Warden the well-known producer attended. The boys were entertained to tea and gifts were presented.

A short tug-of war contest took place, first between the schoolboys and then between the lady visitors. Their wives and lady friends who assisted in entertaining the community and the boys accompanied many of the Rotarian members. A good day was had by all.

Other activities at this time included the provision of entertainment for poor and crippled children in the Mansion House, a concert for the patients of Peamount Sanatorium and donations to St Mary's hospital Cappagh, Temple Street and Harcourt Street hospitals and the Sunshine Home in Leopardstown.

Later that year R.I. opened a European office in Zurich, Switzerland. In 1925 also Council decided to invite Rotary International to hold its annual Convention in Dublin 1927. An illuminated Invitation was designed by Miss McConnell featuring a shamrock in the middle of the Rotary wheel with the Dublin crest at its centre. The Invitation was signed by the President, Past Presidents and officers of the club and by William T. Cosgrave who had succeeded Arthur Griffith as President of the Executive Council of the Irish Free State. The Lord Mayors of Dublin, Belfast, Londonderry and the Presidents of those clubs also signed it. R.I. made inquiries re venues and hotels and the Irish Tourist Board and the Royal Dublin Society became involved in providing information on facilities. Although Pat Montford (President in 1933/34) addressed the Cleveland Convention in 1925 outlining the benefits of holding the International Convention in Dublin. R.I. decided against the invitation and opted instead for Ostend in Belgium.

A few years later, in 1929, the club invited R.I.B.I to hold its 1930 conference in Dublin. However, by that time there were over three hundred and fifty clubs in Britain and Ireland and it was felt that Dublin would not have the hotel capacity to cater for the numbers who would wish to attend. The 1930 R.I.B.I. conference was held instead in Edinburgh.

There had been a number of attempts to encourage businessmen in Cork to become involved in the Rotary movement. Friends and acquaintances of members of the Dublin club who were in business in the southern capital had attended Dublin lunches and dinners and William McConnell had travelled south on a number of occasions to introduce the idea of Rotary. The Dublin club formally established an Extension Committee in February 1926 and on June 15th of that year all these efforts finally paid off. On that evening a dinner attended by some of the leading businessmen in Cork together with members of the Dublin and Belfast clubs was held and a decision was taken to found a club in Cork. Their Charter was presented to their first President, J.J. Horgan, by Sydney Pascall President of R.I.B.I. on September 18th 1926. The Dublin and Belfast clubs jointly presented a gavel to the new club.

In November 1927 William McConnell reported that the club had surrendered the lease on the their Grafton Street office and taken a new one at 12,13,14, College Green at a rent of £20 per annum. This arrangement lasted only two years. By April 1929 they were on the move again, this time to 12 Westmoreland Street where a lease was signed with Mr. Bewley. A brass plate bearing the name of the club was affixed and a letterbox ordered. The club was to remain there for many years.

The Dublin club's Extension Committee continued its work and on June 21st 1928 a club was chartered in Limerick. Unfortunately the new Limerick club did not thrive. Speakers were hard to come by and meetings began to be cancelled for lack on interest. Intensive efforts by the Dublin and Cork clubs and District officers helped to stabilise matters for a while but eventually in June 1932 the club surrendered its Charter. The feeling at the time among Rotarians was that the conservative element in the local Catholic Church had exerted its influence and brought about the club's demise. As a relatively new organisation on the Irish scene Rotary, in the eyes of some, had become confused with other organisations where oaths and secrets were the norm. It was to take efforts over many years before these prejudices could be set aside and Rotary could begin to make strides in Ireland. With one exception, Drogheda (1946), it was not until the 1960s that the Rotary movement in the Republic of Ireland began to expand at a rate similar to Northern Ireland.

In the autumn of 1929 William McConnell its Hon. Secretary, founder member and past president informed Council that he intended resigning his membership as he was emigrating to the United States and would join the New York club. As McConnell had been paid a secretarial allowance that enabled a member of his staff to work part-time on club affairs it was felt necessary that a paid Secretary should be appointed. Eddie Taylor was interviewed and appointed with an annual salary of £50. He was also elected as member with his annual subscription being paid by the club. Eddie continued in that role until 1956 and he manned the Westmoreland Street office from 10.30am to 12.30pm from Monday to Friday. The members bought an antique grandfather clock for presentation to the retiring Hon. Secretary.

With R.I.B.I. expanding it became necessary for administrative purposes to divide it into districts. In 1918 Ireland was designated District 6, while by 1920 it had become District 8. There was a move in 1923, following Partition, to divide Ireland into two districts. Irish Rotarians, north and south, petitioned R.I.B.I. to maintain unity on the island and it was agreed that the new district should be 16, embracing the whole island. Ireland became District 116 in 1957 and 1160 in 1991.

As the decade drew to a close the Dublin Club decided to adopt the Standard Club Constitution offered to it by R.I.B.I. As a club formed before 1922 the Dublin Club had the option to retain its own Constitution so long as it was judged compatible to general Rotary principles. The decision of the club on October 29th 1929 to adopt the Standard Constitution can be viewed as the final step in integrating our Club into the Rotary family world-wide.

[1] *The famous Jammet's Restaurant occupied the same premises for over thirty years. Subsequently Judge Roy Beans and Lillie's Bordello have occupied the building.*

[2] *The R.M.S. Leinster operated by the City of Dublin Steam Packet Company carried mail and passengers between Kingstown and Holyhead. On the 10th October 1918 it was struck by two torpedoes fired by the German U-Boat U.B. 123. It sank off the Kish Rock with the loss of 444 of its 700 passengers and crew.*

[3] *Community singing was commonplace at U.S. Rotary Clubs and at International Conventions held there. It was a completely new concept to Rotarians from outside North America and has never quite caught on here to the same extent as across the Atlantic.*

[4] *The Unknown Warrior was selected from four bodies exhumed from different Great War battlefields in France. He was taken, with much pomp and ceremony, by road, sea and rail to London and interred in the Abbey on November 11th 1920 in the presence of King George V and representatives of every facet of British life. The Cenotaph in Whitehall was unveiled on that day also.*

[5] *At that time the Belfast Club had its own magazine, the Flywheel and Cogs carried information on the Dublin and Cork clubs only as well as items from R.I.B.I. and R.I. This changed the following year when Cogs became 'The Official Organ for the Rotary Clubs of Ireland'.*

Group photo District Conference 1927

Chapter Twelve

Paul Harris calls

'Of all the things we think, say or do:
Is it the TRUTH?
Is it FAIR to all concerned?
Will it build GOODWILL and BETTER FRIENDSHIPS?
Will it be BENEFICIAL to all concerned?
Rotarian Herbert J. Taylor

1928 was a momentous year in the life of the Dublin Club. On Wednesday 5th May of that year Paul Harris, the founder of Rotary, travelled south from Belfast to a joint meeting of the Dublin and Cork clubs. Strangely enough, there is no mention of his visit in the minutes. We are indebted to the Dublin correspondent of 'The Rotary Wheel' for a description of the event that appeared in the July edition of the R.I.B.I. magazine.

'**What a chance Paul Harris missed and how much he gained thereby. He came upon us so silently and so suddenly, spoke a few words and was gone from among us with such great speed, that even now we think of him as more of an apparition than the living founder of the great moral movement of which we are so proud to be a part. He lost the acclamations of a record meeting, and the hospitality that Irishmen love to lavish on their honoured guests: but he gained on balance, because he left with those who met him at lunch the precious memory of a man worthy of the cause that he made his own for so many wearying years. A great cause and a lowly man. Rotary is too big now to suffer permanent damage, even from its founder, but it is easy to imagine the heartbreaking disillusion which would burst over us if a trace of the charlatan or the egoist or the spellbinder had been discovered in Paul Harris.**

The only regret that we have in the Dublin Club is that we did not rise quickly enough to the frenzy of hero worship: in fact, however, the welcome was as cordial and sincere as warm hearts make it though it lacked the volume because of the unexpected nature of the visit. We know now that Paul would spurn any that dared to worship him.

Before he left, the members of the Dublin Club presented Paul Harris with a shillelagh in honour of his visit. After his visit to the Club, Harris met William T. Cosgrave President of the Executive Council. There was also time for him to listen to proceedings in the Dail from a seat in the Distinguished Strangers' Gallery before going to the North Wall Quay for an overnight sailing to Liverpool. At the quayside nearly all the members of the Dublin club gathered to bid farewell to their guest'.

Over the years friendships developed between the members of the different Irish clubs and this led, quite naturally, to a desire to get together each year. The first District Conference attended by representatives of the three clubs in the District (Dublin, Belfast and Londonderry) took place in 1925. The Belfast Club organised it and the venue was Newcastle, County Down. There was no Conference in 1926 because the General Strike in Britain had caused the postponement of the R.I.B.I. Conference to September and it was felt that the Irish Rotarians would not want to travel to two events in the same month. The Dublin club organised the 1927 District Conference and it was held in the Grand Hotel Greystones County Wicklow. One hundred and twenty eight delegates attended representing four clubs and it was adjudged a great success socially. On the financial front, however, matters were not quite as rosy. The Council at its November meeting in 1927 decided to sell £50 of its holding of British War Bonds to make up the £30 deficit incurred on the Conference and a further shortfall incurred in entertaining foreign visitors during the previous year. The District Conference continued on an annual basis, apart from 1939 and 1940, when due to the outbreak of war it was not held.

Golf matches were held between the Dublin and Belfast clubs from 1914 with Londonderry joining in the early 1920s. This has developed into a full-blown golf competition that is now held each year in conjunction with the district conference.

Quite another interaction between Rotarians took place in 1930. An internal dispute in the Kensington club in London resulted in the expulsion of its Hon. Secretary who subsequently took a High Court action against the club. The judge found in favour of the club and awarded costs against the former member. The latter then filed for bankruptcy and the club was saddled with a debt of £1,300, which it had no funds to meet. With the approval of R.I.B.I. the Kensington President, Sir Charles Mander, wrote to all the clubs in Britain and Ireland requesting assistance. After some consideration, Council decided to send a cheque and eventually with the aid of many other clubs the debt was cleared. The Board of R.I.B.I. expressed the hope that if a similar situation should arise in the future that the club would get in touch with the governing body before taking action. This suggestion has been acted on and over the years R.I.B.I. and its Secretariat has been able to act as mediators in situations which could have had similarly unhappy outcomes.

A more happy development in London around the same time has resulted in increased mobility for blind and visually impaired people. In 1931 the wife of E.J. Johnston, a past president of London's West Ham club, suggested that the club present the borough's four hundred and fifty blind residents with a white stick so that they could navigate the streets more easily. The club enthusiastically endorsed the idea and shortly after the entire London District 13 adopted it. By 1935 over one hundred clubs in R.I.B.I. including the Dublin club had 'white stick' community projects and the idea soon spread throughout the world. Rotary then passed the project onto the various organisations for the blind in individual countries.

In 1934 a group of Dublin businessmen including our own member Dick Archer founded the Mount Street Club. Dick had joined in 1920 with the classification of 'Private Motor Cars'. The Mount Street Club had premises at 81, Lower Mount Street and very early in its existence it purchased a 130-acre farm at Larkfield in Clondalkin County Dublin

Photo taken at the 1931 District Conference held in Dublin. From left (back row): George T. Clampett past president Dublin, George E. Smyth, W.W. Blair-Fish Editor The Rotary Wheel (official magazine of R.I.B.I.), Reginald H. Keatinge Conference hon. Secretary. From left (front row): Herbert Scholfield president R.I.B.I., Fred Summerfield Dublin District Chairman, past president Dublin and Kevin J. Kenny president Dublin for £3,600. It was a non-political and non-sectarian organisation and its members under the guidance of the founding directors were self-governing. To be a member it was a condition that you should be an unemployed man and within two years they had three hundred members. All the members worked, either on the farm or in the club's workshops in Mount Street. In return for the work performed they received 'tallies' that enabled them to purchase the products of other members' toil. No money changed hands. It provided gainful employment and gave new hope and self-confidence to its members. When a member became employed he ceased to be a member. The Dublin Rotary Club provided some of the seed capital that helped set up the Mount Street Club and, each year, well into the 1960s it contributed to its ongoing expenses. In addition the Dublin Club provided presents and a party for the children of the Mount Street members at Christmas.

From time to time, members were encouraged to speak at lunches, particularly on topics relating to their business. Members also, because of their position in Dublin civic life were required to address public gatherings. While some took naturally to this exercise, others found it difficult and this lack of facility in public speaking tended to inhibit their enthusiasm for becoming involved in club and civic affairs. In 1928 the club started a 'Speakers Circle' that was designed to introduce members to the art of public speaking, give them practice in a friendly and non-threatening environment and to give them the confidence to speak in public. The meetings were held in 42 Grafton Street, the business premises of Richard Keatinge, classification Decorator, who became President in 1936/7. We have an account of one of the meetings of the Circle recorded in Cogs:

The Speakers Circle[1]

The Seventh Meeting of the Speakers Circle was held on Tuesday evening at 42 Grafton Street. The Summary of the Sixth Chapter of the course was considered after which impromptu speeches were made.

The subject on which each member was to speak had previously been written out on a card and put into a hat. The members then

drew numbers and in order proceeded to the rostrum, drew a subject out of the hat and spoke for five minutes. Some of the members, before their turn, felt considerably nervous and feared that they would not be able to speak for one minute. However, to the delight of the speaker and audience, every member was fully able to occupy the minutes allotted to him.

The speeches were on such different subjects as Civic Week, Keep to the left, Town Planning, Should hospitals be supported by the State, Commercial Aviation, Is a knowledge of first aid to the injured necessary and should it be taught by the State, Should War be outlawed, Clean Milk, and Bridge Accommodation.

At the conclusion of the meeting it was interesting to hear the enthusiastic way the members spoke of the benefits that they realise that they are getting from the course.

At the next meeting the subject was 'Success'. Each member had to write a paper on this subject, but he had to make his oration from memory without the use of notes. Criticism of what the speaker intended to say and how he said it was then in order. The papers were examined during the week and criticised by Rotarian Smyth who reported the following week.

At a business lunch in December 1930 the club decided to introduce a new classification for membership – 'Foreign Government Service'. This apparently was the first time that this particular classification had been offered in Rotary and the club's action was subsequently endorsed by R.I.B.I. Up to that time representatives of foreign governments could join under the classification 'Diplomatic Service'. The United States Minister, the Hon. F. Sterling had joined in 1928. It appears that the introduction of the new classification was intended to allow several diplomats to join a club. Following on from this, in June 1931, Maurice Goor[2] Consul General for Belgium, E. Eriksson Swedish Consul and William Peters British Trade Commissioner were elected members.

Christmas gifts and entertainment for children in the Dublin hospitals continued with 'Father Christmas' making his appearance for the first time in the minutes in December 1930. The Christmas trees that had up to then been provided by club member Ireton Jones classification nurseryman were, for the first time that year, presented by Viscount Powerscourt from his Wicklow estates. In addition, each year, hundreds of poor children were entertained in the Mansion House at Christmas time. Throughout the 1930s the club brought over a hundred poor and crippled children each year to the Gaiety pantomime. In 1936 it was decided that:

All Rotarians looking after the children at the Pantomime should get an 'attendance'.

In the early thirties also, funds were raised to send over a hundred poor boys and girls from Dublin for a holiday in the foothills of the mountains above Bohernabreena. These two-week holidays were organised by the Fresh Air Fund and at the weekend Rotarians and their wives and lady friends journeyed out to entertain the children with sweets, presents and games.

A regular feature of the charitable work of the club at this time was the annual summer outing for poor boys to Donabate strand in north county Dublin. In the summer of 1928 one hundred and fifty boys were brought in twenty five cars, a bus and a covered van and there was:

no casualty, even of the mildest character. Luckily, the estimate of the committee that each boy would drink six bottles of gas-water was falsified.

Sandwiches, chocolates, sweets, cakes, biscuits and mineral waters were provided and the boys were looked after by twelve Rotarian stewards and a contingent of Sea Scouts. There were lots of games, races and prizes and '**A good day was had by all**'.

In the years since 1923 the political situation in Ireland had stabilised. In the mid-twenties deValera and his followers had broken with Sinn

Fein and in 1926 he had founded a new political party, Fianna Fail. The new party was forced to change its policy of not entering Dail Eireann by legislation introduced by the Cumann na nGaedheal government following the assassination of Minister for Justice Kevin O'Higgins T.D.. Following the general election in early 1932 Fianna Fail took power with the support of the Labour Party. A snap election in 1933 gained Fianna Fail an overall majority and they continued in power until 1948.

A process of disengagement from ties with Britain was begun by Kevin O'Higgins T.D. then Minister for External Affairs in negotiations resulting in the Statutes of Westminster in 1926. The effect of this agreement between Britain and the other members of the Commonwealth was to confer sovereignty on the Dominions, including the Irish Free State. DeValera continued this policy and effectively sidelined the Governor General, George V's representative in Ireland. Furthermore, he withheld the land annuities[3] and this resulted in Britain imposing tariffs on imports from the I.F.S. The economic war that ensued caused great hardship to Irish farmers and business generally. Taking into account the widespread unemployment and economic disruption brought about by the total collapse of share prices on the New York Stock Exchange in October 1929 the 1930's generally were a tough time to be in business.

The big event in 1930's Ireland was the Twenty-first Eucharistic Congress held in Dublin from 21st to 26th of June 1932. The Council decided:

'Not to hold a Reception but that visiting Rotarians be invited to lunch'.

Members of the club, acting in their personal capacity, were involved both in attending and organising the events that took place during the Congress. Fred Summerfield, who had become Hon. Secretary in 1930 following the departure of William McConnell, was a member of the Traffic and Transport sub-committee of the Congress as was P.J. Lawrence who had been President in 1921/22.

In 1932, also, Herbert J. Taylor, a member of the Chicago club was asked to try and save a near bankrupt aluminium company. The company had no money, low employee morale and was the subject of ruthless competition from other companies in similar circumstances. Taylor used his Rotary grounding in business ethics to produce a twenty-four-word code of conduct that he used to guide all his daily business decisions. He applied this Four Way Test, as quoted at the beginning of this chapter, to all his dealings with employees, customers, dealers and suppliers and he turned the company's fortunes around. Over the next fifteen years the company paid out over $1 million in dividends and built up an asset value of $2 million. The R.I. Board officially adopted the Four Way Test in 1943 and when Herb Taylor became R.I. President in 1954 he donated the copyright to R.I. It has since been translated into over one hundred languages.

Despite the club's best efforts politics intervened in 1931 with the decision of the board of R.I.B.I. to invite H.R.H. the Duke of Kent to be its Patron. The invitation was issued, apparently, without consulting the constituent clubs. The Dublin Club Council protested and asked to be excluded from the patronage, all to no avail. Michael Rowan who had been president in 1925/27 felt compelled to write:

The Secretary,
Dublin Rotary Club
12 Westmoreland Street
Dublin

Dear Sir,

I wish to tender my resignation as a member of the Dublin Rotary Club. I deeply regret having been forced to adopt this course, but the recent action of the Board of R.I.B.I. in appointing a Royal patron without consulting the affiliated club leaves me no other option.

I would like to express my gratitude and appreciation for all the favours and honours which my brother members have so

abundantly conferred on me. The break which I am obliged to make at this stage leaves many pleasant memories behind it.

I wish you to convey to the committee my best wishes for the future welfare of the Dublin Club.

Believe me

Yours very sincerely
M.P. Rowan

Some years later when the Duke was being married, R.I.B.I sent a letter to its clubs inviting them to contribute to a wedding present for the Royal couple. They did not intend to send it to Dublin but, in error, they did. Strenuous efforts were made to have the letter returned unopened but the Hon. Secretary, Fred Summerfield, brought it to Council on November 11th 1934. Having discussed the matter, at length, it was decided that any gift should be made on behalf of the Rotary Clubs of Great Britain and Northern Ireland. R.I.B.I. was informed of the Dublin club's wishes. The Duke continued as Patron of R.I.B.I. until his death in an aircraft crash in Scotland in 1942. No other member of the British royal family has assumed that role since that time.

A ballot of members took place in the autumn of 1932 following which it was decided to transfer the lunch meeting back to the Metropole, a venue that they had been forced to abandon with its destruction in 1916. A new building had been constructed and a cinema and restaurant replaced the previous hotel on the site in O'Connell Street

A major difficulty reared its head at the December 30th meeting in 1934 when Council considered that fact that the R.I. Convention in 1935 would be held in Mexico City. The problem was that since a civil war in the 1920's there had been killings of priests and nuns and a persecution of the Catholic Church generally. These events in Mexico caused widespread revulsion across the world and the Dublin club evidently felt that Rotary would be sending out all the wrong messages if it went ahead with its plans for the 1935 convention.

It was unanimously decided to warn R.I. headquarters to walk warily as regards the holding of conventions in Mexico City and further that a cable should be sent to R.I.

Copy of cable.
Dublin Club views with great concern holding Convention Mexico City and hopes Board will prevent any action that would have repercussions similar to five years ago[4]

At the April Council:

This matter was thoroughly discussed and no reply having been received to the cable sent in January it was decided to send the following cable:

Further to our cable of January. Impossible to exaggerate difficult position of Catholic Rotarians because of holding Convention in Mexico. Dublin Club representative of all creeds now sends further emphatic protest and expects Rotary International to give no official recognition to the Govt. that has given such offence to a large section of Rotary membership. Cable reply stating what steps have been taken to prevent repercussions similar to six years ago.[4]

Later that month R.I. cabled a reply:

Position of Rotary as secular, non-religious, non-political organisation is being clearly set forth. Future of Rotary depends upon maintaining that position.

The Dublin club took no further action.

The Silver Jubilee of the foundation of Rotary was celebrated in February 1936 with a dinner in the Gresham Hotel attended by Eamon deValera T.D. President of the Executive Council of the Irish Free State and Alfie Byrne T.D. the Lord Mayor of Dublin. All went well until the very end when the band did not play the National Anthem. This caused much comment in the newspapers the next day and the President, Oswald Jamison, felt obliged to write to Mr. DeValera:

At the meeting of the Club Council, at which I presided, it was desired to tender to you our sincere thanks for the courtesy you so generously extended to our Rotarian visitors from other countries who attended the Silver Jubilee Dinner in the Gresham Hotel. Your kindness to them on that occasion in giving them so prolonged an audience is very much appreciated.

I should inform you that through an unfortunate oversight the proceedings at our dinner did not conclude with the playing of our National Anthem, and the Council of the club ask me to offer our apologies to you as Head of State and to assure you that by an unanimous decision of the Council such inadvertence will not recur.

Two new artefacts made their appearance in the thirties. In 1934 a board with all the names of past presidents inscribed thereon was presented to the club by the Irish Independent newspaper. An easel was ordered so that the board should be displayed appropriately. Its whereabouts, today, is unknown. 1938 saw the arrival of the President's chair, presented by the then Immediate past President Tom Grehan. Happily it is still in use having been refurbished successfully a few years ago.

High quality speakers continued to be recruited for the luncheon meetings and in many cases the newspaper reporters who were usually invited to attend also faithfully recorded their words of wisdom. The poet F.R. Higgins in May 1934 cogently expressed his views with regard to the relationship between the arts and the commercial classes.

'Culture is not expressed and preserved, as the parish politician says it is, by the agile feet of a champion step-dancer; nor by expert palm of a handball player. It is expressed through the head and the artist is its priest.

Our cast-iron businessman – largely the shopkeeper- is given a position of weight in the nation out of all proportion to his importance; while the poet, as the cultural representative, is

entirely disregarded and without any consideration as to his eminence in racial affairs. Indeed the businessman, the shopkeeper, does not recognise the poet as a national asset, or even as an equal; he does not even appreciate poetry. He has no time to nurture his spiritual nature with pure poetry, simply because the world is too much for him. …… I do definitely indict the shopkeeper'

There is no record of what the members thought of this bucket of cold water on their sensibilities but I suspect that they did not forget it too easily. There is no record of any other poet being asked to speak at a luncheon meeting.

PP Frank Tate who had just begun working in his father's company Lemon's Sweets in O'Connell Street remembers passing by the Metropole on his way to lunch in Woolworth's in Henry Street. He could not but notice the large automobiles drawing up to the kerb each Monday and the rather well dressed gentlemen who alighted. On inquiry, a friendly Commissionaire in the Metropole informed Frank that the Dublin Rotary Club was meeting there. It was to be another ten years before Frank joined the august gathering.

The International Day on November 22nd 1937 was an auspicious occasion. Attended by representatives of France, the United States, Switzerland, Belgium, Czechoslovakia, Chile and Britain the theme was 'Steps to World Peace'. Dublin member, Oswald Jamison chair of the International Services committee told the gathering that there were now:

Over 500,000 members of Rotary all working together for the development of peace, friendship and goodwill throughout the world.

In reply Mr. Cudahy, United States Minister, said that:

That some of them could speak intimately on the subject of war. He had never seen a soldier yet who was not the greatest advocate of peace.

Unfortunately the message of peace did not get through to all parts of the world and as the 1930s unfolded totalitarian regimes began to take control in many countries. In October 1938 all Rotary activity in Germany ceased and the clubs were disbanded. Twelve months later, R.I. reported that a similar fate had befallen the Italian clubs. The clouds of war were gathering again.

[1] *The Speakers Circle seems to be a carbon copy of the proceeding at a Toastmasters meeting. Toastmasters was founded in the United States in 1924 and the first club was not established in Ireland until 1959. It is possible that the Rev. J.E. Hutton, who ran the Circle, had attended a Toastmasters club in the U.S. or had obtained a manual from someone who had.*

[2] *Maurice Goor is the paternal grandfather of our current member John who with his wife Magsie has hosted our successful annual charity Barbeque at their home Annacrivey House, Enniskerry for over twenty years.,*

[3] *The Wyndham Act (1903) and the Birell Act (1909) were the last in a series of legislative measures enacted by the Westminster government designed to end the agitation for land reform that had bedevilled Irish politics since the 1860s. A Land Commission was established to acquire and redistribute land and by the end of 1914 nine million acres had been transferred from its former owners. These were to be compensated by annual payments (annuities)*

[4] *In 1928 a Spanish bishop issued a letter entitled 'Good Catholics cannot belong to Rotary Clubs'. This theme was taken up by Rome and led to similar warnings by bishops in Spain, The Netherlands and Quebec in Canada. The authoritative Vatican journal* **Civilita Cattolica** *sharply criticised Rotary based on an alleged link between it and the Freemasons. Priests were banned by the Vatican from joining Rotary despite a statement from R.I. that 'it had no connection with Freemasonry and that religious discussions were forbidden'. Again in 1951 the Vatican issued a decree stating that Catholics could not be members of Rotary. It took a lot of time and effort on behalf of Rotary to heal these divisions and it was not until John Paul 11 became Pope in 1978 that a harmonious relationship developed.*

Chapter Thirteen

Emergency

*'Everything here is perfectly abnormal: for the first time
since the Battle of Clontarf we are neutral'.*
Dublin Opinion

In September 1939 Germany invaded Poland, and Britain and France who had guaranteed Poland's independence declared war on Germany. Russia who had signed a non-aggression pact with Germany the previous month contented itself with invading the defenceless Poles from the east and by October that country was partitioned and Europe settled done to nine months of what came to be called the phoney war.

The Irish Government's response to events in Europe was to adopt a policy of neutrality, declare an Emergency and to take onto itself special powers to deal with the unfolding situation.

The General Council of R.I.B.I. passed the following resolution:

'To record the Council's view that it is now clear beyond doubt that Great Britain and France are fighting in this war for the preservation of precisely those principles to which Rotary is dedicated,'

R.I.B.I. also decided that for the duration of the conflict conferences should not be held and that office holders should continue, where practicable, to hold their offices for the duration of hostilities. It was noted that this was in conformance

with the practice of the House of Commons and Municipal Authorities.

In the Dublin Club, however, events progressed as usual with 500 children being fed and entertained in the Mansion House in December

1939 and Santa Claus bringing toys to children in five Dublin hospitals and the Sunshine Home in Stillorgan. By 1942 rationing had begun to bite and there were some difficulties in obtaining food and toys for the Mansion House event. These, however, were overcome and throughout the 1940s the Dublin Club continued with its Christmas programme. In the early 1940s also the club began to provide the children of the members of the Mount Street Club with toys at Christmas.

1940 began quietly enough but by May Germany had overrun Holland and Belgium and by June France had surrendered and Britain had, with difficulty managed to evacuate most of its army from the continent although they had lost almost all their equipment. It was thought likely that an invasion of Britain was imminent.

On June 27th the Hon. Secretary received the following telegram from R.I.B.I.:

'Urgent, would you favourably consider Eire Rotarians joining British Rotarians in joint request to District Council to convene immediate meeting of District Council in Belfast to receive R.I.B.I. delegation to discuss possible initiative by Rotarians re imperative united Irish action in present imminently dangerous international situation jointly threatening Eire, Northern Ireland and Britain. Please wire reply. If favourable will immediately request District Chairman to convene meeting leaving you to contact Cork Club.'[1]

After consultation with the President, Vice President and some past Presidents the Hon. Secretary Fred. Summerfield sent the following letter recorded in the Minutes in reply.

As soon as I received your long telegram yesterday, suggesting a meeting of the Irish District Council etc. I got in touch with the incoming President and vice President and past Presidents of the Dublin Club and subsequently saw a prominent official of the government here.

It was unanimously agreed that for reasons that it is not wise to explain in a letter, it would be dangerous to adopt your suggestion as the matter you suggested for debate is one that must be left to the Governments to handle.

At the same time, we would like you to feel that we appreciate the sentiments that prompted you to make your suggestions but, of course, the position of the Dublin and Cork Clubs is unique in the R.I.B.I. area and we have to be careful at all times that we make no move that would cut across the Government's attitude.

The Hon. Secretary also reported as to his interview with a highly placed Government official.

In December 1940 the members decided to move their luncheon to the Aberdeen Hall of the Gresham Hotel and that the cost of the lunch should be three shillings.

The position of the club in the civic life of Dublin was further evidenced by the invitation from the newly appointed Archbishop of Dublin John Charles McQuaid to attend his Episcopal Consecration in the Pro Cathedral on December 29th 1940. The club was represented by its Vice President Vincent O'Hare.

Speakers at lunch continued to provide stimulating material for the newspapers. In May 1941 J.B.G. Mathieson addressed the lunch on the subject of Education in Ireland. The Irish Independent reported that:

It was at the Rotary Club luncheon held in Dublin on Monday last that Mr. Mathieson declared, among other things, that in Ireland, education is still in its infancy, most of our schools are worn out or in want of repair, the National Language is quite obsolete and inadequate to present day life, the country is rapidly becoming illiterate in two languages and that teachers who resort to the cane prove, ipso facto, that they do not know their job.

He went on to state that

Segregation of the sexes (in education), could only result in an erroneous outlook for both boys and girls upon one another, and

make their immediate post-school period a most critical time wherein readjustment almost never takes place, with disastrous results.

It transpired that co-education had been condemned by Pope Pius XI in his Encyclical 'Divini Illius Magistri' and the Rotary Club was attacked in both the 'Irish Catholic' and the 'Irish Independent; for giving a platform to Mathieson for his outrageous views. The President and Hon. Secretary both issued statements disassociating the Club from the views expressed; these were published and the matter was closed.

The early 1940s saw some internal problems surfacing in the Dublin Club. In the late 1930s William McConnell returned from New York. Initially, the club conferred Honorary membership on him and when this was declined he was accepted as a past service member. In the eight years that he had been abroad the membership of the Dublin Club had changed considerably. Many of the original members had retired or died and as in any vibrant organisation new members had joined and had become active in committees and in directing affairs.

McConnell began writing letters to the Hon. Secretary, Fred. Summerfield and others, sharply criticising club officers. None of these letters are in the file, but they were taken seriously enough for President J.J. Keane to convene a special meeting of Council together with Past Presidents (with the exception of McConnell) in November 1939 to deal with the matter. The minutes record that:

'That this meeting is of the opinion that all the suggestions made in Past President William McConnell's letter are such that can be properly be dealt with by Club Council and therefore the Club Council is asked to deal with these. The Meeting regrets the tone and spirit in which criticisms of the Officials of the Club have been voiced. The Meeting is of the opinion that in furtherance of the general harmony of the Club and its future wellbeing, the matter must now be considered as closed.

At the next meeting of Council various items were dealt with under the general heading 'Wm. McConnell's letter'. These included an opportunity for the Council to report to members at a private meeting of the club. Furthermore Secretary Edward Taylor (a) had his salary increased by three guineas to £83.3.0, (b) was entitled to speak at club meetings, (c) a list of the members of Committees would be posted on the club board and (d) that changes in membership should be formally notified to the club.

At the May 1941 AGM more difficulties in relation to McConnell emerged. President Arthur Pearson expressed great unhappiness that canvassing had taken place in regard to the election of Council members. A special meeting of Council and Council elect together with past Presidents was called on June 11th.

In the course of the discussion it was pointed out that unfortunately no member of the Roman Catholic faith had been elected to the Council, a repetition of what happened the previous year. Arising out of discussions on this point all present were satisfied that it just happened and that no organised action had brought about such a result.

Past President Wm. A. McConnell admitted that he had issued slips to some members canvassing votes for specified members for election to Council but considered that he had not acted irregularly.

Having heard that some canvassing had occurred for election to Council those present deplored and condemned such action and were strongly of the opinion that it was contrary to the spirit of Rotary. Further they agreed with the expression of view that should such canvassing occur in the future the member concerned should be asked to resign.

It was further agreed that the members present would do all in their power, at the luncheon meetings, to develop that good fellowship which is the basis of Rotary. Bearing in mind the delicate position of the Roman Catholic members nothing should be tolerated which might make their membership impossible.

McConnell continued his letter writing, however, and in August 1941 Council had to deal with his objection to the election of Arthur McCabe to the vacant classification of Auctioneer. The decision by Council to elect him had been unanimous and McConnell wanted this set aside by a General Meeting of the Club. The Minutes state that the Council considered that:

'The election had been carried out with all due regard to the Constitution and to correct procedure and that Rotarian McConnell had no grounds for such an appeal. Already two specially convened meetings of the Club Council and Past Presidents had unanimously decided that Rotarian McConnell had been acting for some time in a manner calculated to create discord and at variance with the spirit of Rotary.

On the President's suggestion it was agreed that no further correspondence should be entered into but that a further meeting of the Club Council should be held after lunch on Monday September 1st, to which Rotarian McConnell would be invited, so that the President could convey to him verbally the final decision of the Council in the matter.'

At the Council meeting held after lunch on September 1st McConnell was left in no doubt as to the feelings of its members:

To allow an appeal to the Club would necessitate bringing to light the fact that since his return from America a few years ago Rotarian McConnell had indulged in various activities which had caused him to be censured by special meetings of the Council and the Past Presidents of the Club. A general discussion followed, in which many members expressed themselves strongly on the subject of Rotarian McConnell's activities.

He was informed that he was definitely out of step with the rest of the Club, and some members of the Council suggested to Rotarian McConnell that it would be better for Rotary if he were to resign from the Dublin Club. Rotarian McConnell did not indicate that he was prepared to do this. The meeting terminated whilst members were still expressing their feelings of opposition to his recent actions.

It should be remembered that this was the Council whose election McConnell himself had engineered the previous May.

In July 1941 Germany invaded Russia and as the year ended Japanese bombers attacked the United States fleet at anchor in Pearl Harbour in Hawaii without warning. Following the declaration of war between the two states, Germany declared war on the U.S. and Britain at last had the ally for which it had long yearned. It was to be some time, however, before Britain could take advantage of this new relationship. In early 1942, Japanese forces took control of Southeast Asia having defeated the British, French, Dutch and U.S. forces stationed there. Singapore fell and Australia was under threat. This was truly a world war. The war ended in 1945 with the defeat of Germany and Japan. The Club sent £100 to the Red Cross in response to their European Relief fund.

While the war raged there were thousands of Rotarians from all over the world stationed in London. Taking advantage of this, the London Club and District 13 in 1942 organised a conference to plan for peace. In addition to Rotarians, ministers and diplomats representing twenty-one countries attended it. A forum was set up for the exchange of ideas on culture, education and science and after the war had ended this group evolved into the United Nations Educational, Cultural and Scientific Organisation (UNESCO).

During the war new clubs had been chartered in Ballymena (1943), Larne (1944), Newry (1944) and Armagh (1944). Suitable gifts were sent from the Dublin club in each case. In 1946 Drogheda was chartered and Felix Hughes reported that

'He had presented the President's badge to the Drogheda Club on behalf of the President and members of Dublin.'

In November 1945 Council learned that the Gresham Hotel could no longer put its Aberdeen Hall at the disposal of the club for their

Monday luncheon. It did not take long to decide that the Royal Hibernian Hotel in Dawson Street should be the new venue and the first lunch was held there in June 1946. The Hibernian was to remain the Dublin Club's luncheon venue for the next twenty-five years.

On 27th of January 1947 Paul Harris, the founder of Rotary died. For forty years he had been the organisation's roving ambassador and had brought the Rotary message to all five continents. At the time of his death there were over six thousand clubs in seventy-eight countries with over three hundred thousand members. This was a truly great achievement. His wish was that any member or club that would like to mark his passing should make a contribution to the Rotary Foundation.

The idea for the Rotary Foundation had come from Arch Klumph who had been president of the I.A.R.C. in 1916/17. The Depression of the 1930s and the second World War had had the effect of curtailing contributions to the Fund, but following Paul's death donations flooded in from all over the world. In 1948 the Fund was able to award eighteen Rotary Foundation Fellowships (later called Ambassadorial Scholarships). By 1948 nearly two million dollars had been donated and the next year thirty-seven graduate students from twelve countries were awarded scholarships. Today the Foundation administers the largest privately funded international scholarship programme in the world. In addition it is to the forefront in spearheading other programmes involving the eradication of polio, Group Study Exchanges, Matching Grants and many other initiatives.

In 1957 Rotary Foundation introduced the idea of a Paul Harris Fellow. This Fellowship could be purchased by an individual as a means of contributing to the work of the Foundation. In Ireland the practice is for the club to purchase the Fellowship and then to bestow it on a chosen member. In January 1978 President Robin Hall presented the club's first Paul Harris Fellowship to PP Joe Hamilton who was District Governor that year. Since then successive presidents have bestowed Fellowships on fifty-three members of the club and two non-Rotarians: Joan Liuzzi the widow of our late member Paul and Alice Leahy the founder of the charity 'Trust'.

In 1948 Fianna Fail who had been in government for the previous sixteen years were defeated at a general election and a coalition headed by W.J. Costello of Fine Gael took office. The following year Ireland was declared a republic and all links with the British Commonwealth were severed.

In September 1949 the club had a high profile speaker at lunch. This was Dr. Noel Browne[2] Minister for Health. He was, in fact, Ireland's first full Minister with responsibility for health, which had previously been assigned to a Parliamentary Secretary, attached to the Department of Local Government and Health. Dr. Browne's talk to the club was extensively reported in the newspapers of the following day:

The facts in respect of Tuberculosis were the subject of an interesting talk yesterday by Dr. Noel Browne for Minister for Health in an address to the Dublin Rotary Club. Here are some points from Dr. Browne's talk.

At some time in the future it is the hope of the medical profession that TB and cancer can be treated by chemotherapy methods. Meanwhile research, which is steadily being pursued, must be supplemented by more improved facilities by way of up-to-date surgery and the provision of conditions most favourable to medical treatment and patient recovery.

The cost of maintaining one person for a year is between £200 and £250. The death rate in Ireland for each 1,000 from TB in 1911 was 34. In 1948 it is 10. Comparable figures for Denmark are 3, for Norway 6, Sweden 5 and Holland .37. Eighteen months ago 1,000 people were waiting for beds in sanitoria. Since then approx. 1,700 beds have been provided and it is hoped that this will be increased to 2,000 by the end of the year.

Dr. Browne disclosed that in addition to the provision of these beds by adaptation, contracts were coming up for the provision of regional sanitoria in Galway, Dublin, Cork and Waterford.

In the next eighteen months the demand for thoracic surgery has gone up to such a considerable extent that one thoracic surgeon then operating had to be supplemented by the appointment of two others and shortly there would be two working in Dublin plus one in Cork, one in Limerick and one in Castlerea and one in Monaghan.

The standard of treatment, equipment, medical personnel in the three major sanitoria in St. Mary's Dublin, Mallow and Castlebar was unequalled in Europe. The services were absolutely free, were run by the Public Health Authorities and were becoming the best of their kind whether public or voluntary

The Minister also spoke of the use of Mass Radiography mobile vans throughout the country and the expanded use of the preventative BCG vaccination.

Free Service

Dr. Browne had a word for the free medical service[3] observing that TB treatment under the Local Health Authority was completely free and that in addition allowances were payable to the dependants of sick persons. 'I have not yet seen a sound reason why this procedure should be so readily conceded by the medical profession in relation to TB and Venereal Disease and yet should be so unacceptable in relation to any other disease. I am certain that the passing of currency notes between a patient and his medical practitioner can scarcely affect the value of the treatment, which the practitioner has made available to the patient.

Vote of Thanks

Professor Thomas Whelan proposed this. He referred to the search for a cure for TB that was ongoing. Lack of funds was a major inhibiting factor in the search for a cure. Professor Whelan went on to observe that in this country it is easier to get funds to fight Partition and Communism than it is to get money to help in finding a cure for disease.

In October 1950 the Vocational Committee reported to Council on the difficulties that it was experiencing:

A Hobbies Exhibition was doubtful and the Royal Dublin Society was unable to offer accommodation for a Rotary Meeting Place, as they were unable to fit in all the existing applications. Vocational School chiefs did not appear to be particularly interested as classes were already full and there is a Waiting List.

On a happier note the Council approved the expenditure of £7.10.0 for the purchase and posting of 240 Christmas cards to be sent by the club to all those Rotarians from other clubs who had visited the Dublin club during the previous twelve months.

There were, however, storm clouds on the horizon and as the next decade unfolded our club was to face the greatest crisis in its history.

[1] *The telegram from R.I.B.I. should be seen in the context of the very real fear in Britain that an invasion by Germany was imminent. Although Winston Churchill had become Prime Minister in May he had yet to stamp his authority on his Cabinet and peace feelers were being tentatively made through neutral Sweden by officials of the Foreign Secretary, Halifax. The three ports at Berehaven, Lough Swilly and Spike Island in Cork Harbour that had been retained by Britain under the 1922 Treaty had been handed over to the Irish authorities two years previously. Churchill, in particular, felt that the loss of these facilities was detrimental to the efforts of the Royal Navy to protect convoys and successfully prosecute the war at sea. Churchill wanted the ports returned to British control for the duration of the war.*

[2] *Dr. Noel Browne, a medical doctor by profession, had survived TB (his eldest sister Eileen had died from it). He joined the newly established party, Clann na Poblachta in 1947 and was elected a T.D. for Dublin SouthWest in the 1948 General Election. He was one of only two Clann na Poblachta TDs in the Inter party Government led by W.J. Costello of Fine Gael. (The other C. na P minister was its leader, Sean McBride who was appointed Minister for External*

Affairs). Browne dedicated himself and his department to the eradication of TB. He took the capital sum that had accrued from the Irish Hospital Sweepstakes and set about building and fitting out a series of sanitoria throughout the country. The isolation of TB sufferers in sanitoria, the introduction of the new drug streptomycin and a mass X ray campaign to catch the disease at an early stage all combined to reduce dramatically the incidence of TB in the community.

[3] These comments by Dr. Noel Browne concerning a free medical service are an early indication of his thinking on this subject. The Inter Party Government fell in 1951 following Browne's abortive attempt to introduce the 'Mother and Child' scheme. Vehement opposition by vested medical interests supported by the hierarchy of the Catholic Church led to his resignation as Minister.

The visit of Rotary founder Paul Harris to the Dublin club on May 1928. From left: Wm. Findlater (founder member and president 1913/14), William McConnell (founder member and president 1923/24), unknown, Bryan Cooper (president1927/28), Paul Harris, Reginald Keatinge (president 1936/37), J.R. Coade (founder member, first hon. Treasurer and president 1916/17), D. Keatinge, Walter Beckett (Uncle of PDG Horner Beckett and president 1925/26) and Tom Grehan (president 1937/38).

'Commodore' the late Paul Liuzzi and his wife Joan lead the Rotary flotilla on the Shannon during a fellowship visit to the region.

At an Aquabox fundraising event in the River Club in Temple Bar Dublin in 1994 were (from left): Rotarian Wyn Beere, Gill Evans beside her husband PP Peter and Paul Liuzzi.

Colour plate 1

A photo montage of the Euromeeting in Dublin in 2007. Descending from left top: a song from the Swedish club, the troupe of entertainers in City Hall, Rotarian Frank Bannister, a lecturer in TCD, shows visitors around Trinity College, the Cyprus club's traditional dance, Dublin City Manager John Tierney addresses the group in Dublin's City Hall, Irish traditional entertainers in Dublin Castle and PP Kevin McAnallen the organiser of the Euromeeting bids farewell to the guests.

Colour plate 2

At the Shelter Box collection outside the Church of the Sacred Heart Donnybrook were (from left): the late Kent Maytham, Patrick White, Brian Dobson, Derek Griffith, PP Tony Keegan, Jim Bourke, Robin White, Patrick's son, a friend and Richard Kavanagh another friend of Robin's.

Colour plate 3

Florrie Amber Keegan with Santa Claus in the Children's Hospital Tallaght.

Golden Jubilee Banner.

Ethna Fitzgerald, the first lady president of the Rotary Club, Dublin in 2000/2001.

Colour plate 4

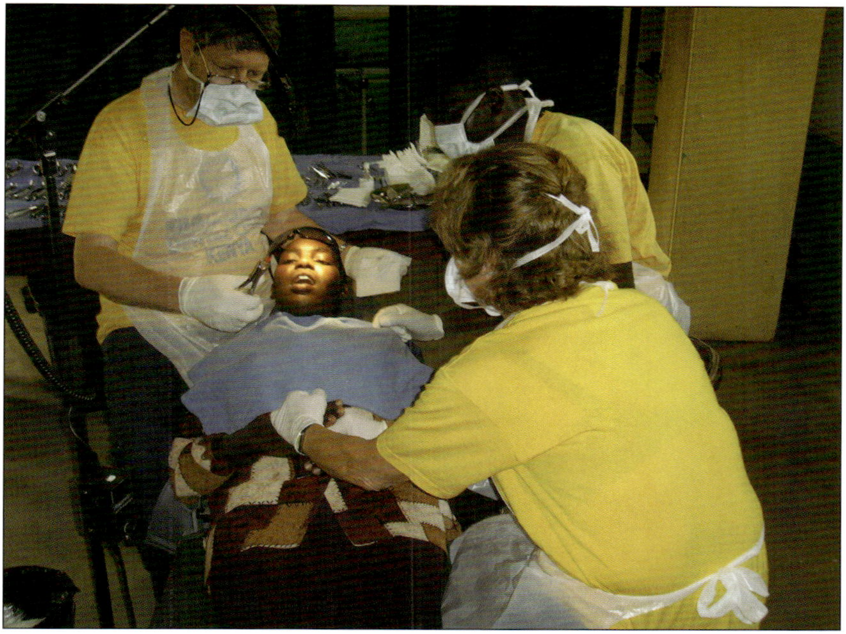

Dental Surgeon Rotarian Peter McGonigal at work in Kenya assisted by his wife Kate, a Registered General Nurse.

HIV Unit at Kilimambogo hospital.

Colour plate 5

Picture of past presidents of the Dublin club with President Guy Johnston taken on the roof of Jurys Hotel outside the Martello Room on the first Monday in July 2003. From left (back row): PP Ted Corcoran, PP Ken Hunt, PP Tony Gannon, PP Denis Boothman, the late PP Michael Cagney, PP Sean Donohue, PP Alan King, PP James Gorman. From left (front row): the late PP Peter Evans, PDG Horner Beckett (president 1956/57), the late PP Jo McGough and President Guy Johnston.

Celebrating Rotary's Centenary in Dublin Castle in February 2005 were (from left) Rotarian Alan Harrison, Madeleine Beckett with her husband PDG Horner and our then newest member Rotarian David Booth.

Colour plate 6

Christmas card sent from Malta to members of the Rotary Club, Dublin in 1915 by their member Dr. Edwin Fannin who was serving there with the Royal Army Medical Corps. The flags bear no relationship to the written message.

Magsie Goor and Musicians before the BBQ in Anacrivey House.

Colour plate 7

Colour plate 8

Members of the Rotary Club, Dublin pictured at the Grand Canal Hotel on the first day of the Club's 100th year: 1 Jim Bourke, 2 Assistant District Governor PP Ted Corcoran, 3 Denise Leahy, 4 Kenneth Carroll, 5 President Tony Seery, 6 Sargeant at Arms Maeve Turner, 7 Past District Governor PP John D. Carroll, 8 Hon. Secretary Stefano Vaiani, 9 PP Peter Evans, 10 PP Paul Loughlin, 11 Paolo Zanni, 12 Fred Duffy, 13 Peter Ferguson, 14 Donald Gordon, 15 Frank Bannister, 16 Bernadette Mulvey, 17 PP Alan King, 18 Pamela O'Loughlin, 19 Peter McGonigal, 20 Derek Griffith, 21 Martin Elsasser, 22 Bertie Finegan, 23 PP Tom O'Neill, 24 David Horkan, 25 Aldo Aletti, 26 PP Ken Hunt, 27 Brian George, 28 Brian Taylor, 29 President Elect Randal Gray, 30 Geraldine Mackey, 31 PP Michael Larkin, 32 Mary O'Rafferty, 33 Liam Yendole, 34 PP Willie Widmer, 35 Vice President Mark Doyle, 36 Allan Kilpatrick, 37 David Booth, 38 PP Paul Martin, 39 Valerio Potti, 40 Michael Boyle, 41 Patrick White, 42 PP Tony Keegan, 43 Immediate Past President Victor Hamilton.

Colour plate 9

From Left: Eavan Ryan, Hannah Loughlin, Jessica Sweetman and President Paul Loughlin at his presidents night in the Masonic Hall 2006.

Herbert Park - Croquet – following instruction in the finer points of the game (from left): Catherine Bourke, PP Kevin McAnallen, PP Alan King, Wyn Beere and the late PP Peter Evans.

Colour plate 10

Group Study exchange team 1988 on canal barge.

Colour plate 11

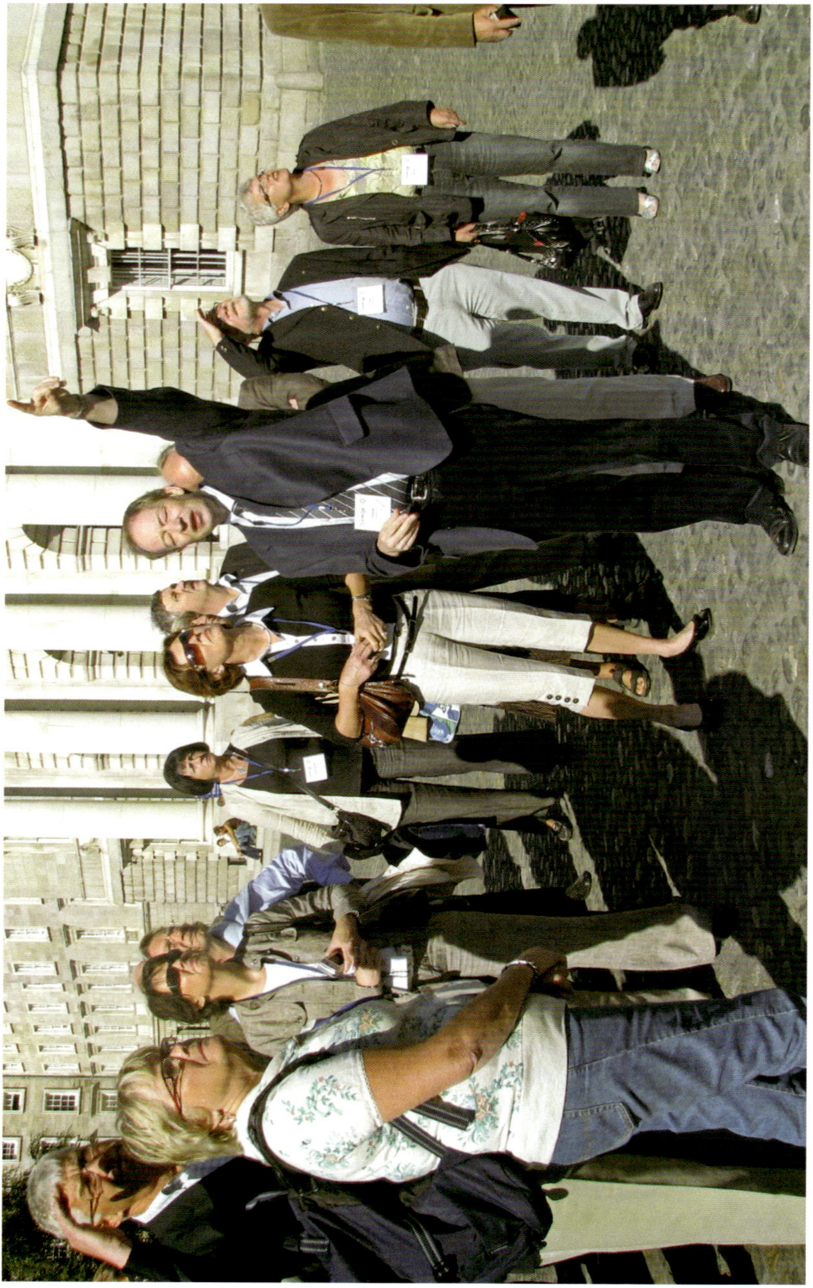

Frank Bannister guides Euromeeting visitors around TCD 2007.

Colour plate 12

Rubber Duck Race on the Dodder 2007.

Colour plate 13

BBQ Montage. Dublin Rotary Club `Olympic` BBQ raises €10,000 for club charities.

Dublin Club President Jo McGough presents new colours to 20th Batt. FCA 1988.

Colour plate 14

Beginning the Wicklow Way in Marley Park, Rathfarnham. (from left): Derek Byrne, Paul Dempsey, PP Tony Keegan, PP Alan King, PP Victor Hamilton, Donald Gordon, Joe Long, Jim Bourke, Brian George and PP Kevin McAnallen.

Colour plate 15

Past presidents Kevin McAnallen and Victor Hamilton pictured at Cape Finisterre in Northern Spain. Both had completed the Camino de Santiago de Compostelo from St. Jean-Pied-de-Port on separate occasions (Victor twice) and they walked together the three days from Santiago to the Cape. The literal meaning of Finisterre is 'the end of the world'. In centuries past it was considered to be the end of the known world.

District Governor Edwin Dunlop presents Tyrone Crystal to President Mary Robinson with Dublin President Finbar Ambrose centre.

Colour plate 16

Chapter Fourteen

Toasts, Stones and Stamps

'Rotary – a philosophy that seeks to reconcile the need to provide for oneself with the central objective to share what one has with others.'
Past Rotary International Director Sabino Santos

When the Rotary movement was founded in 1905 the original Chicago Club had felt that there was no particular need for a written constitution – a gentlemen's agreement was deemed to be sufficient. Soon, however, it became apparent that something more definite was necessary. As other clubs were formed it seemed quite natural that they should adopt the Chicago constitution as their own with variations suited to their particular local circumstances. By 1915 there were over two hundred and fifty clubs with constitutions that varied in one way or another from the original Chicago document. Obviously this was a situation that could not be allowed to continue. If clubs were to be permitted to set their own rules, aims and objectives, then there would be fragmentation and the spirit and ethos of Rotary would be diminished to such an extent as to be, in time, practically invisible.

Accordingly, a sub-committee was appointed by the I.A.R.C. and they drew up a standard constitution that was adopted by delegates at the 1916 Convention in Cincinnati. The adoption of this constitution would be mandatory on all clubs founded after that date, while existing clubs would have to have all amendments to their constitutions approved in writing by the I.A.R.C (R.I.). Gradually, all the early clubs agreed to adopt the standard constitution although here and, even after over one hundred years, there are still some anomalies[1].

The actual reasons for joining and remaining a member of Rotary varied likewise. The idea of Rotary that Stuart Morrow brought from San Francisco, that members should benefit each other commercially, had by the time the Dublin Club was founded in 1911 been superseded in Chicago by the addition of Community Service. Similar accidents of history shaped the members of many early clubs in their attitude to what precisely Rotary meant to them.

To address this difficulty successive Conventions set down objects and aims so that the essentials of what Rotary meant could be distilled into easily remembered phrases. By the 1951 Convention in Atlantic City there were over 7,000 clubs in 83 countries with 341,000 members. Aims and Objects of Rotary as we know them today were agreed at that time. They are:

The development of acquaintance as an opportunity for service.

High ethical standards in business and professions, the recognition of the worthiness of all useful occupations and the dignifying by each Rotarian of his occupation as an opportunity to serve society

The application of the idea of service in each Rotarian's personal, business and community life.

The advancement of international understanding, goodwill and peace through a world fellowship of business and professional persons united in the ideal of Service

Meanwhile, back in Ireland, matters were taking a serious turn. The club archives contain a substantial file discreetly headed 'Toasts at District Functions'. In 1951 there were nine clubs north of the Border and three – Dublin, Cork and Drogheda – south of it. From the time that the District Council was established in 1918 it was customary to hold a Dinner in connection with District Council meetings and at the District Conference. A Toast to 'Ireland – North and South' reflecting the fact that District 16 encompassed the whole island would usually be proposed at these functions. Because of the Second World War and shortages and rationing all District functions were held south of the Border between 1937 and 1949 and, unfortunately, over time the Toast was attenuated to just 'Ireland' with no unfavourable reaction from anyone.

In 1950 the District Conference was held in Portrush, County Antrim and at the dinner the toast to 'Ireland' was proposed by the District Chairman (Governor) Kenneth Graham of the Cork club and honoured. The following day the Belfast Telegraph carried the heading '**TOAST OF KING IGNORED BY ROTARY AT PORTRUSH DINNER.**' Senior past presidents of the Belfast club were determined that such a discourtesy to their monarch would not recur and with the overwhelming support of their members they proposed the following motion at the District Council meeting in March 1951:-

'That at any District Conferences and Assemblies the customary toast of the country in which the meeting is held shall be honoured'.

At a later meeting of the Council in July of that year Senator Fred Summerfield the Honorary Secretary of the Dublin club asked for an interpretation of this resolution. Belfast President Malcolm McKibben told him that he had been instructed by his club to propose the resolution and that there was no doubt what it meant. It meant that the Toast to the King be honoured at District meetings in Northern Ireland and that the toast should be the Republic of Ireland at meetings in Southern Ireland. Fred did not accept this interpretation and deplored the introduction of politics into Irish Rotary. When the Northern delegates insisted on this interpretation Fred left the meeting as a protest and asked that this fact be recorded. Despite this, the Minutes were passed and this proposal was seconded by another member of the Dublin club the Rev. L Callaghan.

There ensued long and tortuous negotiations beginning with an attempt by Dublin at the District Council in October 1951 to have the motion rescinded. This attempt was rejected and a resolution passed that the motion be replaced with a Gentlemen's Agreement in exactly the same terms. Thereupon the Dublin delegates withdrew as instructed by their club. As a result of several meetings of the members of the Dublin Club it was agreed to put this matter before R.I.B.I. and R.I. so as to ascertain whether a change of District or being directly affiliated to R.I. could be arrived at constitutionally. A letter of April 1952 to R.I. set out the position, explaining that as matters stood the Dublin Club was unlikely to remain in association with the northern clubs and faced the prospect either of severing its connection with District 16 or the possible break-up of the club. The advice of R.I.B.I. was sought with regard to the club's position in the event of their secession. The club also wrote to the President of R.I.B.I. asking for his assistance in having all toasts at District functions omitted or having existing toasts replaced with one to Rotary International. The Officers of the Dublin Club pressed their case further at a meeting with the President of R.I.B.I. adding that they already had had a number of resignations because of the controversy. R.I.B.I. replied that this was a matter that could be properly settled by District 16.

In May 1952 Senator Fred Summerfield resigned his membership of he Dublin Club. He had been President in 1929/30 and Honorary Secretary from 1930. The reason for his resignation was revealed in a subsequent news item that appeared in the 'Irish Press' on December 9th.

Senator F. M. Summerfield a past president of the Dublin Rotary Club and its honorary secretary of nearly twenty three year standing states that he resigned from Irish Rotary in May as a protest against the introduction of political toasts in Irish Rotary

In December of that year the Lord Mayor of Belfast, Alderman James Norritt, who was a member of the Belfast Club, was reported in the 'Sunday Press' as stating that:

'All we in the northern area want is that the toast of the ruler of the territory in which the District meetings take place be honoured. In Holland, should we meet there, we would pledge a toast to the Queen of Holland'.

At the lunch meeting of the Dublin Club the next day its President D. Gillespie felt obliged to issue the following statement:

Fellow Rotarians, you may have seen in an Irish Sunday newspaper yesterday a reference to Rotary.

I would like it to be known that though a approach was made to both the Hon. Secretary and myself no statement was made by the Dublin Rotary Club on this matter and indeed some of the statements that appeared were most inaccurate.

As regards the statement quoted as being made by Alderman James Norritt, Lord Mayor of Belfast who is a member of the Belfast Rotary club but is not an official of the club it seems to be to be ill-timed and, if I may say so, not helpful to the cause of Rotary.

His analogy in saying 'should we meet in Holland, we would pledge a toast to the Queen of Holland' bears no comparison to the present situation here. I would point out to Alderman Norritt that Holland is another country.

Here we are dealing with one country (though at the present time there happens to be two administrations). District 16 of Rotary is the whole of Ireland, north, south, east and west.

At a District Council held in the Shelbourne Hotel Dublin in March 1953 the Dublin Club suggested that a special sub-committee should be appointed to help come up with a solution to the intractable problem of toasts. The sub-committee duly reported in May of that year with the recommendation that there should be no formal dinners at District functions thus obviating the need for a toast. This compromise was rejected by a majority of the members of the District Council who would accept nothing else except the enforcement of the Loyal Toast at all dinners held in Northern Ireland. A similar proposal put forward by R.I.B.I. was also rejected later in the year. R.I. also indicated that they would not intervene and that they would not support the Dublin Club's proposal that they should be directly affiliated to R.I.

At all times during the controversy the President, Council and Officers of the club consulted the members before embarking on any course of action. Sometimes this was done by secret ballot and at other times at special general meetings. On every occasion majority support was forthcoming for the policy adopted by the officers and Council of the club.

Faced with this impasse, Council decided in July 1954 to completely withdraw from all District activities. In a ballot seventeen members declared that the club

Should now submit and comply with the terms of the District Council resolution, which for three years we have been trying to have annulled.

A further thirty members agreed with the proposition that

The Dublin Club should no longer co-operate with any District activities

Thirty-one members decided to leave any decision on the matter to the Council and five papers were spoiled. Membership at the time was around one hundred and thirty so it can be calculated that forty-seven members did not exercise their democratic right to vote.

In any event, Council decided to withdraw from District. Delegates were instructed not to attend District Council meetings, orders for the District magazine Cogs were cancelled and no information concerning the activities of the Dublin club was to be supplied. District was instructed to exclude Dublin from the Roster and R.I.B.I. and R.I. were informed of the club's decision.

It should be mentioned that during this time of controversy cordial relations still continued to exist between Dublin and the northern clubs. Its President, Vice President and two past presidents represented Dublin at the Charter Night of the new Lisburn club in October 1954 and, as was customary, we presented a gavel to their first President.

It was not until 1957 that the matter began to be resolved. In that year the same Malcolm McKibbin who had been Belfast President in 1951/2 was District Chairman and he approached the Dublin President Eddie McCabe suggesting that there should be no formal meals and therefore no toasts at District Council meetings. Unsurprisingly, this was acceptable to the Dublin club and we resumed our involvement at District level. With the expansion of Rotary in Ireland it became impossible to accommodate all delegates and their partners at District Conference Dinners and the practice grew up of individual dinners being held instead of a formal banquet. The problem of controversial toasts ceased to exist and normal relations between all Rotarians on the island of Ireland were resumed.

In the midst of all this controversy Rotary celebrated its Golden Jubilee. In the early years, Chesley Perry, the I.A.R.C. Secretary operated out of a borrowed office in Chicago. After some years he was able to rent office space in Downtown Chicago. By the early 1950s it became obvious that a dedicated building to house the central administration of the Rotary movement was required. A search began for a suitable building and in 1955 R.I. settled on Evanston a university town just north of Chicago where they bought a 50,000 sq. foot facility[2].

In August of that year the Dublin President, Walter Griffiths, received a letter from George R. Means, Secretary of R.I., explaining that at the approach to the front of their new headquarters there was a spacious plaza about 40 feet long by 30 feet wide. This walkway was to be paved with stone blocks on both sides. The idea was that each country where there was a Rotary club would provide an indigenous stone and it would be engraved with the name of the club and country and the date of the club's foundation. There were to be eighty-nine stones in total. The letter was sent to Griffiths as the president of the first club in Ireland to seek the club's co-operation in contributing a stone that would be representative of the Rotary Club of Dublin as well as Ireland.

With Council's approval he replied saying that the idea was excellent and that we intended to send over a slab of Connemara marble. He added:

My Council and I think it advisable to make clear that we are sending the stone in accordance with your request namely 'a stone

that will be representative of the Rotary Club of the city of Dublin as well as Ireland. We understand that the Dublin Club as the first club in Ireland is the only club to which your request has been made.'

The R.I. Secretary confirmed that understanding as correct, and that the Rotary Club of Dublin was the only club in Ireland to which the suggestion had been made. He went on to say that a similar suggestion had been made to each of the other countries in which Rotary Clubs were located. Griffiths replied, thanking him for confirming that ours would be the only stone from this island.

He must have had his doubts, for shortly afterwards in a conversation about other matters he asked the Belfast President John Morrow if it was true that his club was ending a stone to Evanston. He confirmed that Belfast was indeed sending a stone and added that R.I. wanted a stone representing Northern Ireland and had asked Belfast to provide it on behalf of the other North of Ireland clubs. Morrow added that it seemed that Dublin was doing something similar for all the clubs in Eire. He went on to remark that it would do no harm to Evanston to have a stone from each side of the Border. Griffiths replied that this might do no harm to Evanston but he was afraid that most people here and many in Northern Ireland would deplore that fact that Ireland was not represented in one piece. He then wrote to Evanston asking 'if Dublin was the only club in Ireland to which the suggestion had been made, how was it that Belfast had been asked for a stone also?' Evanston replied that the list of eighty-nine included Ireland and Northern Ireland and they thought that the two areas were separate: there was no intention to mislead. Griffiths replied that Ireland should be represented by one stone and that Dublin was the one to supply it. He asked for a list of clubs sending stones and the precise form of inscription. In reply he was told that the list of clubs contacted included Dublin Ireland and Belfast Northern Ireland. Later he was informed that the precise inscription on our stone would be 'Ireland Dublin 1911'. The total cost of our stone including transport by Cunard liner was £25.14.3.

To celebrate Rotary's[3] fiftieth birthday the Dublin Club organised a banquet in the Royal Hibernian Hotel on February 22nd attended by Alfie Byrne T.D. Lord Mayor of Dublin, one hundred and twenty four Rotarians and their wives, diplomatic representatives from eleven countries and Minister for External Affairs, Liam Cosgrave T.D.

Replying to the toast 'Our Guests' the U.S. Ambassador W.H, Taft said that as an international organisation he knew how important Rotary had become. The very fact that it was international meant that they had a free world and a free press. The Minister for External Affairs who also spoke said that he saw the goodwill the Rotary had succeeded in establishing throughout the world as a significant factor in promoting better relationships between peoples.

To commemorate Rotary's Golden Jubilee the club decided that they would finance the fitting out of a wing of the Civics Institute Nursery in Marylands off Cork Street in Dublin. This was to be called the 'Rotary Room'. The cost was £230 and this included ten tables, forty metal cots with mattresses, forty children's chairs, cutlery, overalls, Montessori equipment and decoration. A plaque recognising the contribution of the Dublin club was erected.

Other service projects, in addition to the usual Christmas gifts to the children's hospitals, included the presentation of two rocking horses to the Orthopaedic Hospital and a programme of visits for secondary school students to industrial premises to acquaint them with the world of work. At the opening of a new Out Patients Department at the National Children's Hospital in Harcourt Street Mr. W.H. Anderson Chairman of the Hospitals House and Finance Committee thanked the club: -

through its president Desmond FitzGerald for all the work it had done for children in the hospital.

While the club was celebrating Rotary's Jubilee and dealing with its difficulties with District, another matter arose that nearly brought it to its knees financially. Ernest Reid-Smith vice-president of the Wirksworth Club had joined in 1953 with the classification of past service and became Chairman of the International Committee and a member of Council in 1955. In October 1955 Ernest Reid-Smith and his Committee proposed and got approval from Council for a project entitled 'Rotary World Stamp Pool'. The idea was that each Rotary Club in the world would be contacted and asked to send us used postage stamps. These would then be made up into packets and sold on to Rotarian philatelists throughout the world. The proceeds were to be divided between the Foundation Scholarship scheme and our own project for assisting University students. All clubs and District Governors/Chairmen were circularised and the stamps began to arrive.

By early 1956 nearly one thousand letters and some eighty thousand stamps had been received. Soon administrative problems began to emerge involving sorting, cleaning, finance, and correspondence. However, in May of that year, Ernest, who appeared to be handling everything himself, was able to mount an exhibition of four thousand letters and a quarter of a million stamps so far received.

By early 1957, during Horner Beckett's presidency, Council had become seriously perturbed to learn that there were three million stamps in stock with only half a million sorted. There were long and agonised discussions at general and Council meetings on how best to deal with the situation by, for instance, employing temporary stenographic assistance. The Pool was flooded with stamps and Ernest's own attic was overflowing. Finally, in November of that year, following a report from Dr. Paul Singer[4], and in the face of some resistance from Ernest and his Committee, Council decided to begin disposing of the stamps in bulk lots. The following January, with Ernest unable or unwilling to provide a coherent account of the situation, a sub-committee was appointed to wind up the project. While this was under way an interview with 'Ernest Reid-Smith the Chairman of the Dublin Rotary Club' was published in the March 4th edition of the 'Evening Herald' in which he extolled the virtues of the project that had become a debacle.

In May 1959 the sub-committee was at last able to report that the Stamp Pool had been wound up with all the stamps sold for £55, leaving the club with two filing cabinets worth £20 and a deficit of £253 to be written off. When you consider that, at the time, the annual subscription was £7 this figure is in the region of £10,000 in today's money.

In October 1956 Eddie Taylor who had been a member of the club and its paid Secretary indicated that he wished to retire. Eddie who had served the club for twenty-six years was presented with a wallet of notes and at the next agm was elected an Honorary Member. Council decided to insert the following advertisement in the Dublin morning papers:

DUBLIN ROTARY CLUB

Requires part-time services of

L^{ady} S^{ecretary}

Unusually attractive post for cultured lady over 30 with an interest in world affairs, and having thorough knowledge of shorthand and typing.

Half-day attendance required for 5 days a week. Salary £150 p.a. Apply in writing only to

**THE ROTARY CLUB
12 Westmoreland Street Dublin.**

Following interviews, Miss Maureen O'Reilly was appointed Secretary the following January. Miss O'Reilly was by all accounts a charming and efficient lady who had the rather useful attribute of being able to 'pour oil on troubled waters' when the need arose. The club office was decorated and a new desk and an addressograph machine were purchased.

In May 1957 President Horner Beckett led a large delegation of Rotarians from the Dublin club to the R.I. Convention in Lucerne Switzerland. This experience, for many the first that they had of Rotary in action at International level, was to lead to a greater emphasis on service in the Dublin club in the coming decades. So ended a very difficult time for our club.

[1] Up to a few years ago the Belfast club had seven elected members of Council rather than the standard six.

[2] Rotary International remained in this building on the corner of Ridge Avenue and Davis Street for thirty years until it too became too cramped. In 1985 they bought the eighteen-storey building at 1560 Sherman Avenue in Evanston for less than $24million. R.I. rented out the excess space and soon paid off the mortgage. They still occupy this prestigious facility today.

[3] By 1955 there were 8,313 club with 392,628 members in 89 countries.

[4] Paul Singer was a continental expert philatelist who arrived in Ireland in the early 1950s. He had an impressive personality and was blessed with boundless self-confidence. He persuaded Desmond Shanahan a principal in the long established Shanahan's Auctioneer in Dun Laoghaire to set up a stamp dealing business with him as Managing Director .The business initially prospered, early investors obtained an excellent return and as word got around more and more people wanted to get involved. It was, however, too good to be true and following a robbery the business collapsed. Singer and Shanahan were charged and while Singer managed to get himself acquitted on appeal, Shanahan was sentenced to fifteen months in prison. Following his acquittal Singer disappeared abroad and most investors lost all their money.

Chapter Fifteen

Golden Jubilee

'Some of you present here today might be alive to celebrate Dublin Rotary's first centenary. I ask those of you who may have had that experience to remember to tell those who may be gathered together of how you saw Irishmen of all creeds and political views, from north and south, with many visitors from our neighbouring island across the Irish Sea and distinguished representatives from Europe and America assembled here to pledge together their continued determination to work together as brothers for the happiness of all peoples and for peace among nations'.
An Taoiseach Sean Lemass T.D. speaking at the club's Golden Jubilee Dinner.

After many years of effort the Vocational Committee led by Desmond Kilroy finally managed to mount a 'School's Exhibition of Hobbies, Arts & Crafts'. This was an enormous undertaking by the club and involved over three hundred and fifty students from forty-three schools. It was opened by the Lord Mayor Catherine Byrne and took place in the Metropolitan Hall Lower Abbey Street from December 30th 1958 to January 2nd 1959. The exhibits were divided into fourteen classes and included photography, knitting, needlework, basket working, ceramics, leather and metalworking, model making and doll dressing. The Honorary Adjudicators were the Hon. Desmond Guinness, the well-known architect Michael Scott and Miss Lillian Mitchell. Amazingly, the Exhibition turned in a small profit thanks largely to sponsorship from twenty-two companies.

In November 1958, William McConnell, the grand old man of Rotary died. McConnell whose brother-in-law Stuart Morrow had brought the Rotary idea to Dublin from the United States in 1911 was the last remaining founder member of the first club in Europe. During his forty-seven years of membership he had seen many changes, not all of which met with his approval. Despite many offers by the Dublin Club he had refused to accept honorary membership, as this would have prevented him from having a vote at meetings. He was active right up until his death and Rotarians throughout Britain and Ireland and beyond mourned his passing.

The club marked its Golden Jubilee in 1961 with celebrations extending over three days. On Monday February 13th Frank Aiken T.D. the Minister for External Affairs hosted a reception in Iveagh House, on Tuesday 14th a Banquet was held in the Shelbourne Hotel and the following day Jack Lynch T.D. Minister for Industry and Commerce opened an International Poster Exhibition in the Brown Thomas Little Theatre in Grafton Street.

The attendance at the Banquet included Cllr. Maurice Dockrell T.D. the Lord Mayor of Dublin, An Taoiseach Sean Lemass T.D., E.G. Breitholtz first Vice-president R.I. representing the president of R.I., J. Ed. McLaughlin, the R.I.B.I. President John C. Pride and Jacques Giraud Chairman of the European, North African and East Mediterranean Rotary Council. In addition to the presidents of London and Belfast there were presidents and vice presidents from twenty other clubs. A cheque for one thousand guineas was presented to Professor J. F. Cunningham Chairman of the Medical Research Council for cancer research. As Sean Lemass took his place, army trumpeters and drummers sounded the Taoiseach's salute. Eight Aer Lingus airhostesses showed the five hundred guests to their places.

Proposing the Toast 'Ireland' An Taoiseach Sean Lemass T.D. noted that of the seventeen rotary clubs in Ireland, fourteen were north of the border.

'Everybody here will understand if I extend to the representatives of these clubs a special greeting and welcome.

He went on to say:

I hope that those guests who have come here from abroad for the first time will have no difficulty in understanding the Irish people. I do not think that you will find us very complicated or different from other people. The rapid improvements in international communications are helping to reveal the comforting fact that people are very much the same the world over. This is the case notwithstanding differences of colour, language or social custom, and that the great majority of them are decent folk who have no other desire than to live in harmony with their neighbour and to garner in peace the fruits of their labours.

Today, when distances between continents and cities can be measured in hours instead of miles, when men and women of all races were coming nearer to one another, not only in time but in ways that they think and act, we should be capable of rising to more rational conduct inspired by our discovery of the essential unity of the human race.

The growth in understanding that the person from the next parish or the next country or the farthest corner of the earth is not necessarily our enemy, whatever the political leaders may try to tell them, must help to develop in time a new hope in the world that the constant danger of war may at last fade away before our civilisation is destroyed by forces which man has learned to release but have not yet acquired the wisdom to master.

Tell them you saw it

Some of you present here today might be alive to celebrate Dublin Rotary's first centenary. I ask those of you who may have had that experience to remember to tell those who may be gathered together of how you saw Irishmen of all creeds and political views, from north and south, with many visitors from our neighbouring island across the Irish Sea and distinguished representatives from Europe and America assembled here to pledge together their continued determination to work together as brothers for the happiness of all peoples and for peace among nations.

Group photo at the 1964 district conference in Killarney with district chairman Felix Hughes and his wife Christine centre front row. Felix was Dublin president in 1947/48 and hon. Sect.1952/64. District Secretary Horner Beckett and his wife Madelaine are second and third from the right front row.

Fifty years hence that may either be a vague memory of lost possibilities or a commonplace of human relations hardly worth mentioning. Tell them that we this evening, in so dedicating ourselves, thought of these things as the highest aims of human endeavour on earth'.

Walter Douglas, president of the Dublin Club, welcomed all the guests who had come to celebrate the club's centenary. He especially welcomed the presidents of Belfast and London who would celebrate their own 50th birthday later that year.

Long-serving members of the club have told me that An Taoiseach Sean Lemass used the occasion of the Dublin club's Jubilee celebrations to initiate contacts with Rotarians from Northern Ireland and sounded them out as to whether it would be possible to improve relations between north and south. Over the next few years civil servants from both administrations kept in touch with each other and these contacts were to lead eventually to the historic meeting between Northern Ireland Premier Terence O'Neill and Sean Lemass four years later in January 1965.

The club continued its involvement with the Marylands Centre by funding redecoration work, repairs to a fence and the presentation of Easter Eggs to the children each year. Other projects undertaken were the provision of a mini-bus for the transport of handicapped children, organising a film show for the prisoners in Mountjoy Gaol and an outing for elderly people to Greystones. Christmas hampers and bags of coal were provided for the needy and Santa Claus delivered a selection of toys to children in hospital while the club delivered twelve Christmas trees provided by Mrs. Slazenger of Powerscourt. Recreation equipment was provided for children in seven Dublin hospitals and a Silver Cup was presented for a blind boy's chess competition. Used office equipment was given to Cappagh Hospital to assist in the vocational training of patients.

In the 1960s there was no directory of accommodation available for elderly people in the Dublin area. Anyone requiring such information would have had to phone whatever nursing homes they knew of and make inquiries as to availability, cost and services provided. The Community Services Committee led by Kent Maytham decided to rectify this unsatisfactory situation and with the assistance of students from T.C.D. they produced the first 'Register of Accommodation for Elderly Dubliners.' The publication listed the names, addresses, telephone numbers and contact persons at over eighty nursing homes in the greater Dublin area. With twenty-five sub-headings detailing the type of accommodation available, its cost and the services provided this was the first, and for nearly twenty years thereafter, the only publication of its kind. This invaluable directory was distributed free of charge to health care professionals, solicitors, social workers and every organisation that had some interaction with the elderly. A copy of the publication was presented to Erskine Childers T.D. Taniste and Minister for Health. Erskine had himself been a member of the club in the 1930s when he was working for the Irish Press. The Directory was re-printed and up-dated several times up to 1986.

The international aspect of Rotary was very much to the fore at this time. Many members of the Dublin club made contact with Rotarians on the continent of Europe and arrangements were made for their children to spend the summer months with Rotarian families in France, Germany and the Benelux countries. They, in turn, would send their children to Ireland where Rotarian families here would look them after. Foreign languages were perfected: and contacts established that have proved beneficial to all concerned to the present day.

In 1959 President Joe Jennings led a party of Dublin members to the District Conference in Killarney. On this occasion they decided to take a different route and travelled via Shannon Airport where they had lunch with its General Manager Brendan O'Regan. There were two consequences of this luncheon. Firstly a Rotary Room with a Visitors Book was established at Shannon Airport (there was already a similar facility at Dublin Airport put in place by the Aer Lingus Deputy General Manager Rotarian James Gorman) and, secondly, the idea of Rotary was reintroduced into the south-west. Following on from this visit Dublin past President Eddie McCabe and Rotarians from the Cork

Club visited Limerick on a number of occasions and spoke about Rotary and how it operated to groups of businessmen. Eventually on July 8th 1963 the Limerick Shannon Club was chartered at a dinner attended by many Rotarians from north and south.

Following on from this the Dublin club also undertook similar work in its own area and clubs were founded in Dun Laoghaire(1965)[1] and Dublin North(1969). The establishment of both of these clubs required the District Cartographer to redraw the boundaries of the Dublin club to take account of its new neighbours[2]. The Monaghan club was founded in 1967.

Following on from the World Stamp Pool debacle and the expenses associated with the celebrations of the club's Jubilee in 1961 the finances were not in good shape. Accordingly at the 1963 AGM the annual subscription was raised from eight to ten guineas and the Entrance Fee was doubled from two to four guineas. Four years later finance was still a problem and the possibility of closing the club's office in Westmoreland Street was mooted. This suggestion met with opposition from members who thought that such a decision would result in loss of face for the club as, apparently, only four clubs in R.I.B.I. had offices and two of them were due to close when their lease ran out. Two years later Miss O'Reilly informed Council that she felt unable to continue as Secretary. The club presented her with a television set in recognition of her twelve years of service and the club office was closed in 1970.

Severe difficulties arose between R.I. and R.I.B.I. in the 1960s. When the British Association of Rotary Clubs (B.A.R.C.). was established in 1914 the clubs in Britain and Ireland looked naturally to that body for direction and guidance. The disruption of communications during the Great War reinforced the feeling that clubs in these islands, where Rotary was flourishing, should deal with their own affairs themselves. The position of the B.A.R.C. was regularised at the Los Angeles Convention in 1922 when they submitted their proposed constitution and bylaws, which were ratified. At the same time the name was changed to Rotary International in Great Britain and Ireland. At the time it was the only territorial administrative unit in R.I. and fearing that others might follow this example the 1927 Convention in Ostend forbade any such units in the future.

In the mid 1960's, strong objection was raised to R.I.B.I's. status and the matter was vigorously debated at the R.I. Council on Legislation in Toronto in 1964. The fear, again, was that other regions might demand similar status and the Rotary spirit might be diluted. After endless meetings and sub-committees it was arranged in 1966 that District Chairmen in Britain and Ireland should henceforth be District Governors and that dues from clubs should be shared taking into account the administrative duties performed for R.I. for R.I.B.I. Some differences remain: throughout the world clubs are governed by their Board of Directors while in Britain and Ireland it is the club Council that runs the club. R.I.B.I. remains a strong unit of Rotary and four of its past presidents have served as R.I. presidents.

There was more controversy in 1967 when in March of that year John Edmund Doyle; a Solicitor who had joined in 1964 gave a talk at lunch on the topic of 'Communications'. This rather anodyne title gave no clue to the furore that would follow.

Knights and Masons urged to Co-operate

Better understanding between peoples could be encouraged by interdenominational schools which existed so freely elsewhere, said John Edmund Doyle District International Service Convenor of the Dublin Rotary Club speaking at a club lunch in the Royal Hibernian Hotel.

Mr Doyle, speaking on 'Communications', said that he looked forward to the day when there would be communication between the Knights of Columbanus and the Masonic Order leading to mutual charitable works.

Mr Doyle, who is a lawyer, prefaced his talk by emphasising that he was giving his own personal views and was not speaking as a

Rotarian. He asked the members present to study their reaction to his suggestions about the Knights and Masons because it should be the test of their awareness of and true desire for unity between men of goodwill.

Talking on contraception, abortion and divorce he went on to say that it behoves the 95% Catholic population of this country to make it clear to State authorities that the State was in error in demanding that these teachings should be enshrined in a Constitution binding even one person who was not a Catholic.

The Irish language was costing the country £30m a year, the language that as he had learned it and knew it was the language of fishermen and small farmers. Modern Gaelic was a different tongue: a concoction of words adapted artificially within living memory by those not content with compiling dictionaries. They had with savage disregard for the science of semantics invented words, abandoned grammatical rules, altered spelling and recently they had thrown overboard the Gaelic script beloved of scholars.

Now they would have Mother Ireland prostituted by Gaelic gigolos to produce a bastard medium. This was being done with Gestapo-like methods by self styled Gaelgoiries who culled their ill-gotten gains from a Government that lacked the courage to reverse itself on this topic in the light of the advancing technological world.

Mr Doyle said that the greatest single advantage that we had going into Europe was our knowledge of the English language. It was also the greatest single advantage of those who emigrated to the United States. Yet, he said, many children leaving school had not got as good English as had their parents: they were inclined to blame this on the teaching of Irish.

Short Term

Speaking of religion, Mr Doyle said that it would soon be recommended that clerics should not hold office for life. He made the suggestion that all clerics in all churches be appointed to a particular office for a term of five to ten years. This would remove problems such as asking them to resign.

He also spoke about communications between Christians and those who were called pagans and he quoted a theologian who said that there was no direct pipeline from heaven to the Pope. He urged them to remember that the words 'Love thy neighbour' meant all peoples.

People of plural societies which were so rapidly developing in the world today would have to break down barriers of international, inter-racial and inter-religious ideas. They would have to communicate between each other not as transcendental phenomena but as extremely commonplace realities.

He said that he had found Rotary to be a truly catholic organisation with a higher proportion of tolerant people than in many other organisations and this was particularly true of Rotary International. The function of Rotary International was to serve as the promotion of better understanding between people.

Although some members complimented him on his talk there was a hostile reaction from others. District Governor Joe Jennings, who sat in on the Council Meeting that considered the matter, said that he had discussed with John Edmund the content of his talk and had asked him not to repeat it at other club meetings. The DG felt that its content infringed on the Rotary constitutional rule that 'party politics and sectarian religion shall be excluded from all proceedings of the club'. John Edmund took a different view, however, and the talk was given to other clubs in the District. As the original address to the Dublin club had been reported in the newspapers a lively correspondence ensued in the Letters Page of 'The Irish Times' where John Edmund defended what he had said in his personal capacity. A past president who had resigned in protest was induced to withdraw his resignation,

Apart altogether from the Rotary Foundation Ambassadorial Scholarships, many clubs have set up schemes of their own. In 1920 the Atlanta Georgia Club in the U.S.A. established an educational foundation to put children who required such assistance through college. By 1940s hundreds of students had graduated through the aid of such scholarships. In the 1950s the Georgia scholarship scheme was extended internationally and the Dublin club nominated graduate students to undertake post-graduate study in the U.S. A number of these were successful in obtaining scholarships including some children of members. In 1966 we were informed, through District, that R.I. had decided that from then on Foundation Scholarships would be confined to those who were not children, step children, grandchildren, mother, father, brother or sister of a Rotarian. While this restriction came about because of the tax laws in the United States it would apply worldwide. This news was not well received in the club.

In the spring of 1965 Brian Hillery was nominated by the club for a Georgia Scholarship and shortly afterwards he was offered and gladly accepted the scholarship. He was co-sponsored by the Atlanta based West End and East Point Rotary Clubs. Brian told me about the life-changing year he spent in Georgia. His own words tell the story.

'I was met on arrival by the President of the West End Rotary Club and his family and I enjoyed Rotary hospitality in their home for several days before going to the University of Georgia. On my first day on campus I attended an American Football thriller – the University of Georgia Bull Dogs beat the University of Alabama by just one point. The teams were preceded by the two hundred strong Redcoat Dixie Band led by long-legged, baton twirling majorettes – an exciting and colourful first day.

I enrolled in the Master of Business Administration programme and, after four terms, graduated in September 1966 achieving first place in the MBA class. Several of the subjects were at the cutting edge of business education and I was able to put these to good use later in my academic career in University College Dublin.

Rotary hospitality made the transition from Ireland to a great year in the United States much easier. For example, during the Christmas break alone, I had over a dozen invitations to stay in

Rotary homes in addition to other frequent visits during the year. I addressed both sponsoring clubs and was elected Rotary Student of the Year in May 1966.

In addition to Rotary I made numerous friends at the University. The 1960's saw considerable political and social change in the United States and it was a privilege to be able to be able to be part of debates on the Vietnam War and the Civil Rights Movement.

All in all, the Rotary Scholarship provided an invaluable opportunity and led to a life and career-changing experience for me from which I benefited hugely. I shall be forever grateful to the Rotary Club, Dublin for nominating me for the scholarship.'

Brian's experience of the Rotary scholarship has been replicated by tens of thousands of young people throughout the world. Rotary provides the greatest number of privately funded scholarships of any organisation each year and their value in giving life-changing opportunities and improving international goodwill and understanding cannot be over estimated. Brian[3] joined the Dublin club in 1969 and was International Convenor for some years. During the 1970's the International Committee held an annual reception in Newman House for foreign students attending university in Dublin and many students from abroad were entertained to our luncheon meetings.

Meanwhile back in Ireland the partition of the island in 1922 did not lead to harmonious relations between the unionist and nationalist population in what had become Northern Ireland. There were sporadic outbreaks of trouble in the nineteen thirties, forties and fifties.

In the late 1960's following Civil Rights marches, extensive rioting and bloodshed took place. With armed groups organising, the British army was brought in to maintain order and Direct Rule from Westminster was introduced in 1972. For over thirty years since then there has been carnage affecting both nationalist and unionist populations. After various abortive attempts, a Power Sharing coalition of unionist and nationalist politicians has been in place since 2007. During all these years, despite many atrocities committed by the extremists on both sides, the Rotary movement in Ireland has maintained its unity and was and is one of the few cross community organisations on the island of Ireland. At all times excellent relations have existed both at a personal and at club level between the Rotarians on both sides of the border.

On a happier note, in May 1967 President Tom McMurray presented Dick Archer who had joined in 1920 with two 'beautiful pipes'. Dick had the distinction of having met Henry Ford and was the first to import Ford cars into Ireland. As the decade ended, man ventured outside the earth's atmosphere for the first time. On Monday July 21st of that year Neil Armstrong became the first person to set foot on the Moon. Space travel was possible and who would know where that would end.

[1] *The Dun Laoghaire club founded Bray in 1972 and they, in turn, founded Wicklow in 1988. Dublin Fingal was founded by Dublin North in 1979.*

[2] *On the initiative of Stanley Leverton, a past president of the London Club, at the Scarborough Conference of R.I.B.I. in 1931 new clubs were allowed to be formed in the same 'well-defined trade or commercial centre' as existing ones. Up to that time each city or large town would have been entitled to have just one Rotary club. The legislation giving effect to this was ratified at the St. Louis R.I. Convention in 1943. This change required that a District Cartographer be appointed to delineate the boundaries of clubs in the same urban area.*

[3] *Dr.Brian Hillery joined CityBank in Dublin following graduation from Georgia University. In 1967 he joined the staff of the Graduate School at University College Dublin and served as Professor of Industrial Relations and Human Resources until his retirement in 2001. He holds PhDs from U.C.D. and Oxford. He served in the Dail and Seanad from 1977 to 1994. He is currently Chairman of Independent News and Media and a Director of the Central Bank.*

Chapter Sixteen

Community Service

'The Rotary Foundation Scholarship-a life-changing experience'.
PP Paul Loughlin

As we have noted over the years, attendance at lunches was not always good. With a membership of between a hundred and twenty and one hundred and forty the average number at lunch rarely exceeded fifty. Many members had joined the club because socially and commercially it was the done thing to do so. Luncheons were convivial and relaxed affairs and the need to finish precisely on time was not as imperative as it is today. One of the principal concerns of many members at the time was that the president should move on as quickly as possible to second grace so that they could light up their cigarette or cigar. From the time it was founded, attendance competitions had been held, cups presented, cards and letters sent to remind members of their obligations with varying degrees of success. By the 1970s there was about a sixty percent attendance at lunches.

In 1972 our Attendance Officer was Robert Hirsch, a native of Austria. In the late 1930's Robert was the owner of the Hirsch Ribbons factory in Galway and he was instrumental in helping a fellow countryman escape the Nazi terror. Georg Klaar, a seventeen-year-old Jewish young man had, with Robert's encouragement, applied to the Irish legation in Berlin for an entry visa. If obtained, this would have allowed him and his family to travel to Ireland where he was to work for Hirsch as a ribbon-weaver despite having little or no knowledge of the trade. The Irish Minister in Berlin was Charles Bewley[1] an anti-Semite and a staunch supporter of Hitler, who was a most unsuitable person to represent Ireland in Germany. The visa was approved in Dublin and sent to Bewley but he deliberately delayed countersigning and issuing it. Eventually through the intervention of his brave German secretary the family were able to leave for Ireland.

Whereas Georg made it to Galway, his mother and father were not as fortunate. While waiting in Berlin for the visa to be signed Georg's father accepted a job in Paris and while his mother travelled to Ireland with her son she pined for her absent husband and soon rejoined him in the French capital. Six months later the Germans invaded France and the Vichy authorities handed them over to the SS and they died in Auschwitz.

A major event in the 1970s was the decision of the Irish people to join the European Economic Community[2]. The United Kingdom and Ireland formally became members of the EEC on January 1st 1973. Since then the Community has been enlarged until today the European Union consists of twenty-seven states encompassing most of Europe. Originally an economic grouping of countries successive treaties have resulted in a movement towards a federal organisation with more and more power being given to Brussels.

Over the years the Community Services Committee has been the most active of all the club committees. Our archives hold their Attendance Book from 1956 to 1980 and it indicates that they were a vibrant and dedicated group of men. Most meetings took place at around 6.30pm either in the hotel where the club met for lunch or the Hibernian United Services Club on Saint Stephens Green.

Sheltered Shopping began in the spring of 1973 when three hundred elderly, disabled and infirm people were taken to Dunnes Stores Cornelscourt in the evening. There they were presented with a voucher, assisted in their shopping and Dunnes gave them a hamper. After refreshments and entertainment they were driven home. In succeeding years the venues changed to the H. Williams Supermarkets in Rathmines and Dundrum until in the 1980 and 1990s when the venue for a number of years was the Dunnes Stores supermarket in Kilnamanagh near Tallaght. The Dunne family took a personal interest in these events and were often present themselves. Some of the leading entertainers of the day gave freely of their time to provide entertainment for the hundreds of participants.

Throughout the 1970's, Christmas trees were provided each year from the Archer estate near Lough Dan. In addition to the usual toys and Santa Claus for the National Children's Hospital around one hundred and fifty hampers were distributed. Another annual event was bringing fifty elderly people for a coach drive to Glendalough or Mount Usher Gardens in Ashford County Wicklow with afternoon tea. Travellers' children from their school in Milltown were brought to the Gaiety pantomime and entertained at Halloween Parties. A concert was arranged for the Old Men's Home in Northbrook Road. And a bell-call system was installed in Kilcroney Old People's Home. Lady Wicklow's holidays for Belfast children was supported financially and Playform Bricks and tricycles were presented to the National Association for Cerebral Palsy for their school on Sandymount Avenue.

In 1976 the Vocational Committee organised the first series of Mock Interviews for final year secondary school students. These are designed to give the students some idea of what it is like for them to be interviewed for a job. In the first year the club provided members to undertake this task in four schools: Marian College Ballsbridge, Saint Andrew's College Blackrock, Loreto Abbey Dalkey and Sallynoggin Comprehensive School. The procedure was that each student prepared a letter and a C.V. beforehand as if they were actually applying for a job and they were then interviewed accordingly. Marks were awarded for the letter, the C.V. and the interview. Indications as to how their technique and presentation could be improved were given. The first year over one hundred and thirty students were interviewed and each year thereafter this excellent and worthwhile project has been continued.

The first Group Study Exchange (GSE) teams were organised in 1965 between districts in California and Japan. The programme was such a success that it soon spread around the world. The way it works is that a district selects a Rotarian as team leader and then four to six people between the ages of twenty-five and forty who are not Rotarians, but would make excellent goodwill ambassadors. Rotary Foundation then matches this team with a district in another country and pays all the travel expenses. For four to six weeks the host district takes the visiting team to points of interest and arranges for them to visit schools, courts, civic leaders, businesses and Rotary clubs. They live in Rotary homes, dine together and visit those in the same trade or profession as their own. A team from the first host district then visits the district from where the original team came and the same procedure is followed.

The first reference to GSE in the club Minutes came in 1976 when the club's selection to participate in this scheme was accepted by district. The team travelled to Kentucky in the United States and the U.S. team came in Ireland later that year. With the co-operation of the Dublin North club accommodation for the incoming team was arranged and there were meetings with President O'Dalaigh and An Taoiseach Liam Cosgrave T.D. as well as visits to industrial facilities.

The 'Troubles' in Northern Ireland continued to cast a dark shadow and in 1974 bombs were detonated in Dublin and Monaghan killing many people. The following year, the Belfast Club set up the Harmony Trust in conjunction with International Voluntary Service. This was a cross community project taking children out of Ireland on holiday and was initially under the chairmanship of PP Harry Corscadden. So that the children could continue to meet in a relaxed environment Glebe House close to Strangford Lough was purchased. The Dublin club supported this worthwhile project with substantial funds over a number of years. The Trust and Glebe House continue to provide a centre for people affected by the 'troubles' to meet, learn, play and develop contacts that would help ease the conflicts engulfing them.

We have seen how from the very early days of Rotary, Women's Rotary Clubs were formed although they did not last too long. Many clubs, particularly in the United States had unofficial Ladies Committees that co-operated with the their men-folk on suitable projects. These were colloquially known as Rotary Anns. The name came about when Californian Rotarians chartered a train to take them to the 1914 Houston Convention. At that time it was customary for only men to attend such meetings. On this occasion the wife of the San Francisco President Ann Brunnier accompanied her husband. Her presence was such a novelty that all the men wanted to be introduced to her and as the journey progressed they named her their 'Rotary Ann'.

Rotary had publicised the arrival of the West Coast train and there was great excitement when it arrived at its destination. There was a large crowd including the wife of Guy Gundaker from Philadelphia who was also named Ann. When the West Coast Rotarians discovered that they had two Anns they carried both shoulder high along the station platform singing a song they had composed about their 'Rotary Ann'. The name caught on and for over sixty years thereafter the ladies of Rotarians both in the U.S. and on this side of the Atlantic were known as 'Rotary Anns'.

Over the years the wives, sisters and daughters of the Dublin Rotarians had assisted in various projects, particularly visiting and entertaining children on the Club's annual visits to the Children's Hospitals. In 1923 the vice-president of R.I.B.I. suggested at a meeting of the Manchester Club that the wives of club members should consider setting up a women's club. Following on from this the wife of the Manchester president issued an invitation to other spouses and on the 15th November of that year an exploratory meeting was held. The following January 10th the first meeting of Inner Wheel took place in Manchester and Margarette Goulding was elected chairwoman. The idea took hold quickly in Britain and six years later there were so many clubs that they had to be organised into districts.

The first Irish Inner Wheel club was Belfast, founded in 1931. In the 1960's the nearest Inner Wheel club to Dublin was in Drogheda and wives of the members of Dublin Rotary Club visited them to get an idea of the type of work they undertook. After a lot of preparatory work it was decided to found an Inner Wheel club in Dublin and in 1971 the Club held their Charter Night in the Ballroom of the Royal Hibernian Hotel. The then president of the Rotary Club, Dublin, Alan King, presented their first president, Christine Hughes, the wife of our Honorary Secretary Felix, with her Chain of Office. From their foundation the Dublin Inner Wheel Club have been active both in supporting the work of the Rotary Club, Dublin and undertaking their own projects. They immediately took charge of packing the Christmas parcels and also played an important role in the Sheltered Shopping project. Christine served as Inner Wheel's District 16 Chairwoman in 1975/76. In 1971 'Cogs' reported that the Dublin Inner Wheel Club was running a Meals on Wheels Project. Each Wednesday 25 meals were prepared and members of the Dublin Rotary Club delivered them to old and needy people. Today, there are twenty-four clubs in District 16 and the Dublin Inner Wheel Club meets on the first Tuesday of each month in the National Yacht Club Dun Laoghaire.

From the time that Foundation Scholarships began to be awarded in the late 1940's there was a steady stream of incoming graduate students to Ireland and to Dublin. In some years there were two or three studying at TCD and/or UCD. Mentors were appointed to liase with them and, where appropriate, accommodation was found. They attended club lunches and the District Conference as our guests, told us about their home town and their hopes and aspirations. The ability to provide a scholarship depended ultimately on the amount the district subscribed to Foundation. In the first twenty years our district sent thirteen scholars abroad, mostly to the United States but also to France, South Africa, Canada and Sudan. Michael Kehoe, nominated by the Dublin club secured a Foundation scholarship in 1965/66 and attended the University of California Los Angeles. In 1973/74 Adrian Masterson, also nominated by the Dublin Club was awarded a scholarship to attend Harvard University in Cambridge Massachusetts.

In 1969 Paul Loughlin, then completing a M.Litt. in Education at TCD heard, through a friend John Kelleher[3], about the existence of the Rotary scholarship. John himself had been an Ambassadorial Scholar from the Rotary Club of Sheffield and had attended Tulane University in Kentucky. Having discovered the whereabouts of the Dublin Club through Dick Biggar, a friend of his father's, who was a member, he wrote and was interviewed by a District panel that included Joe Hamilton who was subsequently President of our club in 1973/74 and District Governor in 1977/78. Paul was unsuccessful, but afterwards Joe told him that he had done a very good interview and that he should re-apply the following year. Taking him at his word, Paul did just that and was successful in obtaining a scholarship to Emerson College Boston to study Mass Communications. At the 1970 District Conference in Killarney he met Mary Taxis, an incoming scholar from Pennsylvania. They struck up a friendship and travelled together, in his father's Opel Kadett, to many clubs throughout Ireland where Mary spoke about her homeland and Paul about his upcoming course in Boston. Joe Hamilton arranged all their travels and took a personal interest in their welfare.

In September 1971 Paul travelled to Boston and enrolled in Emerson College. At that time the Vietnam War was at its height and there were many veterans among his fellow students attending under the G.I. Bill. The experience was, as they say, a real eye-opener and a stimulating introduction to world affairs at first hand. While there he spoke to seventeen Rotary clubs in Massachusetts, Rhode Island and New Hampshire and attended the District Conference in Boston. The troubles in Northern Ireland were at a particularly violent stage while he was in the U.S. and his stay coincided with the Bloody Sunday killings. It was a difficult time to be speaking about Ireland abroad and the necessity to provide a balanced account of events in Ireland while being true to his own principles was to prove of immense value to him in his future career.

As he was completing his course at Emerson, Paul was offered a job as Lineup Editor on CFCF television in Montreal Canada. He remained there until 1980 when he returned to Dublin where he has worked with and for RTE ever since. When I spoke to Paul about the effect that the Foundation Scholarship had on his life he told me that it was for him a life changing experience.

Back in Dublin he met our own member Dudley Engert who had been president in 1981/82. Dudley told him that it was now 'pay back time'. Dudley invited Paul to join the Dublin club in 1994 and he was our president in 2005/06.

The 1970s saw another club allied to Rotary formed in Dublin. Probus began in the mid 1960s in England and is 'an organisation designed to provide a meeting point for retired business and professional men and women who appreciate the value and opportunity of meeting others in similar circumstances'. The first Irish club was formed from the Bangor Rotary Club in 1971 and the Dublin club founded Dublin South Probus and presented their first president, Dr. J.B. O'Regan, with his chain of office in 1973. Probus clubs usually meet on a weekly basis and there can be a speaker at some meetings. Today there are one hundred and seventy four clubs in Ireland with nearly five thousand members. There are three hundred thousand probarians throughout the world.

In 1975 the Club invited the representatives of the Freemasons and the Knights of Columbanus to address the club in November and December respectively. Consequently, on November 17th the Deputy Grand Master of the Grand Lodge of Antient, Free and Accepted Masons of Ireland, Dr. Maurice Henry Redmond O'Connell, addressed the club. He was followed the next month by Sean Patrick Bedford the Supreme Knight of the Knights of Columbanus. At each talk representatives of the Masons and the Knights were present. Summing up, then President Michael Larkin said that 'if the speakers had changed scripts, except for the dates and names, we would not have noticed any difference between them as their good works are so similar'. Both talks were well received by the club members. Subsequently a meeting involving the two organisations and Rotary was organised with a view to providing jobs for school leavers. It is not known what outcome, came from these endeavours.

In March 1977 our luncheon speaker was the Gay Rights campaigner David Norris. The Dublin Club was quite advanced in giving a platform to Mr Norris at a time when there was quite vehement opposition to any notion of gay rights. He spoke passionately about the position of gay people in Irish society at that time.

Laws Against Homosexuals an Open Incitement to Hatred

The laws against Homosexuality in Ireland are both an insult and an open incitement to hatred said Mr. David Norris Chairman of

the Irish Gay Rights Association at the Rotary Club of Dublin lunch.

Mr. Norris called for law reform[4] as an absolute priority although he personally was not afraid of the law and would welcome a prosecution, as it would afford him the chance to challenge the law, constitutionality.

It was no longer acceptable to deny employment on the basis of religion but it was apparently permissible to get an otherwise satisfactory employee out of a job because he is 'one of them'.

There was no real reason why the average gay person should be regarded as a less than reliable employee and Gay Liberation could only have a beneficial effect on Irish industry. Once the homosexual was valued on the basis of individual achievement the energy deployed in subterfuge and concealment could be engaged more productively.

This talk by David Norris was one of many given during the 1970s on matters of topical interest and exemplified the club's vibrancy and relevance to society in general. Although it was not marked by any fanfare the one-thousandth member joined the club in October 1978 during John D. Carroll's presidency. In that year the club had one hundred and twenty-six members.

As the 1970's ended the major event in Ireland was the visit of Pope John Paul the Second. Elected the previous year he was the first Polish Pope and the first to visit Ireland. Father Tom Fehily PP of Porterstown, near Clonsilla, had joined the club in 1978 with the classification of Religion-Roman Catholic and in 1979 the Archdiocese of Dublin appointed him chairman of the committee tasked with organising the papal visit. The club played its part by providing forty-two cars to transport dignitaries during that extraordinary week.

[1] *Bewley was educated in Oxford where he converted to Catholicism. He was Irish Minister to the Vatican before he was appointed to Berlin*

in 1933 and he served there until July 1939 when he was recalled to Dublin. He chose not to return, thus effectively firing himself from the Department of External Affairs. While in Germany he was drawn into a belief in the Nazi State and its trappings and his confidential reports became increasingly clouded by the Nazi party line. After the war he settled in Italy, wrote a biography of Hermann Goring and died in Rome in 1969. Conversely, the Bewley family in Ireland were most supportive of Jewish refugees and marginalised people generally. Following the Second World War legations headed by Ministers began to be upgraded to Embassies headed up by Ambassadors.

²*The European Economic Community (EEC) was established by the Treaty of Rome in 1957. The original members were Belgium; France, Italy, Luxembourg, the Netherlands and West Germany .The first expansion took place in 1973 when Ireland, the U.K. and Denmark joined. Greece became a member in 1981 while Spain and Portugal joined in 1986. With the fall of Communism East Germany joined West Germany as a member in 1990. The biggest expansion took place in 2004 with the accession of Malta, Cyprus, Slovenia, Estonia, Latvia, Lithuania, Poland, the Czech Republic, Slovakia and Hungary*

³*John subsequently produced the acclaimed Strumpet City, became Controller of Programmes at RTE and recently retired as the Director of the Irish Film Classification Office.*

⁴ *Following a lengthy campaign by David Norris and the Campaign for Homosexual Law Reform the Irish laws prohibiting homosexual activity were, in 1988, declared to be in contravention of the European Convention of Human Rights. In 1993 homosexuality was decriminalised and laws were enacted outlawing discrimination based on sexual orientation. Norris was elected to Seanad Eireann representing Trinity College Dublin in 1987 and has so represented them to date.*

District Governor John D. Carroll with his late wife Bosco at his Conference in Kenmare in 1983.

Chapter Seventeen

75th Anniversary

'Never has it been so important that Rotary in District 116 keep all its lines of communication and friendship open. Rotary has no corporate political image nor can it adopt one. The privilege of each Rotarian is that his own views and convictions are sacrosanct. At all costs Rotarians should avoid polarisation either within their clubs or in the District. Rotarians in R.I.B.I. and throughout the world are looking at District 116 with concern and sympathy'. District Governor Horner Beckett 1971.

Since our District was established, the Dublin and Belfast Clubs have each provided fourteen District Governors[1] (Chairmen). The early district meetings were purely of a social nature and it was not until 1924 that a formal meeting of representatives of Dublin, Belfast and Londonderry clubs took place in Ye Olde Castle Restaurant in Belfast. The first meeting of the District Council for which minutes survive took place in the Dublin Club's offices on 5th April 1928 when representatives from Dublin, Belfast and Cork Clubs attended. With the exception of the war years between 1939 and 1945 the Council has met on a quarterly basis. Since the Second World War six members of the Dublin club have served as head of district. These are V.J.O'Hare (1946/47), Felix Hughes (1964/65), Joe Jennings (1966/67), Horner Beckett (1971/72), Joe Hamilton (1977/78) and John D. Carroll (1983/84). Their Conferences were held in Bundoran, Killarney twice, Galway, Killarney and Kenmare. The Drogheda Club was chartered in PDG V.J. O'Hare's year while PDG Felix Hughes had the pleasure of presenting charters to Newtownards, Sligo and Dun Laoghaire. Carrickfergus was chartered during PDG Joe Jennings year and Castlebar received its charter from PDG Joe Hamilton in November 1977. PDG John D. Carroll presented charters to Bandon in August 1983 and Limerick Thomond in May 1984.

The Dublin club was also involved in organising a new club in the city centre. Dublin Viking held its inaugural lunch in March 1980 and received its charter from R.I.B.I. president Eric Firby at a dinner in the Gresham Hotel in September 1980. The club met for lunch for some years and in 1994 they decided to become a Breakfast Club and they now meet at 7.30am each Friday morning in Buswells Hotel, Molesworth Street.

In 1978 a group of Rotarians from district 116 including Liam Yendole (Senior Active), Dudley Engert (Engineering Marine) and Michael Larkin (Management Consultant) attended the R.I. Convention in Tokyo, Japan. On their way back to Ireland they stopped off in Bangkok and visited Rotary clubs in that city and in Pattaya on the coast 165km to the south. Father Ray Brennan, a Redemptorist priest, was the president of the Pattaya club and after the meeting he invited them back to his home. This turned out to be six or seven small wooden buildings and there they found an American nun nursing about thirty small babies with some local help.

Father Brennan was the breadwinner, soliciting financial help from the owners of local night-clubs and lecturing in philosophy in Buddhist monasteries. Six years before, in 1972, Father Brennan had been asked to assist temporarily at the local Saint Nikolaus church. Opening the church one morning he found a newly born baby lying on the ground. He was taken aback by this, but decided to take the infant to his home and care for it. Word got around about his generosity and more and more babies began to be given to him by unmarried mothers who had no possibility of looking after their children themselves.

When the Irish Rotarians returned home, they informed the forty clubs in Ireland, through district, about the work that Fr. Brennan was doing in Pattaya. The response was amazing, and in a short space of time £37,000 had been collected. Fr. Brennan was invited to come to Ireland to receive the cheque at the District Conference in Galway. He told members that he had never handled a cheque of that size before and went on to explain that he intended to build an Orphanage to provide secure accommodation for the young children in his care. Thus began an association with Fr. Ray and Pattaya that lasted for many years.

The Orphanage expanded rapidly covering a huge area with schools, a medical centre, Buddhist temples and is now the largest institution of its kind in Thailand. In gratitude for the help that he received from Ireland Fr. Ray presented a diamond and sapphire broach that is worn by the wife of our District Governor. Fr. Ray died in 2003 but the legacy of his work lives after him in the form of a Children's Village, a Vocational School for Disabled Children, a school for blind children, a Day Care Centre and a children's home.

Throughout the 1970's and the 1980's the conflict in Northern Ireland affected all parts of the island. It is a tribute to the friendships and sense of service that Rotarians north and south developed over many years that the unity of the district was maintained in often very difficult times. The words of District Governor Horner Beckett quoted at the beginning of this chapter spoken in 1971 when he was chairing a District Council meeting are a testimony to the level of commitment of Rotarians at that time.

In 1980 Fergus O'Brien and John Carson, Lord Mayors of Dublin and Belfast respectively, undertook a tour of cities in the United States to emphasise the goodwill and co-operation that existed between north and south in Ireland. Co-operation North[2] who's Chief Executive Joe Greevy (Trade-Industry Development) had joined our club in 1977 and subsequently became President in 1988/89 supported their highly successful visit. While on a visit to the Belfast club in 1981 our then President, Michael Larkin (Management Consultant), conceived the idea of following up the Lord Mayors' visit with a two-week tour of Rotary clubs in the United States. This would be undertaken by himself and Gordon Millington (Civil Engineering – Consulting) the Belfast President. Gordon having agreed to the proposal, the trip took place in June 1981. Dr. Brendan O'Regan Chairman of Co-operation North, who again provided funding, accompanied them.

Over the two-week period they visited six clubs and a District Assembly. Both presidents spoke at each and emphasised that though they came from different communities they had much in common. Both supported the resolution of difficulties through peaceful means and both encouraged inward investment to the advantage of all the peoples on the island of Ireland. The largest club they visited was Houston; the world's largest, with over 800 members. They also visited Chicago No. 1 and the District Assembly in Dallas, Texas that had representatives from 50 clubs. The U.S. Rotarians were amazed at the good relations between Michael and Gordon (many clubs had been wondering how they could seat them in such a way as to avoid conflict) and, together, they achieved much in advancing understanding about Ireland north and south. They also showed that Rotary in Ireland was a powerful force for good.

At his Conference in Kenmare in 1983 District Governor John D. Carroll (Catering Contracting) spoke for many at a time when, as now, we were struggling to find a way through an economic recession:

'We spend a lot of time assuring ourselves, telling ourselves what a great organisation we are, but we should remind ourselves seriously, at this time, that our motto is 'Service Above Self'. The Rotary man is no ordinary man because his opportunities are extraordinary. Each of us has many talents, some of us use them, and some of us don't. We have got to give, and if you withhold you are cheating because we have all got these gifts. So, when you go home, please bring some of the enthusiasm from this conference with you and apply in your everyday life some of the messages that we are trying to communicate to you.

There can come a day for every man when his foundations are shaken and the world is dark and there seems nothing to live for, but when everything else is gone the sense of duty remains. The value of a person lies not in their social status but in their efficiency. The true value lies in the contribution a person can make to their community. The true aristocracy lies not in lineage, but in service. All social claims are valueless and baseless unless they are backed by usefulness to the general community. The important thing about any person is not their ancestry, but their potential for the future'.

These words are as valuable today as they were over twenty-five years ago.

In the early 1960's, R.I. began to develop the idea of forming a Rotary style club for boys and girls in secondary schools. The first Interact club was launched in 1962 in a High School in Florida U.S.A. An Interact club is not a stand-alone organisation but is always allied to and mentored by a Rotary Club. The first Interact club established in Ireland was in Newry in 1971 and the Dublin club founded an Interact club in 1979 during John D. Carroll's presidency. Our current member, Kenneth Carroll (Contract Catering), John's son, was its first president and in its two-year existence it undertook a sponsored climb of the Sugarloaf and other fundraising efforts. The money raised helped purchase a special chair for dialysis patients in the Meath Hospital. By their nature, Interact clubs have a transient membership and despite the best efforts of our members PDG John D. Carroll and Dr. Robbie Nichol (Trade Associations-Industrial Improvement) our first Interact club folded in March 1981.

Since that time, our club has established Interact clubs in secondary schools including Sion Hill, Blackrock and Marian College, Ballsbridge. For a number of years the Sion Hill club ran a series of talent contests entitled 'Search for a Star'. The Sion Hill Interact club chose their own charities and over the years, through their successful concerts, they raised money for the Rape Crisis Centre, the Somalian Famine Appeal, Cairde[3] and Aids sufferers. The teacher who had responsibility for the Transition Year programme and who was of great assistance to the Dublin club in identifying suitable students for participation in the Interact club was Mary Hanafin who afterwards went on to became a T.D. and Minister for Education. The Marian College club also staged a concert in 2008 and raised Euro 1,300 to assist chicken farmers in Zambia. In 2004 the Dun Laoghaire Rotary took on responsibility for the Sion Hill Interact Club while we continue to mentor the Marian College club.

As Interact grew in popularity, Rotary clubs noticed a gap in the chain of service to the community. In the late 1960s the first Rotaract club catering for young adults in the 18-30 age group was founded in Charlotte, North Carolina U.S.A. The Larne club was the first in Ireland to foster a Rotaract club while Dublin followed suit in June 1976. The Dublin Rotaract club undertook much useful work at a Hostel for Battered Wives and bringing children from a local Orphanage to the Zoo. Other projects included painting and decorating old people's homes and hosting a R.I.B.I. Rotaract conference in Wesley College in the late 1970s. Our club currently mentors a Rotaract club based in University College Dublin Belfield.

In the 1980s two graduates nominated by the Dublin Club were successful in obtaining an Ambassadorial Scholarship. Valerie Furlong went to New Jersey where she was hosted by the Glassboro club in 1982/83 and Maria Marnon attended Ohio State University in Columbus Ohio in 1986/87. Interestingly, Valerie married a native of Glassboro and settled in the United States.

The Dublin Club celebrated its 75th anniversary in February 1986 with a luncheon attended by President Hillery in the Royal Hospital Kilmainham on Saturday February 22nd. There was a District Council meeting held that afternoon in the RHK and in the evening a fork supper and dancing rounded off the day.

To mark its 75th year it was decided to undertake the fitting out of a room in the newly built Interpretative Centre on the Bull Island north of Dublin. UNESCO had designated the three and a half-mile long Bull Island with its world famous bird sanctuary as a Biosphere some years previously. Each year thousands of Brent Geese spend their winter here. A building was constructed with funding from the EEC and Dublin Corporation with an upper floor of 1,000 square feet. The club provided display panels and visual equipment for this floor to create a facility exhibiting the wide variety of birds that nest on and pass through the Bull Island. Specialist groups and the general public have used this facility over the past twenty-five years. In 1990 the Dublin Club produced a video for the Centre showing the birds and wild life in the area. The Interpretative Centre is still in use today and a plaque notes the club's involvement.

Mock Interviews continued to be undertaken by members and by the 1980s we were providing this service for thirteen secondary schools. Another project was the donation of £1,400 to the National Rehabilitation Institute following a Gala Night at the Gaiety Theatre featuring the Rathmines and Rathgar Musical Society's production of Gilbert and Sullivan's Princess Ida. All the usual projects continued: the Guide to Accommodation for Elderly Dubliners was reprinted and updated, twenty-eight Christmas Trees were presented to hospitals and other institutions and a Multiple Sclerosis centre in Sandymount was provided with TVs and filing cabinets. Other projects included senior citizens outings and support for the Brabazon Trust in its work of providing sheltered accommodation for the elderly.

In 1986 the first Safari Supper was held. This involved members and their wives eating a starter course in one home, a main course in another and dessert and coffee in a third venue. With most couple involved providing both food and participating in the event by attending other homes it was an exciting and stimulating event. Fellowship, good fun and money raised for charity has made the Safari Supper one of the highlights of the Rotary year.

Another highlight is the annual Barbeque. The first one was held in 1989 in John (Machinery – Distributing) and Magsie Goor's wonderful home outside of Enniskerry. Since then this has been an annual themed event enlivened by the Suzuki children's orchestra, raffles and auctions of everything from weeks in holiday homes to paintings and boat trips. During the past twenty years, tens of thousands of euro have been raised by the Community Services Committee at this annual event.

Another project of the Community Services Committee in the 1980s was bringing young people from Children's Homes on outings. In 1989 thirty children between the ages of three and fifteen were brought to the Wax Museum, the Savoy Cinema and McDonald's. Another outing was undertaken to Mosney.

Readers may remember that in the early years of the Dublin Club a lady applied to join and was turned down for membership because:

The Board of Directors (of the I.A.R.C.) was not in favour of the admission of women members and that there was no wish on the part of any Club that a woman should be admitted.

By the 1970's views were beginning to change and motions from clubs began to appear on the agenda of the Council on Legislation[4] asking that women be allowed to join Rotary. Although all such motions were defeated, each time they gained a greater amount of votes and it appeared to be inevitable that, over time, women would be admitted. However, in 1978, the Duarte club in California admitted three women as members. As this was in direct contravention of their constitution they were suspended from membership of R.I. This, in turn, prompted legal action from the Duarte club and after appeal and counter-appeal the lawsuit ended up in the U.S. Supreme Court. In 1987 the Court found in favour of the club as Californian law precluded establishments from discriminating or refusing to provide service on the basis of gender, race, colour, religion or national origin. At the 1989 Council on Legislation a motion was passed removing the word 'male' from the Rotary Constitution.

The position then was that while all U.S. clubs could not by law refuse membership on the basis of gender it was open to clubs outside the U.S., subject to their own laws, to allow women to join. Each club would have to decide for themselves. On May 29th 1989 the Dublin Club debated the matter and on a motion proposed by Mark Doyle (Civil Law Practice) and seconded by PDG Horner Beckett (Senior Active) by a vote of 27 to 11 it was decided to allow members to invite qualified women to become members.

The following November, Major Sheina Henderson of the Salvation Army was elected as a Honorary member and in 1991 Her Excellency Margareta Hegardt, the Swedish Ambassador to Ireland, was elected an ordinary member with the classification of Foreign Government Service. Rotary was entering a new and exciting phase in its development.

[1] *Up to 1966 the head of a district in R.I.B.I. was called Chairman. As part of the settlement of outstanding differences with R.I. the title became Governor in 1966.*

[2] *Co-operation North was founded in 1979 by Dr. Brendan O'Regan and a group of like-minded businessmen who realised that for Ireland to succeed both economically and socially there needed to be better relations between Northern Ireland and the Republic of Ireland. They developed sensitive programmes that brought together people from both traditions north and south. Although, today, conditions in Northern Ireland have greatly improved there are still communities that are polarised and, for them, suspicion rather than friendship is the norm. Now named Co-operation Ireland, the organisation continues to work to assist these communities in participating in cross community and cross border projects.*

[3] *Cairde is a community development organisation that works to tackle health inequality among ethnic minority communities.*

[4] *The Council on Legislation, Rotary's democratic body for reviewing and changing its constitution, meets every third year. Each club is entitled, through its district, to propose amendments to the existing constitution.*

Pictured at the Killarney District Conference in 1970 were (from left) Joe Hamilton then convenor of the district Foundation committee and later president of the Dublin club in 1973/74 and district governor in 1977/78, Mary Taxis incoming Rotary Ambassadorial Scholar, Graham Alford of the Dublin club and Paul Loughlin outgoing Rotary Ambassadorial scholar and president of the Dublin club 2005/06.

Immediate past president Peter Evans presents the chain of office to incoming president Finbar Ambrose July 1993.

Chapter Eighteen

Polio Plus

The membership of any club is made up of four bones:
The **Wish Bones** who spend most of their time wishing someone else could do the work.
The **Jaw bones** who do all the talking and very little else.
The **Knuckle Bones** who knock everything and anybody who tries to do anything.
The **Back Bones** who get under the load and do all the work.
Anon.

Since its foundation in 1905 the membership of Rotary has grown at a steady rate. There have been times when due to wars and recession the growth has not been as strong as other times. By 1996 there were 1.2 million members throughout the world in 27,640 clubs in 154 countries. The membership of R.I.B.I was 62,965 in 1,799 clubs. Women, who had begun to join in the late 1980s, accounted for 60,000 worldwide. Of that number there were 2,150 in Europe and 925 in R.I.B.I. It was this membership that was going to have to face its most challenging project.

The Polio Plus campaign has been described as 'Rotary's Finest Hour'[1] and would nearly deserve a chapter all to itself to do it justice. From its earliest years many Rotary programmes catered for the needs of crippled children and in most cases they were crippled because they had contracted 'infantile paralysis'. Little was known about the cause of epidemics that destroyed the lives of tens of thousands of children throughout the world, except that the condition took no account of race, class or ethnic origin. Rich and poor alike were struck down. Even Franklin Delano Roosevelt[2], the son of one of the richest families in the United States was its victim.

In Ireland, there were sporadic outbreaks of the disease throughout the 1940's and the 1950's. It is estimated that as many as 15,000 cases of polio were treated in the 1950's in Ireland. The major outbreak was in Cork in the summer of 1956. Following a public outcry civic and community life was brought to a standstill and all sporting events cancelled.

The first breakthrough in combating this scourge was to identify the poliomyelitis virus and to discover that it enters the body through the mouth and attacks the nerves in the spinal cord. When the flow of impulses from the brain is interrupted the affected muscle fibres shrivel and die. In 1955 the United States licensed a polio vaccine developed by Dr. Jonas Salk. This was administered by injection. By 1960 Dr. Albert Sabin had produced an oral vaccine. Following on from this a mass vaccination programme was undertaken across the industrialised world and tens of millions of children were inoculated. Even so, in 1969 when man walked on the Moon for the first time, 60 million children were born with no protection against the disease.

In 1978 R.I. created a new programme entitled ' Health, Hunger and Humanity' (3-H) to focus the attention of clubs throughout the world on the needs of underprivileged peoples. Through contacts with the World Health Organisation, UNIFEC and the U.S. Centre for Disease Control, R. I. began to develop a strategy designed to combat and finally eradicate polio from the world. Up to then, only one infectious disease, smallpox, had been eradicated by mass vaccination.

The Polio Plus campaign was officially launched in 1987 with the aim of finally eliminating polio from the world by Rotary's centenary in 2005. Clubs and individual Rotarians contributed hundreds of millions of dollars to the project and throughout the 1990s large swathes of Asia, Africa and Latin America were certified to be polio free. Rotary has provided funds, volunteers, advocates, transport, food, accommodation and logistical support to enable eradication to become a reality. By Rotary's 100th birthday there were still about five countries in South East Asia and Africa where polio was still endemic. This situation is largely due to religious and cultural misconceptions about the nature of the vaccine.

Over the past twenty years the Dublin club has contributed tens of thousands of pounds and euros to help make Rotary's promise a reality and Rotary clubs throughout the world have raised $1.3b since 1987. As we reach our 100th anniversary the Gates Foundation[3] has given $200m to the Polio Plus campaign and challenged Rotary clubs throughout the world to match it and this is what we are working towards at present.

From the time that the Club Newsletter, 'Cogs', was taken on by the district that were a number of short-lived attempts to provide a periodic in-house resume of the club's activities for its members. It was not until the mid-eighties that the 'Dubliner' began to appear on a quarterly basis. From 1993 it became a weekly publication with PDG Horner Beckett and Peter Ferguson (Architecture) as joint editors. It is now published each week both in hard copy and is circulated through E-mail to all members. The current editors are Frank Bannister (Information Technology), Fred Duffy (Computer Manufacturing Consumable), Denise Leahy (University Lecturer) and Alan Harrison (Legal Services).

The Youth Leadership Competition, a district project, was launched in 1993 and over the years, the Standard Life Insurance Company and Marks and Spencer have sponsored it. Confined to secondary school students from 15 to 18 years old it seeks to identify young people with latent leadership qualities and to encourage them to realise their full potential. The way that the competition works is that the club chooses a number of secondary schools in its area and with the co-operation of the Careers Guidance teacher identifies those students with leadership qualities who would like to take part. Members of the club conduct interviews in each school and the school winner goes forward to the club final. There a student is chosen to represent the club in a regional final where three are picked as winners. With ten regional finals a party of around thirty travels to Strasbourg where they join students from other E.U. countries in a Euro Scola parliament. The gathering is conducted along the lines of the European Parliament with sub-committees reporting back to the general assembly on a number of topics. The whole concept of meeting other young people of their own age and sharing and debating with them has proved an enriching experience for those involved

The Postal Survey, operated by Price Waterhouse Coopers began in 1993. It is designed to give an independent measurement of the efficiency and quality of the postal service in Ireland. Members act as receivers or droppers, note the times and dates of delivery and posting and forward same to PWC. Each transaction attracts a small amount of money that is credited to the club's Foundation account at district level. The Dublin club has taken part in this project from its inception.

Fellowship has always been an integral part of the Rotary philosophy. We have seen how our founder, Paul Harris, put this concept at the centre of this thinking when the first club, Chicago, was founded. Over one hundred years later friendship is still very much an integral part of how any club goes about its charitable work. In the mid 1990s Peter McManus who had joined in 1989 with the classification Cosmetics Distributing and Finbar Ambrose (Financial Services), who had joined the same year, began walking in the Wicklow hills. Both had retired and their love of the outdoors brought them together. Each week they plotted a different course through Wicklow's many mountains, hills and valleys. Around the same time they organised less strenuous weekend walks for other members and their families. Hill walking became a regular feature for members of the Dublin Club.

A unique experience for Peter and Finbar occurred in August 1999 when, on Percy's Table at the summit of Lugnaquallia they witnessed the eclipse of the sun. This would have been an amazing experience anywhere but at over 3,000 feet above sea level with just the two of them there it was truly inspiring. The intrepid pair were joined in 2001 by Alan King (Accountancy) and Tony Keegan (Periodical Publishing). Although Peter died in 2002 and Finbar in 2010, the walking group has continued to roam the Wicklow hills each Tuesday in all weathers. There are regularly between five and ten members and friends on the walks and in August 2008 a group of five climbed Carrantuohil (3,414 feet), Ireland's highest mountain. The Wicklow Way from Marley Park in Rathfarnham County Dublin to Clonegal in Carlow and back has been completed on a number of occasions. In April 2007 the group travelled to Cyprus on a walking holiday organised by Kevin McAnallen (Interior Construction). Victor Hamilton (Vehicle Leasing) who was president in 2008/09 has completed the Camino de Santiago de Compostelo from St. Jean-Pied-de-Port twice and Kevin who joined the club from Dundalk (president 1994/95) has completed it once.

Other fellowship events included a special lunch in the Royal Hospital Kilmainham in October 1993 where the guest speaker was Edsel Ford the great grandson of the original Henry and the holding of the R.I.B.I. conference in Dublin in April 1999. On the sporting field Tony Gannon (National Fisheries Development), who had been our president in 1986/87, was a member of the 2000 Irish Rotary golf team that retained the Jubilee Cup at Saint Andrews in the annual R.I.B.I. competition.

In the mid 1990s also, we organised a chess competition for primary school children, sponsored by the E.S.B. It was a success both in the number of schools participating and in raising the level of self-esteem of the youngsters taking part. A Drugs Guide compiled with the assistance of An Garda Siochana was distributed to parent-teacher associations in fifteen Dublin secondary schools. It set out clearly the drugs in common usage, their physical symptoms and dangers that could occur.

One of the biggest projects that the Dublin Club ran on the 1990s was Aquabox. The Aquabox comprises three simple components – a rigid 75 litre plastic container, a re-usable carbon activated filter and a dispensing tap. The container is filled with whatever water can be found locally and is initially strained manually through a muslin cloth to remove floating detritus. A single 10gram purification tablet is then added and after two hours potable water may be drawn through the filter and tap. Enough tablets are provided with the Aquabox to provide 1100 litres of drinking water. Developed by the Wirksworth Rotary Club, Derbyshire it was adopted by R.I.B.I. as project in the early 1990s.

The Dublin Club decided to back the project and Paul Liuzzi who had joined the club in 1989 with the classification of Water Treatment led the International Committee in raising funds to purchase the Aquaboxes. Funds were raised by collecting outside churches at weekend with the permission of the local clergy. A particularly successful collection took place outside of St. Michael's Church in Dun Laoghaire where our Honorary member the late Mons. Tom Fehily was Parish Priest. Here we were allowed to address the congregation during the weekend masses and over IR£10,000 was collected. This enabled Aquaboxes to be sent immediately to the Save the Children Fund for distribution in Bosnia and Croatia. These Aquaboxes provided approximately 1.4 million cups of pure water. When Paul Liuzzi died suddenly in 1996 other members continued the project well into the 21st century.

Other projects at this time were £17,000 raised in 1993 to assist the Salvation Army in their building and fitting out of their Granby Row Centre and a similar amount in 2000 for the children's charity Barnardos.

As we have seen, each year since 1915 members of the Dublin club have been providing toys and entertainment for the children in Harcourt Street Hospital. In 1998 the hospital transferred to a brand new complex in Tallaght that it shares with the Adelaide and Meath hospitals. So in December of that year Santa Claus a.k.a Peter Evans (Oil Refining) re-routed his sleigh to the western suburbs of Dublin and continued a tradition that has brought happiness to sick children at Christmas for over ninety years. Peter was our president in 1992/93 and each Monday he introduced us to a litany of patron saints, most of whom existed, whose special qualities and achievements enlivened our lunches.

The year 2000 saw the first organised club trip to the continent of Europe. In previous years members had travelled to R.I. conventions but in the Millennium year President Ethna Fitzgerald (Conference Organiser) led a party of twenty-six Rotarians and partners to lunch at the Paris club. After lunch, together with some Parisian Rotarians, they were received by the Irish Ambassador and his wife at the embassy and entertained to afternoon tea.

[1] *'A Century of Service'* by David C. Forward.

[2] Roosevelt became the 32nd President of the United States in 1932. He died in office in 1945.

[3] The Gates Foundation, established by Bill and Melinda Gates in 1994, has the aim of enhancing healthcare and reducing extreme poverty throughout the world. It has the additional object of improving access to educational opportunities and Information Technology in the U.S.

Chapter Nineteen

New Millennium

'Well done, is better than well said.'
Benjamin Franklin

As the new millennium dawned there were a number of 'firsts' for the Dublin Club. Ethna Fitzgerald took over as president in July 2000, the first lady to hold that office. Her President's Night in March 2001 was held jointly with Joy Duffy, the president of the Dublin Inner Wheel Club, whose husband Walter (Packaging Machinery-Distributing) had been our president in 1985/86. The dinner was held in Saint Patrick's Hall, Dublin Castle, a truly splendid venue for this unique occasion. Just two years later the first husband and wife joined our club. These were Catherine Bourke (Architectural Inspector) and Jim (Economic Development). Both have been active in providing service: Jim has been the convenor of the Community and Vocational Committee and Catherine is currently our Honorary Treasurer. In the same year (2003) Ted Corcoran (Transport - Rail), Dublin president in 2001/02 became the first European to be elected president of Toastmasters International since its foundation in 1924.

In 2001 a decision was made by the club to establish a Trust Fund. A Deed of Trust was prepared and in December of that year the Revenue Commissioners accorded it charitable status and Past District Governor John D. Carroll, Alan Harrison and Tony Keegan were appointed Trustees. Shortly after it was established Kent Maytham (Paper Distributing) endowed the Fund with a substantial donation. The long-term aim of the Trust Fund is to purchase an apartment in Dublin that could be used by an incoming Ambassadorial Scholar and the rent derived from this would be used for the charitable purposes of the club. A number of members have indicated their intention to bequeath funds so that this objective might be attained.

We continued our support for the Jaipur Limb[1] project and sponsored a disabled young person to go on a voyage in the Lord Nelson sail-training vessel. The Irish charity, Bothar[2], was also supported and we began our involvement with the village of Luhimba in Tanzania.

Through his friendship with Michael Carey and their love and appreciation of good wines, Kent Maytham introduced the club to the village of Luhimba in Tanzania. Michael himself had first learned of its existence in the early 1980s and had travelled there and was impressed with the quality of leadership that he found. Michael was a member of the Rotary Club of Wrington and under Michael's leadership the club set about providing the funds to enable Luhimba to undertake a series of developmental projects. At the outset Michael, an engineer by profession, laid down two basic principles: these were that everything that was to be done should be at the request of the villagers and that all monies collected should go directly towards the projects. Over the past twenty-five years the Luhimba project initially led by Michael and latterly by his good friend Paul Temple has provided a blueprint of how developmental aid should be best provided. One of the first projects involved the provision of clean drinking water and schools, a dispensary and irrigation for agricultural production followed this. The Dublin Club assisted in this work by raising over €15,000 through a Golf Classic and other events and after long and tortuous negotiations with Rotary International we managed to obtain a matching grant. This enabled an irrigation project to be put in place that will greatly assist in increasing agricultural output. Our own member Nigel Brown (Geologist), who has since transferred to Montreal along with his wife Bernadette Hunkeler Brown (Foreign Service) persevered through all sorts of difficulties to achieve, finally, the last matching grant that R.I. was to provide in the current straitened economic circumstances.

Through Past President Finbar Ambrose we have developed an ongoing relationship with the Ballybrack Conference of the Saint Vincent de Paul organisation. We support them in their work in relieving the effects of poverty in their area. In particular we assist them in providing educational grants to young people of promise that enables them to complete their education and obtain a qualification.

Other projects include involving our Interact clubs in sponsored walks to help build an extension to a Kenyan school and through our Golf Classics in Dun Laoghaire Golf Club providing funds to help the Housing Association for Integrated Living and Schizophrenia Ireland. In Rotary's centenary year our Golf Classic provided funds that enabled Saint Jude's Home for Homeless Children to purchase a mini bus to bring the children to and from school and sporting activities. We also have undertaken Bag Packing at Tesco's supermarket in the Merrion Centre in aid of Polio Plus and flood relief in Ireland.

The club has also been able to respond promptly to national and international disasters by working with local Rotary clubs in the affected areas. On Saint Stephen's Day in 2004 an undersea earthquake in the Indian Ocean created a Tsunami that killed 230,000 people in fourteen countries with waves of up to 30 metres high. Within ten days we were able to send €3,000 from our emergency reserve fund to assist the victims in Sri Lanka.

In October 2005 an earthquake with a magnitude of 7.6 on the Richter Scale struck the Pakistani administered region of Kashmir killing over 8,000 people and making tens of thousands homeless. Our club was able to obtain a fully functioning Shelter Box tent and with the aid of the local troop of Boy Scouts we set it up outside the church of the Sacred Heart in Donnybrook. With the co-operation of the parish priest, Father Pat Carroll, Brian Dobson of R.T.E. was able to address the congregation at all the masses. A team led by Patrick White (Solicitor – Property Investment and Development) ran the project and the incredible generosity of the parishioners of Donnybrook and of friends of members resulted in over €46,000 being collected in just one weekend. We were able to send this amount together with other funds collected by Rotary clubs[3] throughout district 1160 directly to a Rotary club in the affected region who were co-ordinating relief efforts.

The membership of Rotary in Dublin continued to expand with the formation of a new club, Dublin Central. The Dublin and Cork clubs assisted Dublin North in its foundation. Their inaugural dinner was held in the Hibernian United Services Club on Saint Stephen's Green on Wednesday September 5th 2001. As with most new clubs, the age profile of the Dublin Central members is much lower than that of the existing clubs. They meet each Wednesday evening at the same venue at 6.30pm.

The trips to the continent continued with a visit to Brussels and lunch with the Erasme club in December 2003. The following year the club was invited to join two international groupings of Rotary clubs. Bernard Thienpont, a member of the Oudenaarde club in Belgium, initiated the Rotary Euromeeting. They hosted the first meeting in 2003. The next year's meeting was in Auxerre in the Burgundy region of France and President Tony Keegan led a party of fifteen to enjoy the French hospitality. We were hosted in Rotarian homes on the Friday evening and the next day a coach took us on a short tour of the area with lunch in a vineyard in the nearby village of Chablis. That evening we were treated to a banquet in ancient caverns in the locality during which our president was inducted, as a Chevalier, into the Order of the Three Cups. To achieve this distinction President Tony had to drink, successively, a large cup of red, white and rose wine while appropriate songs were sung. Having survived this rather pleasant ordeal, the next morning, brunch completed the event. Our coach journey back to Beauvais included a particularly pleasant diversion through Paris. The 2005 Euromeeting was held in Iglesias in Sardinia, 2006 in Jonkoping Sweden, 2007 in Dublin, 2008 in Hastings, 2009 in Bochum Rechen in the Ruhr Germany and 2010 in Paphos Cyprus.

The Leonardo da Vinci grouping was established in 1975 by the Rotary club of Florence as an annual international prize to be presented to a young person involved in the study of the sciences, technology, literature and the arts. Among the disciplines recognised and awarded are painting, sculpture, music, geology, architecture, medicine, nuclear physics and the art of the silversmith. Prior to 2005 the event has been hosted by Rotary clubs in a number of European cities including Tours, Vienna, Athens, Wuerzburg, Brussels and Amsterdam. We were invited to join in 2005 when the award was made to the Danish silversmith, Sidsel Dorph-Jensen, in the Goldsmith's Hall in London. The format is similar to that of the Euromeeting except that the Euro 11,000 award is usually presented on the Saturday morning. The 2010 Leonardo da Vinci weekend took place in Vienna and in 2011 the Dublin club will host the Leonardo da Vinci weekend.

Other tours abroad have included opera trips to Rome and Verona organised by our very own Italian contingent led by Stefano Vaiani (Banking-Overseas).

The centenary of the foundation of Rotary was celebrated in the 32,000 clubs throughout the world on February 23rd 2005. The Dublin Club held an ecumenical service of Thanksgiving for the life of Paul Harris and all the other Rotarians who had given service in the past 100 years. The service was held in Saint Bartholomew's Church in Clyde Road Ballsbridge by kind permission of the rector the Reverend Michael Thompson and the Select Vestry. To symbolise the coming of Rotary to Ireland in 1911 a succession of past presidents carried lighted candles forward to the altar rails while the names of all former presidents of the Dublin club were read. The sermon, on the theme, 'Rotary, a Century of Service' was given by our own Honorary member Mgr. Tom Fehily. Afterwards a reception was held in Dublin Castle attended by members, past members and their families. Many other Rotary clubs both in Dublin and throughout Ireland were represented.

Other events around the same time included an ecumenical service organised by the district in Saint Anne's Cathedral in Belfast at which the presidents of the Dublin and Belfast clubs read the Lessons. In March 2005 President Mary McAleese was gracious enough to invite members of the Dublin club together with Lady Presidents and Presidents elect of nineteen Rotary clubs from district 1160 to a reception on Aras an Uachtaran. Afterwards the group took lunch in the Merrion Hotel.

By 2007 the club had had the same luncheon venue for thirty-six years. This was the longest sojourn they had had in any restaurant/hotel. The previous longest stay had been in the Royal Hibernian Hotel where they had lunched between 1946 and 1971. By early 2007, however, it had become apparent that we should shortly have to find a new luncheon venue. Property prices had spiralled out of control and Jurys, the adjoining Jurys Towers and the Berkley Court hotels had been sold for many hundreds of millions of euro. The developer intended to close the hotels and build a mix of high-rise apartments and commercial buildings on the site. Inquiries among other hotels and restaurants in the Dublin 4 and 2 areas did not prove fruitful: they were not willing, in the then climate of expanding business, to dedicate a room to one group each Monday. After a lot of searching we settled on the Grand Canal Hotel in Grand Canal Street and this has proved to be an excellent venue for both our lunches and meetings. Lunch is now self-service and costs €20. In the years since we moved the business climate has changed dramatically for the worse, Jurys is still open, under a new name, and there is little likelihood of any development on the site for many years to come.

The Rotary charity, Foundation, provides Individual Grants to cover the travel costs to enable a volunteer to work on a World Community Service project. In 2008 our member Peter McGonigal, a Dental Surgeon and his wife Kate, a Registered General Nurse, spent some weeks among the people of Kilimambogo north of Nairobi in Kenya. Many were suffering from AIDS and from HIV and Peter found that there was no effective government programme to try and combat the disease. Peter worked as a dentist while Kate who was a member of the International Committee of the Red Cross, and has extensive experience working in Third World countries, assisted him.

The dentistry that Peter practised in Kenya was nearly all of a surgical nature and pain relief: there was little or no restorative work as HIV and Aids are manifest in the mouth as well as the rest of the body. As part of the programme they also worked in remote clinics and parish halls. This entailed packing all their equipment into a 4x4 and setting off for outlying areas. Peter spoke very highly of the work being done by members of the local Thika Rotary club and by nuns working amongst the poorest and most marginalised people in the area.

There have been many happy and slightly scatty occasions in our Rotary club and none more so than the annual Rubber Duck Race on the river Dodder from below the weir at Dartry to the Dropping Well. First run in 2005 it is a great day out for all the family. Whether your duck wins or not there is splendid fun watching David Booth (Linguist), Paolo Zanni (Investment Banking) and their families splashing around in the river while shepherding the little yellow competitors towards the finishing line.

Another happy event was the visit of the former Taoiseach Dr. Garret Fitzgerald to celebrate Past President James Gorman's (Civil Aviation) 90th birthday. Garret gave a witty and entertaining talk in which he remembered arranging an impromptu cartel amongst his fellow job seekers in 1948 as they waited for James, as Secretary of Aer Lingus, to interview them. Garret got the job because, apart from his other excellent qualities, he told us that he was able to recite the PanAm timetable by heart.

In the autumn of 2009 a party of members travelled south to Bordeaux to celebrate the 50th anniversary of the chartering of the Bordeaux Nord club. Bordeaux is known as the Paris of the south and it did not disappoint. A visit to a local vineyard had been arranged and as we sipped the vintage the runners in the local marathon race dashed by serenaded by a jazz band. We met Rotarians from other clubs in Europe and Africa and it was a most enjoyable weekend.

After lunch on the afternoon of Monday 22nd February 2010, the first day of our 100th year all those who had been at the meeting gathered outside at the Grand Canal Hotel for a photo opportunity. Peter Evans(Oil Refining) who is club photographer took the picture on a lovely sunny day and by dint of technological sleight of hand managed to get himself into the photograph also.

[1]Ram Chandra, a local sculptor in Jaipur in India was deeply disturbed by the number of amputees and polio victims whose immobility made them outcasts. In 1966, using simple, cheap materials such as rubber and plastic, he created a prosthesis in collaboration with Dr. Pramod Karan Sethi, an Orthopaedic Surgeon and the inventor of the Jaipur foot. The prosthesis could be prepared and fitted

in forty-five minutes and was so light and mobile that its users could climb trees and pedal bicycles. Rotary quickly supported the devices wide distribution.

[2] Bothar enables families and communities worldwide to overcome hunger and poverty and to restore the environment in a sustainable way. To do this they specialise in improved livestock production and support related training and community development. Sponsors can finance the purchase of livestock that is then sent to families in the developing world to enable them to become self-sufficient.

[3] The Rotary club of Bray, with just twelve members, collected in excess of €46,000 from the people of the town. They pitched their tent on the Main Street and manned the collection points for a whole week.

Having parked his sleigh, Santa Claus entering the National Children's Hospital in Harcourt Street in the 1980s.

Chapter Twenty

Future

'This is the good ship Rotary, notice that it is going someplace, it is in full sail'.
Paul Harris

As the Dublin Rotary Club faces into its second century who can know for certain what the future holds? We currently have seventy-five members and plans are afoot, as they always have been, to recruit more. Pressures on people in business have never been greater and time for anything other than work is at a premium.

Having said that, Rotary offers a unique opportunity to give something back to society while at the same time having an enriching and fulfilling life experience. By working with others towards the common goal of helping our fellow women and men achieve their full potential we become people who are more valuable to business. Friendships that have begun at a Remembrance Tree or a Shelter Box can often blossom into connections in other areas.

While the membership of the Dublin Club is not what it was fifty years ago the membership of Rotary in Dublin has grown considerably. At our fiftieth anniversary there were about 130 Rotarians in Dublin. Today there are upwards of 225 Rotarians all providing service to the community at home and abroad. There are 76 Rotary clubs in District 1160 with a membership in excess of two thousand. There are 32,000 Rotary clubs in the world with a membership of one and a quarter million.

All of this began from the idea of just one man, Paul Harris who wanted to share with others his notion that together people can have more fun than by themselves. The Rotary idea was brought to Europe by William Stuart Morrow who was out of work and trying to earn some money. By these divergent ways, and by many others, Rotary has grown from the germ of an idea to a body that is a partner of the World Health Organisation and is represented in over 190 countries.

It is by continuing to provide Service to the community both at home and internationally that Rotary will thrive. As we come together in friendship to have our lunch let us remember the words of our founder Paul Harris as he pointed to a print of a galleon on his office wall,

'This is the good ship Rotary, notice that it is going someplace, it is in full sail'.

PDG Horner Beckett indicating part of the display in the Bull Island Interpretative Centre to President of Ireland Patrick Hillery while Dublin president Walter Duffy looks on. The Intepretative Centre was fitted out by the Rotary Club, Dublin as part of their 75th Anniversary Celebrations in 1986.

Appendix One

Presidents of the Rotary Club, Dublin

1911/12 J.H. Fleming[#]
1912/13 J.A. Walsh[#]
1913/14 William Findlater[#]
1914   J.P. McKnight[#]
1914/15 R.H. White[#]
1915/16 J.R. Coade[#]
1916/17 R.S. Swirles[#]
1917/18 J.L. Stewart[#]
1918/19 Alfred Fannin[#]
1919/20 Edwin M.Fannin[#]
1920/21 C.McGloughlin[#]
1921/22 P.J.Lawrence[#]
1922/23 WilliamA.McConnell[#]
1923/24 Sir Thomas Robinson[#]
1924/25 J.Walter Beckett[#]
1925/27 R.P. Rowan[#]
1927/28 Major Bryan Cooper[#]
1928/29 L.E.P. Smith Gordon[#]
1929/30 Fred. M. Summerfield[#]
1930/31 G.T. Clampett[#]
1931/32 K.J. Kenny[#]
1932/33 R. K.Hanna[#]
1933/34 P. T. Montford[#]
1934/35 E. K.Eason[#]
1935/36 O. Jamison[#]
1936/37 R. H. Keatinge[#]
1937/38 T. A. Grehan[#]
1938/39 J. H. Aylward[#]
1939/40 J.J. Kenne[#]
1940/41 A. Pearson[#]
1941/42 V. J. O'Hare[#]

1942/43 A. G. Brady#
1943/44 T. R. Beddy#
1944/45 T. H. Mason#
1945/46 P McGloughlin#
1946/47 J. H. Webb#
1947/48 Felix J. Hughes#
1948/49 A. H. Sparkhill#
1949/50 W. J. Costello#
1950/51 T. R. Sparks#
1951/52 J. A. L. Hatch#
1952/53 D. S. Gillespie#
1953/54 John Claude Tonge#
1954/55 W. V. Griffiths#
1955/56 D. Fitzgerald#
1956/57 C. Horner Beckett
1957/58 E. W. McCabe#
1958/59 W. A. Smith#
1959/60 J. J. Jennings#
1960/61 Walter S. Douglas#
1961/62 L. A. Callow#
1962/63 A. D. Bruty#
1963/64 Brendan J. Senior#
1964/65 Frank E. Tate
1965/66 B. J. Fitzpatrick#
1966/67 T. H. McMurray#
1967/68 James Gorman
1968/69 G van de Lee#
1969/70 Earnest A. Goulding#
1970/71 Alan H. King
1971/72 Brian S. Ryan#
1972/73 David Keane#
1973/74 Joseph T. Hamilton#
1974/75 A. G. Pearson#
1975/76 J. A. McGrail#
1976/77 Robert P. Chalker#
1977/78 D. Robin Hall#
1978/79 John D. Carroll

1979/80 James A. Simpson[#]
1980/81 Michael Larkin
1981/82 Dudley P. Engert[#]
1982/83 R. Butler[#]
1983/84 Michael O'Doherty
1984/85 T. B. H. Jameson
1985/86 Walter N. Duffy[#]
1986/87 Anthony O. Gannon
1987/88 Joseph C. McGough[#]
1988/89 Joseph E. Greevy
1898/90 Michael J. Cagney[#]
1990/91 Denis C. Boothman
1991/92 Terence Maguire[#]
1992/93 Peter R. Evans[#]
1993/94 Finbar Ambrose[#]
1994/95 Dick Tuite[#]
1995/96 Sean Donohue
1996/97 Peter McManus[#]
1997/98 W. Barry Wilson
1998/99 Aubrey N. Fogarty[#]
1999/00 Joseph Dunne
2000/01 Ethna Fitzgerald
2001/02 Ted Corcoran
2002/03 W. Ken Hunt
2003/04 Guy Johnston
2004/05 Tony Keegan
2005/06 Paul Loughlin
2006/07 Paul Martin
2007/08 Michael Carroll
2008/09 Victor Hamilton
2009/10 Tony Seery
2010/11 Randal N. Gray
2011/12 Mark E. Doyle

Honorary Secretaries Rotary Club, Dublin

William. A. McConnell#1912-1920
Sealy Jeffares# 1920-1922
Charles McGloughlin# 1922-23
William A. McConnell# 1923-29
Sen. Fred Summerfield# 1930-1952
Felix Hughes# 1952-1964
Martin Mulligan# 1964 –1978
D. Peelo July- November 1978
Martin Mulligan# November 1978 to 1986
Robin Hall# 1986-1987
James Gorman 1987-1992
Tony Gibson# 1992-1997
Niall O'Donoghue 1997-1999
Terence Maguire# 1999-2000
Peter McManus# 2000-2002
Brian Taylor 2002-2007
Stefano Vaiani 2007-2010
Tony Keegan 2010-

Honorary Treasurers Rotary Club, Dublin

James R. Coade# 1911-1915
J.L. Stewart# 1915-1916
F.L. Barrett# 1916-1917
C.J. Joyce# 1917-1920
E.D. Watson# 1920-1921
William Lawrence# 1921-1925
Edmond McGrath# 1925-1928
Henry Staff# 1928-1941
A.H. Sparkhall Brown# 1941-1946
Walter Bowers# 1946-1955
Keith Eason# 1955-1960
Terry Spillane# 1960-1965

Alan King 1965-1969
Martin Tierney# 1969-1973
George Woods# 1973-1990
Peter Carton 1990-1992
Michael Cagney# 1992-1994
Stan Mason 1994-1998
Michael Larkin 1998 -2001
Randal Gray 2001-2006
Finbar Ambrose* 2006-2007
Randal Gray 2007-2008
Mark Doyle 2008-2009
Catherine Bourke 2009-

Paid Secretaries Rotary Club, Dublin

William Stuart Morrow# February to July 1911.
Arthur H. Walkey# July 1911.
Charles M. Coghlan# July 1911 to April 1912.
Eddie Taylor# January 1930-1956.
Miss Maureen O'Reilly# January 1957-1969.

# denotes deceased.

Appendix Two

District Governors District (5, 6, 16, 116), 1160

1918/19 **W. A. McConnell Dublin**
1919/20 J. F. Newell Belfast
1920/21 **Dr. E. M. Fannin Dublin**
1921/22 C. E. White Belfast
1922/23 **P. J. Lawrence Dublin**
1923/24 F. McKibben Belfast
1924/25 J. L. McLoughlin Londonderry
1925/26 W. Malcolm Belfast
1926/27 W. Malcolm Belfast
1927/28 **C. G. McGloughlin Dublin**
1928/29 **C. G. McGloughlin Dublin**
1929/30 D.S. Irwin Londonderry
1930/31 C.G. Lytle Belfast
1931/32 **F. Summerfield Dublin**
1932/33 R.W. Sinnott Cork
1933.34 J. Donaghy Londonderry
1934/35 **Sir T. Robinson Dublin**
1935/36 J.W.T. Watters Belfast
1936/37 D. F. Coyle Cork
1937/38 W. McCarter Londonderry
1938/39 **P.T. Montford Dublin**
1939/40 F. J. Brice Bangor
1940/41 F. J. Brice Bangor
1941/42 F. J. Brice Bangor
1942/43 **R. H. Keatinge Dublin**
1943/44 **R. H. Keatinge Dublin**
1944/45 R. N. Hawthorne Portadown

1945/46 C. E. White Belfast
1946/47 **V. J. O'Hare Dublin**
1947/48 E. Rea Belfast
1948/49 I. M. Russell Coleraine
1949/50 Sir J. H. Norrit Belfast
1950/51 R.K. Graham Cork
1951/52 W.H. Cooper Belfast
1952/53 T. Bloomer Ballymena
1953/54 J. T. Towers Londonderry
1954/55 G. McCartney Bangor
1955/56 A. A. Harding, Belfast
1956/57 H.F. Bell, Coleraine
1957/58 F. McKibben Belfast
1958/59 J Jefers Portadown
1959/60 S. L. Horne Cork
1960/61 H. E. Rugnay J.P. Newry
1961/62 J. Little MBE Belfast
1962/63 T. H. Walker Lisburn
1963/64 P. Maxwell Londonderry
1964/65 **F. J. Hughes PC Dublin**
1965/66 T. S. Duncan Belfast
1966/67 **T. Jennings Dublin**
1967/68 J. Cathcart Larne
1968/69 A. B. Vance Cork
1969/70 R. E. Scott Armagh
1970/71 W. Baillie Bangor
1971/72 **C. Horner Beckett Dublin**
1972/73 T. Trewsdale Lurgan
1973/74 J. S. Tweed Larne
1974/75 C. N. Rountree Omagh
1975/76 J. L. Hill Dun Laoghaire
1976/77 E. S. Leighton Newtownabbey
1977/78 **J. T. Hamilton Dublin**
1978/79 H.T. McIlwaine Armagh
1979/80 N. McVey Drogheda
1980/81 E. Grainger Lisburn
1981/82 M. T. Moylett Dublin North

1982/83 S. J. Martin Strabane Lifforf
1983/84 **J.D. Carroll Dublin**
1984/85 J. K. Magee Belfast West
1985/86 G. F. McGovern Cork
1986/87 R. A. Elliot Portadown
1987/88 S. P. Doyle Sligo
1988/89 B. Ferris Londonderry
1989/90 W. J. O'Reilly Clonmel
1990/91 B. Shields Portadown
1991/92 W. T. Morrow Limerick Shannon
1992/93 M. J. Kelly Dublin North
1993/94 E. A. Dunlop Bangor
1994/95 F. A. Hynes Omagh
1995/96 J. R. Mullen Sligo
1996/97 G. Berkery Dundalk
1997/98 J. Flood Dublin South West
1998/99 A. Laird Cookstown
1999/00 J. E. Lawson Portadown
2000/01 D. P. Fay Athlone
2001/02 R. Warren Tralee
2002/03 J. Grey Cork Bishopstown
2003/04 F. R. N. Arnold Banbridge
2004/05 D. C. Wilson Antrim
2005/06 M. G. Molony Dublin Central
2006/07 J. H. G. Caskie Limavady
2007/08 R. Cosgrove Cork
2008/09 P. Hutchinson MBE Newtownabbey
2009/10 T. Murphy Athlone
2010/11 W. Armstrong Coleraine
2011/12 B. Callaghan Limerick Thomond

Appendix Three

This is the original Constitution and Bye-Laws of the Dublin Club adopted at the General Meeting on 24th May 1911 with amendments from March 1914. These amendments were 'November 1914' replacing March in Section 111 of the Bye-Laws to align the Club to the newly constituted B.A.R.C. and the addition of the Immediate Past President to the Council.

The Rotary Club, Dublin

Constitution

1 – NAME
The name of this organisation shall be The Rotary Club, Dublin

11 – OBJECTS
The objects of this Club are:-
- To promote the business interests of its Members.
- To increase the efficiency of its Members by the exchange of idea and business methods
- To encourage high ethical standards in business and professional life.
- To quicken the interest of its Members in the public welfare, and to co-operate with others in civic and industrial development.

111-MEMBERSHIP QUALIFICATIONS
Any person who is engaged as a proprietor, partner, director, agent or manager in any legitimate business or professional undertaking shall be eligible for membership, provided that no person shall be elected to represent a profession or business already represented by a

Member of the Club. Any Newspaper may, however, be represented in the Club as a separate business.

Should any questions arise as to whether the business of a candidate infringes upon or comes into competition with the business of any member, it shall be the duty of the Council to discuss the matter with such Member, and if it is the judgement of the Council that the admission of such candidate to Membership be an infringement upon the rights of such Member, then the Council shall declare such candidate ineligible. All questions of eligibility shall be decided by the Council.
No undischarged Bankrupt shall be eligible for Membership**.**

Partners of Members and Officers of Companies already represented may, on Motion of such Members, be eligible for Associate Membership and shall be classified as such. Associate Membership shall not carry any voting power and shall cease on the termination of partnership with the Member or connection with such Company, or upon the Member leaving the Club.

V-WAITING LIST

Application for membership may be received at any time in any profession or business already represented; such application shall be filed and constitute a Waiting List, to be considered in the order received when a vacancy shall occur in any applicant's profession or business.

V1-ELECTION TO MEMBERSHIP

Applications for admission to membership shall be made to the Secretary and presented by him to the Council for election. The names of applications for membership which have been approved by the Council shall be made known prior to election at one of the regular meetings of the Club, or at one of the lunch meetings.

V11-DURATION OF MEMBERSHIP

Membership shall endure for life (unless determined as herein provided) or until the Member changes his profession or business, under which circumstances his case shall be dealt with by the Council, with power to adjust his indebtedness to the Club for the reminder of the financial year.

Any Member who refuses or neglects to pay any indebtedness to the Club within thirty days after demand has been made shall be liable to forfeit his Membership.

A Member who is absent for six consecutive meetings of the Club, without having forwarded in writing to the Secretary, an explanation which shall be considered satisfactory by the Council, shall be liable, at the discretion of the Council, to forfeit his Membership.

A Member upon payment of Entrance Fee or Subscription submits himself to the Rules and Bye-Laws of the Club, both as to restrictions enjoined and penalties imposed, and on these conditions alone is entitled to the privileges of the Club.

1X- REMOVAL OF MEMBERS FROM THE CLUB

If any circumstances connected to the conduct of a Member, likely to endanger the welfare of the Club , be brought under the notice of the Council , the Council shall have power, after investigation of the matter (provided that not less than six members of the Council being present), to remove the name of such Member from the Club, and he shall therefore cease to be a Member, subject to the right of appeal to a General Meeting of the Club, notice of such appeal to be made in writing to the Secretary within ten days after the Member shall have received notice of the action of the Council.

X-OFFICERS

The Officers of the Club shall be President, Vice-President, Treasurer and Secretary.

X1- DUTIES OF OFFICERS

It shall be the duty of the President to preside at all meetings of the Council. And to perform such duties as pertain to the office of the President

VICE-PRESIDENT

It shall be the duty of the Vice-President in the absence of the President to perform all duties pertaining to the office of the President.

TREASURER

It shall be the duty of the Treasurer to collect the Entrance Fees and Subscriptions and all other monies due to the Club. and to lodge same intact to the credit of the Club's banking account. All payments to be made by cheque after claims have been passed by the Council, and the Treasurer shall account for same to the Club at its Annual General Meeting or at any other time required by the Council.

The Statement of Accounts shall be audited by two Members of the Club (not Members of Council) who shall be appointed at one of the regular meetings of the Club.

SECRETARY

It shall be the duty of the Secretary to keep a record of all business transacted, send out notices of meetings and to perform such other duties as pertain to the office, or are provided for therein.

X11- THE COUNCIL

The governing body of this Club shall consist of the President, the immediate past President, Vice-President, Treasurer, Secretary (if a Member), and six other members who shall constitute the Council, and whose decision on all matters shall be final, subject only to an appeal to the Club at one of its regular meetings. The Council shall have general control over all Officers and Committees of the Club, and may declare any office or offices vacant. Should a vacancy occur on the Council it shall be filled by the Council from the Club

Membership. Such appointment shall hold good until the next election of officers. Appeal from the decision of all Committees and from the ruling of all Officers may be taken to the Council.

All obligations undertaken by the Council on behalf of the Club shall be obligations of the Club.

X111-ELECTION OF COUNCIL

The Annual General Meeting of the Club shall be held in November of each year, at which all officers and members of Council shall be elected for the ensuing year.

X1V- RELIGIOUS AND POLITICAL SUBJECTS EXCLUDED

No subject of a religious or political character shall be discussed or referred to at any of the Club meetings.

XV-DISSOLUTION OF CLUB

The Club shall be dissolved at a Special General Meeting called for the purpose, and of which at least one month's notice has been given to the Members, provided that on a motion to this effect being duly made and seconded, not less than two-thirds of the members being present, of whom not less than two-thirds shall vote in favour of the resolution.

In the event of its being decided to dissolve the Club, the surplus funds and effects shall be dealt with in such a manner as the Council shall decide.

X1V-AMENDING CONSTITUTION

The Constitution and Bye-Laws shall be amended at the Annual General Meeting, or at an Extraordinary General Meeting called solely for that purpose, a quorum being present, by a two-thirds majority of the Members present, provided that notice of such proposed amendment shall have been posted to each Member at least seven days before such Meeting.

Bye-Laws

1-Meetings

Regular meetings of the Club shall be held once every month on such date as may be decided by the Council.

Special Meetings of the Club or Council shall be called by the President whenever he deems it necessary, or when requested by two Members of The Council. Notices of such meetings shall be posted at least five days prior to the date thereof.

At least twenty four hours notice shall be given by the Secretary to Members of Council of its Meetings.

11-Quorum

Twenty Members shall constitute a quorum at a meeting of the Club; and three Members shall constitute a quorum at a meeting of the Council.

111-Entrance Fee & Subscription

The Entrance Fee for Members shall be £2.2.0 and the Annual Subscription shall be £1.1.0 payable in advance on 1st November each year commencing on 1st November 1914. Any Member joining after May 1ST shall pay 10s. 6d. for the remainder of the financial year.

The Entrance Fee for Associate Members shall be 10s. 6d. and the Annual Subscription for Associate Members shall be 10s 6d payable in advance on 1st November.

1V-Method of Voting

All voting shall be viva voce, or by show of hands, except the election of Members of Council, which shall be by ballot.

Committees

The Council shall have power to appoint such Committees as it may consider desirable.

The President and Secretary shall be ex-officio Members of all Committees.

Appendix Four

Paul Harris Fellows
Instituted 1957

Rotary Club, Dublin

Joseph T. Hamilton* January 1978
C. Horner Beckett January 1980
Martin L. Mulligan* January 1980
Bryan S. Ryan* January 1981
George W. Woods* May 1983
Vincent McAllister* April 1984
Richard G. Tennant* August 1984
Nicholas Martin October 1985
James A. Simpson* July 1986
Michael J. Cagney* June 1987
John D. Carroll June 1987
Walter Duffy* July 1987
Robert P. Chalker* May 1989
Dudley P. Engert* May 1989
James Gorman May 1989
Joseph E. Greevy May 1989
David R. Hall* May 1989
Alan H. King May 1989
Joseph C. McGough* May 1989
Henry Spring* May 1989
William E. Yendole May 1989
Frank Jennings January 1990
Allan Kilpatrick December 1994
Kent Maytham* December 1994
Sean Donohoe March 1995
Michael Larkin September 1997
Joan Liuzzi September 1997

Richard Tuite* December 1997
Peter R. Evans* June 1998
Aubrey Fogarty* June 1998
Barry Wilson June 1998
Frank Bannister March 2001
John Goor March 2001
Tony Keegan March 2001
Peter McManus* March 2001
Cel O'Reilly March 2001
Ethna Fitzgerald June 2002
Ted Corcoran March 2003
Brian Taylor March 2003
Jonathan Pim April 2003
Paul Martin June 2003
Ken Hunt March 2004
Frank E. Tate March 2004
Gerard Uytterhaegen March 2004
Tony Gannon June 2004
Arthur Beatty* June 2004
Finbar Ambrose* March 2005
Hugh Wyndham Beere March 2005
Guy Johnston March 2005
Tony Seery March 2005
Alice Leahy March 2007
Jim Bourke February 2008
Kevin McAnallen# February 2008
Stefano Vaiani February 2008
Tom O'Neill February 2009
Michael Carroll June 2009
Peter McGonigal June 2009
Paolo Zanni February 2010
Randal Gray February 2010
Catherine Bourke June 2010

* Denotes deceased

With sapphire

Appendix Five

Paul Harris Scholarship Alumni

Graduate fellows	Sponsoring Club	Place of Study
1965/66 Michael A. Kehoe	Dublin	Univ. of California Los Angeles U.S.A.
1971/72 Paul F. Loughlin	Dublin	Emerson College Boston U.S.A.
1973/74 J. Adrian Masterson[1]	Dublin	Harvard Univ. U.S.A.
1982/83 Valerie Furlong	Dublin	New Jersey U.S.A.
1986/87 Maria Marnon	Dublin	Ohio State Univ. U.S.A.

[1] *In his MBA year at Harvard one of Adrian's classmates was George W. Bush, the future U.S. President. Later Adrian attended one of President Bushe's Inaugural Balls as his guest.*

Appendix Six

Mellow Memories

At a luncheon meeting on January 1st 1934 T. A. Grehan who had joined the club in April 1911 gave to members his Mellow Memories of Past Presidents. Grehan was Advertisement Manager of the Irish Independent and went on to become the Club's 27th President in 1937/38. His talk was so well received by members that it was ordered to be printed and distributed to all the membership. Hereunder are the words that he spoke that day.

We, Rotarians of Dublin, derive a good deal of satisfaction from the fact that ours was the first Rotary Club in this hemisphere. Rotary, as you know, had its beginnings in the United States, and in the City of Dublin was founded in 1911, the first Rotary Club outside of the American Continent. Whether we have written the name of the Dublin Club broad and high does not really matter so much. Nor is it of great moment whether or not Dublin has deserved the honour of being the venue of the mother club of Europe. Don't let these points worry us.

What does matter and what does stand to the credit of our club is this, that during every one of those twenty-two years, years crammed with world upheavals, Dublin kept the flag of Rotary waving. Through bright periods and through gloomy periods the Club has carried on its work, and President has followed President in one unbroken succession. To that fact surely we can look back with some satisfaction.

Having been a member of the Club since its opening year, it has been my good fortune to have known every one of our Presidents. Assuming your kind permission, it is my intention, this afternoon, to briefly review these men in the order of their year of office. To make this review an excursion in mellowed memories is my earnest desire.

As the total of the years mounts up, the outlines of the past naturally dim somewhat. I think, therefore, that this first day of a New Year is an appropriate occasion upon which to refresh our memories. Here, in my opinion, seems to be a happy moment for us to take a kindly mellow glance back along this lengthening gallery of old friends. I am bold enough to hope that you will listen with interest to an effort at remembrance of this nature.

There have been of course periods of sorrow. It is inevitable that as the years pass away familiar faces pass with them. There may arise, also, that feeling of loneliness that we cannot suppress at the thought that some voices that we used to hear so frequently in this Club and knew so well are stilled forever. Yet, as a continuing member of this Club all these years, I can recall many creditable achievements in true citizenship, initiated, directed and carried through by this Club under the willing guidance of our presidents.

The men we honoured as presidents represented a wide variety of citizenship, a broad field of human activity. It can, also, be said that each of these twenty-two men was of a different mould of mind, a different personality, and had a different method of action and approach. Looking back over the list, however, you will agree that one and all of these represented a very valuable asset in our community.

They were men of integrity; they were men anxious to serve their fellow men. I am sure that they would ask for no higher title to remembrance from us, their fellow Rotarians. So, today, on the threshold of this year, 1934, I ask you to accompany me in spirit on a brief survey of twenty-two men who have served this Club in the highest position at our disposal.

Our first President was the late Mr. J.H. Fleming. This somewhat narrow-cheeked; delicate little man is scarcely remembered today. He had hardly left the chair when death took him from us. He spoke few words, but the few that he spoke were incisive and he spoke them with an abruptness and an absence of fragrance. Fleming completely misunderstood Rotary, which I may say was a fault shared by all of us in the early days of this Club. Fleming was a banker. He must have been an ideal one; I should imagine, at a time when bankers were not too approachable, but were, as now, men of unimpeachable honour. There is this record to the credit of poor Fleming, let us not forget it to his memory: he was the first President of the first Rotary Club in the Old World.

From a monetary man in the person of our first President we passed on to a medicine man in Dr. James A. Walsh, Fleming's successor. Although the shyest, most unassuming of men, our 'little doctor' while in the chair was a tireless worker for Rotary. He did his job in that unostentatious way we colleagues of his liked so much. Isn't it splendid we see him here among us today? Looking him straight in the face before this lunch began, a member said to Dr. Walsh: 'If you looked as well in 1912/13 when you were in the chair as you look today, well you have no cause to worry'. That member spoke the whole truth.

When Dr. Walsh left the chair, the next occupant was responsible for an immediate and complete change in the atmosphere of our meetings. In other words, the helm of our affairs was taken over by the breeziest of skippers. As a matter of fact whom did we find in the seat of the distinguished but one William Findlater.

William Findlater was, and still is, known to many of us as 'Willie'. He was the first of our great ones whom we dared to address so affectionately[1], or, if you will, so familiarly. Of course, the reason was because we felt sure that here was a case where most of us could surely risk it. That eminently historic name of his somehow suggested Scottish entanglements, even, dating generations back. This is probably the explanation of Findlater's well-known piercing shafts of wit. These Scottish entanglements must surely have something to do with Findlater's battery of devastating and delightful bluntness. Once, in a reminiscent mood, he confessed to me, this was in Edinboro' (where, by the way, good Scotsmen are still to be found), that the cream of the Findlater stock came over to Ireland from Scotland and stayed.

Having known the unique head of the Dublin house for a good many years, I believe he told what could not be gainsaid. I was hoping that he would not be present today while I said about him the things that I have just said. Alas he is here as large as life, but it has been whispered to me that he has temporarily lost his voice. I sincerely hope that this is only a momentary loss.

During the reign of William the Findlater we revelled in a beanfest of Findlater philosophy, unorthodox a good deal of it, but alluring all of it. Among Findlater's distinctions-he has quite a number about which he does not speak- was that of almost stunning Sir Harry Lauder in a five minute speech full of cunning humour and delightfully itching sarcasm when seconding a vote of thanks to the great Scotsman, who happened to be our guest here some years ago. Before he took the chair we knew that Findlater would be worthwhile. He certainly was.

While Findlater was our first Dublin President, the late John P. McKnight, who followed, was our first Northern-born President. The distinction between the Dubliner and the Northerner was splendidly evident. McKnight was meticulous, imperturbable and addicted to irritating punctuality. He gave you the impression of being steeped in seriousness. He was not. He had a gift of dry and apt humour of a definitely entertaining nature. McKnight was a valuable asset to the rota of Presidents.

Richard White, McKnight's successor, is somewhat difficult to sketch. His presidential year was a very troubled one outside of Rotary. It had little or no trouble inside, mainly because of White's occupancy of the chair. He was a somewhat reticent man. He had a gift of deep and winning sincerity combined with coolness and good judgement. I am not read up on the things that White did not do, but of one fact about this solid President I am certain. He did not sing – certainly none of us ever heard him even try. Perhaps in that cool, quiet, shrewd way of his he left this kind if thing to the natural born singer, his successor, J, Robertson Coade.

Coade was our only singing President. And couldn't he sing. His year of office happened to coincide with that somewhat disturbing urge to be up and singing that struck these shores from the U.S. and sent us all nearly silly. Happily that wave subsequently receded before too much harm was done. We liked Coade for his golden throat. We liked him because, although an unbending disciplinarian, he was bluff, hearty, good-humoured and full of the business in hand. How many of us wished that we could speak with that ringing, compelling certainty, that splendid directness and that appropriateness of language that always was Coade's. He did his best to make us sing – we were depressing beyond words. Coade gave it up.

Coade's successor the late Robert J. Swirles, may rightly be regarded as one of our most 'fatherly' of Presidents. He had a soft, noiseless, unobtrusive way about him. He loved the Club. He loved Rotary, and it is true to say of him that he was really in love with his beloved Dublin. He never raised his voice above a gentle, conversational tone, so that he was not an orator, but he had an engaging way of saying those precise things he always said so precisely. Swirles going from amongst us left a gap.

The long service Rotarian J. L. Stewart, who followed Swirles, was a man who writes the words 'Stationer Stewart' above his well known premises in College Green – no mean name, I venture to say, to write up anywhere. Stewart is a star among our merchant stationers, but none of us who know this keen business getter could think of him as a 'stationary' person. By no means. A more all-alive, full of movement man in his line in Dublin we do not know.

J. L. Stewart's other claim to memory is that of being the only Scotsman President we have ever had. As befits all true sons of Scotland, Stewart always carried a valuable cargo of caution. As a fervent son of this land of Ireland my honest wish is that this seemingly inexhaustible mine of caution that is Scotland's may never give out and that men out of Scotland, as forthright as J. L. Stewart may never cease to come to us.

There may be some doubts as to the existence of the monster in Loch Ness. A good deal probably depends on the state of one's mind. But of the existence of Stewart none of us have any doubts. He is just a normal sized man of the mildest manner. May his existence amongst us – well above water- long continue.

While Stewart was in the chair 'Safety and Security' was the slogan. None of us knew what the J. L. in Stewart's name stood for, but we all knew what Stewart stood for, and that was hard solid work, perpetual watchfulness in the Club's interest, and a seemingly inexhaustible capacity for taking pains.

Then there came before us Alfred Fannin in Stewart's place. Alfred the Great we have read of. He was a fellow of daring and sincerity. Our one and only Alfred was sincere beyond doubt, but I would not say that he was daring. To us he was Alfred the placid. Alfred was our handsomest President. I will spare his blushes by this very, very brief sketch. That will please him, as I have a conviction that 'honourable mentions' are far from his liking. But before I pass on to his successor, his beloved brother, Dr.E. M. Fannin I must say this of Alfred Fannin, that the conduct of affairs in the chair, like his presence, was distinctly handsome. The epitome of obvious conscientiousness and sincerity – that, I think, would aptly describe President Alfred Fannin.

It is sometimes said of medical men, as of many other men, that they frequently reveal a weakness to be among the select. In other words to be in on all the good things of this world. Rotary is one of these, as you know, and a Rotary President is unquestionably our Legion of Honour. So, in the natural order of things, we selected the second Fannin, Dr. E. M. Fannin for the chair, the only example in our records of two brothers becoming our Presidents.

Dr. Fannin had a fascinating trait which was characteristic of him alone among our Presidents. He was one of these seemingly easy-going, pleasant, in and out, and round about, kind of man that gave you the impression that he was letting things just slide their own way along. You were quite wrong. He may have looked sort of careless and gay, but, believe me, this cheeriest of cheery men was everlastingly all there. And didn't we rank and filers in the Club soon realise it. He was reputed to have a second love –'golf' but not a great deal is known on that point. The medicine that Dr. Fannin gave us from the chair unquestionably did us good.

The man whom succeeded Dr. Fannin was one of whom many of us will speak will real reverence. Many of us regarded him as one of the most intensely human of characters Dublin has yet discovered. Need I say that I refer to the late Charles McGloughlin.

Here indeed was a man apart, a kind man, a man of gentleness, of subtle brain and of penetrating mind. McGloughlin was a deep thinker, probably the deepest, and certainly one of the most practical Dublin Rotary has ever known. He was a tenacious listener, with the result that he had always a complete grasp of the trend of things. McGloughlin's was a mind that was perpetually perfumed with the enduring fragrance of kindly thoughts. Unlike Coade, McGloughlin had a soft, almost murmuring voice, a voice that he rarely used except to offer an opinion or to express a thought, and as you know, McGloughlin's thoughts and McGloughlin's opinions were always a joy to listen to. His passing in the prime of life was a matter of bitter leave-taking for a great many of our people.

Philip Lawrence followed McGloughlin in the chair. Almost immediately, Philip established himself as a good President. His suavity saved us from occasional awkward moments, his common sense, too, was the Club's sure-shield. He could always be counted on to get us safely through troubled waters by pouring oil on them. Philip knew more about oil than any President. I can still quite distinctly visualise his fine, mobile features as he gave us his rulings. When Philip spoke, that was that.

Now let us imagine a brief but noticeable pause in this talk. Something 'big' is about to happen. Two wide lofty doors slowly open. We stare with eager eyes. In there bustles to the chair the most convinced and convincing Rotarian this country has ever known. –William

McConnell, our William the Conqueror in very truth. Gentlemen, can any of you imagine putting the soft pedal on this great man? It could not be done. There is no pedal made that would be equal to the job. Of McConnell let me at once say that no Rotarian ever deserved the Presidential chair so richly, for no Dublin Rotarian- surely few Rotarians anywhere-ever made Rotary such a life study. He surely must have given his whole waking moments to it, and Rotary is admittedly the gainer. None of us ever saw McConnell that he was not either scribbling Rotary notes, writing Rotary minutes or talking Rotary. He was eternally busy on his beloved Rotary. His eagle blue eyes saw instantly everything that a President should see and, I don't mind telling you today -McConnell is in America at present- a good many things he should not see. When he occupied the chair our Club was well known, for McConnell thought of Rotary in hemispheres. And his name and fame as a Rotarian really and truly went all over the Rotary world. As a torchbearer of Rotary he travelled more than any of our Presidents. Another McConnell claim to a niche in the hall of our immortals was the amazing length and the incurable fluency of language in the composition of his Annual Reports. He almost seemed to record the ticking of the clock. With William, a Report assumed something of the proportions of Gibbons 'Decline and Fall of the Roman Empire'. Every iota of Rotary happenings during the year went into these famous reports. Above all others of our past Presidents, Findlater used to look forward to the McConnell reports with almost childlike interest.

So the historic day that Big Bill vacated the chair was given over to a period of relaxation. We sincerely regretted his going, of course. But we felt that we were entitled to a 'breather'.

In a way we got a 'respite' under the baton of Sir Thomas Robinson who followed McConnell. By 'breather' I mean that under the kind but efficient care of Sir Thomas, this placid man of affairs, we Rotary youngsters of the McConnell era felt that we were not 'kept in' so often after school, so to speak. Sir Thomas Robinson brought to the chair one of our best-known public men. As we expected, Sir Thomas showed himself to be a model President. His adroitness, aptness of speech, and perfect control of any attempt of intransigence marked him out as an ideal President. He knew perfectly how to run the school and not only that but under him we imbibed a lot of helpful knowledge which some of us probably needed badly at the time. Sir Thomas was also a true builder in Rotary, as he has proved himself to be in other walks of life.

So too was Walter Beckett, a builder as well as President number fifteen on our rota. Beckett loved his task, but I feel that I am free to say that he detested speech-making. If you do not believe this, search the Dail records. I don't think that in that temple of tireless tongues he ever uttered a sentence. If I am wrong then I must confess that Beckett has deceived a good many of us.

What a difference in many was the intense Dubliner who followed Beckett. I refer to M.P. Rowan –known to Rotary fame as Mickey Rowan. If ever there was a President of this Club who had more to say to us and certainly saw to it that it was said, it was Rowan. He was frequently referred to as 'Kado'. I have never been able to ascertain how this name arose, but I do know that when in the chair 'Kado' was always arising.

He was a ready, resourceful speaker, and during his term he enjoyed the great distinction of being the only President who visited America on behalf of Rotary, and took his mother with him. Rowan's personality was quite original. His methods in the chair were of the same vintage. His activities were many. He was very vital and while he occupied the chair those inside as well as those outside our ranks had no excuse for not knowing what Rotary stood for but also what Rowan stood for.

After Michael Rowan there came to the chair our most amazing President, our biggest President, our most remarkable President, a man that can be truly described as an absolute moving mass of personality, the late and ever to be regretted Major Bryan Cooper.

Bryan Cooper's year was 1927/28. Let us from this Club never forget that period, for it gave us one of he really great lights in our history to date.

It is said of some men that place them in any community they cannot for long be overlooked. We know only too well, and the thought saddens us, that Bryan Cooper was undoubtedly such a man. The captivating music of his charming personality will haunt those of us who knew him as long as we live. Bryan Cooper was undoubtedly a most remarkable, a most loveable Irishman. He was a great Rotarian too, but, above all, he was a great gentleman.

It was truly said of Bryan Cooper that the moment that he entered a room a blaze of brilliant light seemed to turn on. All I will say is that the day he left us for ever a blaze of brilliant lights seemed to have been turned out.

Lionel Smith-Gordon took over from Major Bryan Cooper. Here we had the spectacle of a somewhat frail little man succeeding a man who was by no means frail. But Smith-Gordon's frailty must certainly did not apply to his mental gifts. It is my belief that this man possessed one of the most original, most resourceful, one of the richest minds that has ever been the gift of the President of this Club. While to those who knew him in a casual way his few and far between speeches gave the impression that he was splenetic, perhaps caustic and destructive, yet he was deep down a man with a genuinely constructive outlook. He hated 'blarney'. He was merciless with shallow thinkers. He left Ireland some years after leaving the chair, and I think that we lost in his departure a man who might have risen to great heights in our councils. His talks were always redolent of sound reasoning and of raptured thinking.

Smith-Gordon was also unique among our Presidents in rather a romantic way. He was the only one of our rota who took unto himself an all-American wife. He spoke tersely and, always, he spoke slowly.

That characteristic of Smith-Gordon's was so sharply in contrast to the speed fiend that next graced the chair. I refer to F. M. Summerfield, the ever present, probably the most 'all-in' man ever to rule the roost in this Club. By 'all-in' I do not refer to anything to do with insurance. I refer to human activity in the general sense, for if ever there came into this community a man whose interests are so numerous as to be almost beyond reckoning, it surely is this terrible little 50-cylinder, ten-engined fellow, Summerfield.

He is reputed to have a home in Sutton, but he doesn't sleep there. Summerfield, they tell you down in Sutton, 'never sleeps' anywhere. He has no time. It seems almost believable to those who know this veritable menace to the peace of mankind.

Have you ever worried about his name? I have. I have always been interested in people's names, and this name Summerfield has, quite naturally, interested me a good deal. Once I suspected German entanglements. It surely must be an Irish rendering of Summerfeldt. Of course no sane person would ever accuse Fred of German nationality and upbringing. Germany could not abide a Summerfield however much she could put up with a Summerfeldt. Fred most undoubtedly does not possess a German accent – his command of the German language is a pure myth. Some little time ago I met a man at sea. He was the living image of Summerfield – face, build, accent, restlessness and all. I was so struck with the resemblance that I simply could not resist asking the man if his name happened to be Summerfield.

Very courteously he replied, 'No, sir, it is not Summerfield'.

'Well, will you pardon me if I ask you what your name really is'?

'With pleasure,' said the stranger,' my name is Winterbottom'.

While Fred was our leader he certainly kept his foot on the accelerator.

In this he was different from G. T. J. Clampett, who followed him. You remember that intriguing habit of Clampett's of always staring at the ceiling while addressing the Club. That trait, however, in no way distracted from Clampett's armoury of logic or his fund of enlightened common sense.

Talking of common sense, now I have the pleasure of directing your attention to a sample of it as impressive and dependable as the Rock of

Gibraltar, which Fred Summerfield and I gazed upon not so long ago. Permit me to introduce you to Kevin J. Kenny – our Nelson Pillar of sense and shrewdness.

Kevin and our present Lord Mayor have two significant things in common. Both went to the same school – which was where each learned the disappearing art of hand shaking. But Kevin learned another art –almost disappeared too- that of smiling. I have seen that biggish little man wearing a smile when I knew well that he had good reason to feel in anything but a smiling mood.

Do you know, I would love to be on a sinking ship with Kevin. It would be a gloriously delightful adventure. Kevin would not only smile, but as well he would regale me with a howling best seller of a story, and the sinking feeling would completely disappear. Kevin has a mine of good stories, yet while he occupied the chair there he kept them all to himself. I suppose he somehow felt his position all too keenly to venture into levity. No man is quicker to sense danger than he. While handing us out law and order from the chair I must say that he did it with a perfectly gloved fist. We really liked law and order and, what's more, obeyed because Kevin was the dispenser.

Talking of good stories brings me to the end of my list, and also to the first and only clergyman who graced the chair – the Very Rev. Dr. R. K. Hanna. Like Summerfield, Kenny and many others, Dr. Hanna is, I am glad to say very much with us. He is is one of those men so full of personality that he simply could not for long conceal that delightful genial self of his anywhere. As with McKnight, Dr. Hanna is from the North. Let us hope that the same corner of our island will send us a few more men as racy, as human, and a speaker as this excellent counsellor. In the telling of a good and perfectly fitting story he had Kevin Kenny down and out every time. Dr. Hanna kept the house in the best of humour, and while he laid down the law to us it didn't matter two straws what the lunch fare was.

That concludes my excursion in Mellowed Memories.

I think that it would be nice if all Past Presidents present would stand up for one moment while the Club gives them a good old Irish cheer.

(The following Past Presidents then stood amid enthusiastic applause: Dr. Walsh, William Findlater, J.S. Stewart, Fred M. Summerfield and Kevin J. Kenny).

Before I sit down may I express the hope that when the whirligig of time brings around another cycle of twenty-two years that those men (and maybe women) who will then constitute this Club will be able to look back along that cycle of time with feelings as mellow as I am sure ours are today.

I thank you very much.

---

[1] *In the U.S. Clubs a member could be fined for not addressing a fellow member by his first name. This practice, while promoted by Stuart Morrow in all the Clubs that he founded, was resisted by the more traditional members on this side of the Atlantic.*

Appendix Seven

Remembrance of Presidents Past
An eclectic memoir

By Rotarian Frank Bannister

My first oblique contact with the Rotary club of Dublin was in the late 1980s. One of my colleagues in Price Waterhouse where I worked at the time, David Algeo, was a member, but other than the fact that he disappeared thence for lunch every Monday and that there was something called a safari supper once a year, I had no notion of what Rotary was or did. My first direct contact with the club came courtesy of the Suzuki movement and the coincidence that one of my children learned the violin from the daughter and the other from the wife of a long-standing member, John Goor. One of the Dublin club's most popular annual social events is a bar-b-cue held at the Goor's superbly located house in the Glencree valley just a few miles outside the Wicklow town of Enniskerry. Before the meal, it is customary to drink a glass or two of wine and swat away the midges whilst listening to and watching the Enniskerry Suzuki group, led by John's wife Magsie, perform a short (and peripatetic) concert. Our younger son was one of this crew and along with other proud mummies and daddies we came, we saw and we preened and then took our little darlings home whilst the Rotarians went off to eat, drink and do whatever it was that Rotarians did. In the summer of 1992, just before we headed for home, we were treated to a short thank you speech by the then recently anointed president, the inimitable Peter Evans. Peter stood behind a plinth and announced in his rasping baritone that he was "…the chief Rotarian" and thanked us all warmly for our contribution to the evening's festivities. After that one thing led to another and some months later John Goor proposed me for membership of the Dublin club which I joined in early 1993. Peter was still president and it was his habit to start each meeting with an 'on this day' announcement. These proclamations included nuggets such as "On this day Geraldus of Wales stubbed his toe while getting out of the bath and decided that he would write a history of Swansea football club". To this day I suspect that some of these vignettes were more a product of Peter's fertile imagination than vulgar historical fact, but that may be unworthy. Fact or fiction, they were marvellously entertaining.

Finbar Ambrose who, sadly, died while I was writing this short memoir followed Peter. I did not understand at this stage in my career how presidents came to be (I am still not completely sure how this happens), but one Monday there was a handover ceremony, chains were exchanged, and Finbar moved into the presidential chair. Only people from Cork call their sons Finbar and like all of those from the real capital, Finbar was proud both of his city and of Ford, the company for whom he had worked for many years. Ford had had a long and sentimental association with that city, indeed they probably kept their factory there in operation long after the dictates of economic common sense would have closed it down. Most presidents have a special characteristic or two and one of Finbar's was walking vast distances on a single tank by which I mean the take-both-your-packed-lunch-and-your-packed-dinner kind of walking. Along with Peter McManus (q.v.) and others he was a founding member of what was later to become the Rotary Rangers. Finbar stomped up hill and down dale with seemingly inexhaustible reserves of energy, often leaving far younger Rotarians red faced and panting in his wake. As a senior executive in Ford, Finbar was well connected and managed to persuade Edsel Ford, the then current heir of the Ford dynasty, to visit our club in 1993 at a special event held in the Royal Hospital, Kilmainham. Finbar was also an active member of the Society of Saint Vincent de Paul with a real commitment to helping the less fortunate in our society.

After two happy presidencies, the tenure of Dick Tuite who succeeded Finbar is tinged with sadness. Dick was a man of action. One evening at the annual bar-b-cue, armed only with a skewer of half cooked chicken, he told me as I stood there, plate in hand, that he wanted me to "look after Foundation". Still being still relatively new to Rotary, I had only a vague idea of what Foundation was and I said as much. No matter, I was told, I would soon learn. This, I was to discover, was Dick's style. He belonged to that class of manager who believes in delegation, giving people a challenge and team effort. Tragically, he was diagnosed with cancer during his presidential year something that emerged (distressingly I might add) during that year's safari supper (by this time I had discovered what these were). He courageously completed his year after which he attended meetings as frequently as his declining health would allow. We all hoped for a recovery, but sadly Dick was to die some months later. To add to the tragedy, his wife Patricia was also to die of cancer not long afterwards leaving their four children orphaned. My last memory of Dick is seeing him laid out in his coffin in his own living room where his many friends assembled for his wake and to celebrate his all too brief life. His premature death was a great loss to both the club and the community.

It fell to Sean O'Donohue to take over at this difficult time. Sean was a liftman and was in partnership with his brother in Donohue Lifts. Quiet spoken, courteous and low key, I came to know him quite well over the course of his year as by this time I was (thanks to Dick Tuite) on the Council. I made many a trip to Sean's house in a quiet corner of Mount Merrion on Saturday and Sunday mornings to sort out various items of Rotary business. I cannot say that he made a huge mark on the club, but he kept the ship steady and managed a sometimes vociferous and combustible Council well.

Peter McManus, our next president, was a distinct contrast. Peter always seemed a bit larger than life. He had the boundless energy and charm of the good salesman combined with great wit and a lively sense of humour. This may have been related to the fact that he was in charge of Revlon's operations in Ireland and, if memory serves, it was Charles Revlon who opined that what his company sold was not lipstick, foundation and mascara, but hope. If on a somewhat smaller scale, Peter, like Michael Carroll of whom more later, worked in an office largely manned (if that is the correct term) by women. Peter was energetic and outgoing and had a way of making you feel, even after a short acquaintance, that you had been his lifelong friend. He was, with Finbar Ambrose, a founder of the Rangers and another great walker. A story told about Peter was about how, on one winter walk, he encountered a sheep that had become entangled in some wire by a river. Peter stripped to the waist and, despite the cold temperature, leaned into the water to rescue the distressed animal. After a successful year, Peter too succumbed to cancer not long after his term of office. He was a fine president, but his premature death was, like Dick Tuite's, a great loss.

To be a Manxmen is to be a member of an exclusive club, and we had one (a Manxman that is) in our next president, Barry Wilson. Barry is a large man from whichever point of the compass you chose to approach him for Barry was a man who loved his food. He towered over most of his fellow members and created an imposing presence in the presidential seat where his sonorous tones were well matched to the dignity of his estate. A naval architect by profession and by passion, he was, his late wife Dorrie once told me, a man who enjoyed working with his hands. The thing most members during this period probably remember most about Barry was his speech to visiting Rotarians and guests when, week after week, he would invariably tell them that they were "Almost welcome". Club members were used to this and would break into a wry smile and sometimes the odd ripple of laughter, though the occasional guest was a trifle disconcerted by this rather ambiguous greeting.

In 1998 Aubrey Fogarty became president. Short, bespectacled and bald, he was quite a contrast to Barry both in physical appearance and temperament. Aubrey was a touch on the acerbic side and not somebody who suffered fools (or sometimes others) gladly. Although I always found him entertaining company and we got on extremely well, Aubrey was the way he was and his relationships with some of his officers and committee chairs were at times on fractious side – something I suspect that Aubrey himself would have been the first to acknowledge. Being in advertising, Aubrey was always a good source of trinkets and like a number of other members I acquired a solid supply of Aubrey Fogarty and Associates pens and other paraphernalia during his reign. One of

Aubrey's achievements was to host what was probably the most successful new member's night we have had during my time in the club. On that evening we recruited many new members including Victor Hamilton and Paul Martin, both to be themselves presidents within a few years.

I have to say that my memories of the year of our next president, Joe Dunne, are scant. Joe was, let's say, low key. He was not a man with the type strong personality a club like ours needs in a president. Sadly, Joe was to succumb to Alzheimer's disease not long after his year and this may have been part of the explanation for the lack of the type of buzz during his term in office that other presidents have brought to theirs. The most notable event of his year was probably the launch in Ireland of the successful Aquabox scheme. Unfortunately, another outcome of his year was of the wrong sort as a number of perceived financial problems (not of his making) developed which led to the departure in frustration of one of our younger members. These problems landed, unfortunately for her, on the desk of our next president, Ethna Fitzgerald.

Ethna is a remarkable woman and, apart from Tony Seery, the president whom I have come to know best at a personal level outside of the club. The first important thing to record for posterity about Ethna (and I am sure there will be ample column inches devoted to this in the main part of this book) is that she was the first woman president of the Dublin Rotary club. Shortly after she took office, I attended a Rotary club meeting in Madison, Connecticut. Invited to give a brief talk on the Dublin club, I was asked (rather aggressively) if we had women members and I recall how pleased I was to be able to say not only did we do so, but that we currently had a woman president. Being first woman president alone would have been an achievement, but Ethna also founded a new club in Youghal and was (and continues to be) extremely active at District level. Indeed she would have been District 1160's first female governor had she not chosen to step down just before she was due to take office in order to look after her beloved late husband Alex who was seriously ill at the time. As noted above, Ethna had to sort out a number of financial problems that she inherited from Joe Dunne's tenure. This was a shame as it took up much of even her formidable energy and it cast a shadow over her year. Ethna would sometimes ring me at home in the evening and we would talk over the situation for an hour or so. She was also the person who awarded me a Paul Harris fellowship, for which honour I am most grateful. I expect and hope that she will one day be District Governor and she will be a great one.

Our next caudillo was the inimitable Ted Corcoran. If Ted did not exist, you would have to invent him. Ted combined a career in Rotary with a parallel and stellar career in Toastmasters International of which he elected International President in 2003-2004. A Kerryman and proud of it (they are almost as bad as Corkmen in this respect, but the accent is less hard on the teeth) Ted was, as one might expect, a gifted speaker who had a ready tale, a ready quip and a ready quote for every occasion. Ted's day job (when did he ever get to it one wonders?) was as Head of Safety for Iarnrod Eireann and amongst his many interests was leadership. When he retired from Iarnrod Eireann at the appointed hour, he set up his own business called The Leadership Bus. Why he did not call it the Leadership Train or the Leadership Engine I am not sure, maybe it is something to do with the tradition of Dublin buses travelling in packs. Even though, as an academic, I would consider myself a reasonable experienced public speaker, I still learned a few tricks listening to Ted and I filed away more than one of his anecdotes and quotations for later recycling. At the time of penning this memoir, Ted is Assistant District Governor and unofficial club wit.

One of the curious things about the club is that way that some people become president after only a few years membership whilst others can be members for decades before the heavy hand of history gives them a belt on the shoulder. Our next president, Ken Hunt, fell into this category having been a member for over 20 years before his elevation. Ken is striking to look at. His magnificent head of hair was the envy of several of the more follically challenged members of the club and his face is deep lined and craggy in a way that is more than a little reminiscent of Samuel Beckett. Ken is one of life's gentlemen and was an enormously popular president. Furthermore his golf handicap approximates to mine which I find useful when I need to find somebody who is not going to murder me over 18 holes. Ken's wife Jeanette (who sadly died in 2008) was also active in Inner Wheel.

Guy Johnston, our next president, had been brought into the club by Ken Hunt only a few years earlier and was to be the youngest president in my time. Guy is an action man, energetic and ambitious for the club. He styles himself a Scotsman (from the clan Johnston one assumes) and proudly wore his tartan to club events. He is in the telecommunications business and persuaded his friend Denis O'Brien to be the guest speaker at our Christmas lunch, something which not only drew a large attendance, but was also a fascinating insight into one of leading entrepreneurs as Denis spoke frankly about his own life and experience. Guy was also a man with all the right connections being a member of both Fitzwilliam Lawn Tennis club and the Royal St. George Yacht club, two places I am not in that often, but both of which I had the pleasure of dining during his year. Guy brought great drive to the job and, as a result, had a somewhat different style to other presidents I have known. He certainly raised a lot of money for good causes including one of most successful ever events, a charity Sunday brunch in the Unicorn restaurant owned by one of our members Georgio Casari - an occasion which I know that I attended, but for some reason cannot remember much about.

Tony Keegan is writing this book, so I must be careful what I say here. Tony is a man of many parts and numerous talents, not just as a talented writer and organiser, but as somebody with a profound knowledge of the minutiae of Rotary. He was and is another of the aforementioned Rangers, those men (no women yet) of fathomless stamina, muscular thighs and robust hiking boots. Tony's many interests extend to occasional bouts of song. One of the club traditions is for the president to invite his council members and committee chairs out at the conclusion of his time in office. There have been many memorable moment at these events, but the one which is permanently etched in my memory is Tony's rendition of Bobby Darin's 'Every Night I sit here by my Window' in the basement of the Royal Irish Yacht Club after much alcohol had been consumed by all present including, I have to say, Tony, whenever I hear that song, Tony memorable performance comes to mind. Some presidents, having served their sentence, are content to retire to the backbenches. Tony continues to be one of the club stalwarts, one of those members who, like duct tape, manage to hold things together when otherwise they would fall apart, both a great leader and a great servant of the club.

Our next president was Paul Loughlin. A former Rotary ambassadorial scholar, Paul's day job was as a director the RTE television series Prime Time and particularly Prime Time Investigates, a programme which went some way to making up for the decline in good old fashioned investigative reporting in the printed press. At some stage, while we were still in Jury's hotel, somebody got the bright idea of making wine available for purchase at the lunch. Paul was one of the few members who regularly availed of this service, one presumes that it was for creative reasons. Paul brought a distinct whiff of RTE to the proceedings with a number of guest speakers and even the brief membership of Brian Dobson, a leading journalist and newsreader at the time who, sadly, did not remain a member for long. Paul also demonstrated on one memorable occasion how one serves a banana to Her Britannic Majesty, Queen Elizabeth the Second. This involved attenuating the banana by chopping off both ends before slitting it down its full length and serving it on a plate still partially in its wrapping so to speak. Further demonstrations can be arranged on request I am told.

Like Guy Johnston, Paul Martin became president only a few years after joining. When I was running a student newspaper in my undergraduate days, somebody gave me a job description for an advertising manager as someone with a ready smile, an overbearing manner and an inability to take no for an answer. A more succinct depiction of Paul it would be hard to find. Paul took a sadistic pleasure in getting his fellow members out of their comfort zone as he put it and that usually meant being willing to get out and raise money – often in sub arctic conditions and strange clothing. Paul himself did not seem to have a personal comfort zone or if he did its boundaries were well over the event horizon. He kept members and occasionally guests supplied with a variety of Oirish souvenirs like large green leprechaun hats and "Kiss me, I'm Irish" t-shirts. His enthusiasm and irreverence had us all exhausted at times, but he shook the club up – not least by being one of the first members consistently to refuse to wear a tie to the lunch – a fashion that has never fully caught on, but which is now adopted by a number of members. Paul's son John was one of the founder members and one of the first presidents of the Dublin Central Club that was chartered in 2001.

After Paul the second, we all needed a bit of a breather. Michael Carroll, another CIE man (and a lawyer, but we will overlook that) had a quieter and more consensual style of leadership than his flamboyant predecessor. Michael (and I do not mean this unkindly) always makes me think of a leprechaun. It was not that he looks like a leprechaun, rather his eye seemed to have a permanent twinkle and, as an advert had it, it was the way he would look at you. Michael, God help him, worked in the legal department of CIE - a legal war zone if ever there was one. Like Peter McManus before him, he seemed to operate in an environment richly endowed with female solicitors (in the legal sense). In Michael's case, it seemed that at any given time as if about half to two thirds of these young ladies were in an advanced state of pregnancy, so he spent much of his time in fear of the number of his available troops being severely depleted by childbirth and of having to manage the presidency as well as all the extra work in the office. Somehow, despite babies to the right of him and babies to the left of him, he made it through the year. Having a good sense of humour is a valuable attribute to have as president of the Dublin Rotary club and Michael had to steer some difficult decisions though an opinionated and high powered Council. If at time that wry smile was a mite philosophical, he could be forgiven.

Victor Hamilton took over the chain of office in 2007. Dubliners, or at least a certain breed of southsider, whose journeys took them up and down the Clonskeagh road, will recall Victor Motors, a large Fiat franchise about half way between Ranelagh and Goatstown. Victor is a motor man through and through. He was also, if I can say so without offending other ex-presidents, the best looking president of my time in the club. With a distinguished crop of silvery white hair, he looked every inch the auto executive and might have come straight out of central casting for the movie of an Arthur Hailey novel. I came to know Victor and his wife Jackie on a glorious, if insane, club opera trip to Genoa, when we left Dublin on Friday morning and returned on Sunday afternoon. Fortunately we had one of our Italian members, Aldo Aletti as master of ceremonies, translator, chaperone and guide. Unfortunately the opera on that night was Der Rosenkavalier, a marvellous work by Richard Strauss, but at a tad short of five hours duration (excluding the intervals!) rather hard on those who, like Victor, were not die-hard fans of this particular art form. Being in German with Italian subtitles did not help and Victor was not the only member of our group to struggle to retain consciousness during the third act. Victor also started a fashion for walking the Camino to Santiago de Compostela. On returning, he gave us an account that I recall included the fact that it had given him a lasting appreciation of the virtues of the en-suite bathroom.

Which brings me to the last president in this eclectic memoir, Tony Seery. I was not responsible for Tony joining the club, but I had an indirect hand, in that I introduced Tony to Peter McManus who invited him to join. Peter had been looking for somebody to help with Revlon's IT systems at the time, someone who was not going to charge them an arm and a leg. I told him Tony was the man for the job and it turned into a fruitful business relationship and eventually another Rotarian. Tony and I worked together in Price Waterhouse for many years where, even though I say so myself, we made a pretty good team as our talents in the world of technology complemented each other nicely. We still do some work together for the Society of St. Vincent de Paul. Over the years, my wife Ivy and I have come to know Tony, his wife Anne and their children, particularly their daughters Rebecca and Rachel. If one wanted to describe Tony in a few words it would be loyal, hardworking and conscientious – all attributes that he has brought to his presidency. As a colleague, Tony was always somebody I felt that I could trust totally not just to do things right, but to finish any job he started. He is not, as I think he himself would admit, a natural leader of men, but he epitomises everything that is best in Rotary. A dedicated family man, he has worked tirelessly for the club since the day he joined and hopefully will continue to do so for many years to come.

Our president for our centenary year will be Randal Gray and of his time I cannot yet speak. He takes over a club that has changed a great deal in seventeen or so years that I have been a member. The club today is smaller, less formal, more active and, I think, more intimate and I think more friendly that the one I joined in 1993. Presidents really can and do affect both the direction and the success of the club, but a club does not exist in a bubble and if it is to thrive, needs to adapt to the spirit of the age and we now live in a time where people seem to have less time and volunteerism has suffered as a consequence. Nevertheless, the Dublin Rotary has been lucky to have many fine leaders in my time and the pipeline looks good, at least for the immediate future. By its nature, Rotary tends to be populated by people with strong personalities and being president must sometimes seem like herding cats. A good president has, therefore, to be a good leader. But above all, the presidency is about what Rotary itself is about – service above self. We have been and continue to be fortunate to have so many members who can meet this ideal.

Appendix Eight

Presidents of the Inner Wheel Club of Dublin

1971-72 Mrs Christine Hughes
1972-73 Mrs Mai Kirk
1973-74 Mrs C. Pearson
1974-75 Mrs M. Hall
1975-76 Mrs M. Bamford
1976-77 Mrs V. Ridgeway
1977-78 Mrs M. Beckett
1978-79 Mrs M. Simpson
1979-80 Mrs J. Anderson
1980-81 Mrs H. Hamilton
1981-82 Mrs Mairead Larkin
1982-83 Mrs E. McCabe
1983-84 Mrs Hilary Hamilton
1984-85 Mrs Elinor Johnson
1985-86 Jean Smith-Keany
1986-87 Gill Evans
1987-88 Maureen Boothman
1988-89 Carmel Moloney
1989-90 Frances Thornton
1990-91 Jeanette Hunt
1991-92 Anne Engert
1992-93 Sheila Woods
1993-94 Joyce Maguire
1994-95 Ann Doyle
1995-96 Dorrie Wilson
1996-97 Maura O'Neill
1997-98 Joan Liuzzi
1998-99 Peggy Pim
1999-00 Ursula Mason
2000-01 Joy Duffy
2001-02 Sylvia Tennant

2002-03 Gill Evans
2003-04 Valerie Osborne
2004-05 Maureen Boothman
2005-06 Maura O'Neill
2006-07 Jo Callanan
2007-08 Sheila Hillis
2008-09 Pauline Wrixon
2009-10 Ninni Frisk
2010-11 Joan Liuzzi

L.C. Ritchie and Tom Tate take their name badges prior to lunch in the Metropole Restaurant in 1936.

Appendix Nine

Luncheon Venues

During its hundred-year history the Dublin Club had fourteen different venues for its luncheons. From time to time lunches were held elsewhere but the ones listed below were the settled venues. Council meetings were held in various locations including the Club Offices, President's and member's offices and hotels. Evening meetings were sometimes held in different locations from the luncheon venues, as were dinner dances and official dinners.

Jurys Hotel College Green February 1911-12

Dolphin Hotel Essex Street 1912-13

Imperial Hotel Sackville Street 1913-15 Lunch 2/-

Metropole Hotel Sackville Street 1915-April 1916 Lunch 2/-

Mills Hall Merrion Row May to July 1916

Central Hotel Exchequer Street July 1916 to March 1919 Lunch 2/- - 2/6

Dublin Bread Company (DBC) Restaurant, 3 St. Stephen's Green North   April to July 1919

Kidd's Restaurant 46 Nassau Street July 1919-1924 Lunch 2/6 – 3/6

Clerys Restaurant O'Connell Street (formerly Sackville Street) 1924-1932

Metropole Restaurant O'Connell Street 1932-1940

Greshan Hotel (Aberdeen Hall) O'Connell Street 1940 –1946 Lunch 3/-

Royal Hibernian Hotel Dawson Street 1946-1971 Lunch 5/-, 7/6 (1951), 10/- (1961), 12/6 + 10% (1964), 18/6, £1, £1.60.

Intercontinental (Jurys) Hotel Pembroke Road Ballsbridge 1971 – 2007 Lunch £2 - €15

Grand Canal Hotel Grand Canal Street 2007- to date Lunch €20.

Select Bibliography

A Century of Service, the Story of Rotary International by Daniel C. Forward published by Rotary International in 2003

The Hub of the Wheel, the Story of the Rotary Movement in Ireland 1911-1976 by Terence S. Duncan ACII FCIB Past President Rotary Club of Belfast

Rotary International in Great Britain and Ireland – 'Nice Gentlemen, Really' by Roger Levy published by Continua Productions 1978

The Minutes, Correspondence and Newsletters of the Rotary, Club Dublin 1911 to 2010.

'Cogs', the magazine for District 1160 and District Rosters.

Handbook to the Dublin District published by the British Association 1908

The Story of the Royal Dublin Society by Terence de Vere White published by the Kerryman 1955.

Findlaters: The story of a Dublin Merchant Family 1774-2001 by Alex Findlater published by A & A Farmar 2001

Letters from Dublin, Easter 1916 – Alfred Fannin's Diary of the Rising Edited by Adrian and Sally Warwick-Haller and published by the Irish Academic Press in 1995

Lockout: Dublin 1913 by Padraig Yeates published by Gill & Macmillan 2000.

Mr. Bewley in Berlin by Andreas Roth published in 2000 by the Four Courts Press Ltd.

Doctor of Millions: The Rise and Fall of Stamp King Dr. Paul Singer by Seamus Brady published by Anvil Books.

Newspapers
The Irish Times, Irish Independent, Daily Express

Directories
Thom's

AUTHOR

Tony Keegan joined the Rotary Club, Dublin in 1989 with the classification of Periodical Publishing and served as president in Rotary's Centenary year 2004/5. He is a graduate of the National University of Ireland (University College Dublin) and holds a Bachelor of Arts degree in English, Economics and History. Tony is currently Honorary Secretary of the Dublin Club.